Women's Utopias of the Eighteenth Century

Women's Utopias of the Eighteenth Century

ALESSA JOHNS

UNIVERSITY OF ILLINOIS PRESS
URBANA AND CHICAGO

This book is printed on acid-free paper.

Library of Congress Cataloging-in-Publication Data
Johns, Alessa.
Women's utopias of the eighteenth century / Alessa Johns.
p. cm.
Includes bibliographical references and index.
ISBN 0-252-02841-4 (cloth : alk. paper)
1. Feminism—History—18th century. 2. Utopias. 3. Women—History—18th century. I. Title.
HQ1150.J65 2003
305.42'09'033—dc21 2002151284

For Christopher Alan Reynolds
and Gabriel William Johns Reynolds

Contents

Acknowledgments

For indispensable advice in the dissertation phase of this project I am indebted to my generous mentor, George Starr, and to my perceptive readers, Catherine Gallagher and Hanna Pitkin. Welcome suggestions also came from James Grantham Turner and John Traugott. I am grateful for the intellectual and moral support of colleagues at the University of California, Davis: Catherine Robson, Kari Lokke, Anna Maria Busse Berger, and Gail Finney. Nicole Pohl has been a diligent editor and much-appreciated comrade. I would also like to thank Paula Backscheider, Vita Fortunati, April London, Felicity Nussbaum, Ruth Perry, Lyman Tower Sargent, and Ann Van Sant for advice and support. Betty Rizzo and Barbara Brandon Schnorrenberg kindly lent materials on Sarah Scott. I have also benefited from the efforts of research assistants Scott Herring, Bill Knight, Sharon O'Toole Dubois, and Anjali Williams. And I am obliged to the reviewers for the University of Illinois Press for helpful comments that guided my revisions. It has been a pleasure to work with the University of Illinois Press and with associate editor Mary Giles, and I am especially grateful to Willis Regier, director.

I am indebted to Katharine Spencer and Corky McGuinness for their kind hospitality as I researched in London; Jolanta Moore and the teachers at Rivendell Nursery School for their devoted care of my son; Lawrence Stewart for his loving encouragement; and Emily Albu, Alan Taylor, Anna Maria Busse Berger, Karol Berger, Ana Peluffo, Pablo Ortiz, Catherine Robson, and Jamie Jensen for friendship and unstinting encouragement.

The work on this project began with the support of a Mellon Fellowship in the Humanities, which funded much of my graduate education. A generous grant from the J. William Fulbright Foundation took me to Germany and allowed me to research and write chapter 6; I am grateful to my sponsor, Ina Schabert, of the English department at the University of Munich, for making me so welcome. I would also like to thank the Committee on Research, University of California, Davis, for continued support.

In completing my research I have enjoyed the hospitality of many institutions: the Shields Library, University of California, Davis; the Bancroft and Doe libraries, University of California, Berkeley; the Huntington Library, San Marino; the Beinecke Library, Yale University; the British Library, London; the Bodleian Library, Oxford University; the Universitätsbibliothek, Heidelberg; and the Staatsbibliothek and Universitätsbibliothek, Munich. The idea for this book occurred to me in an inspiring niche of the New Library at the Villa I Tatti, Florence.

I thank the Huntington Library for permission to quote from the Montagu Papers and the Massachusetts Historical Society for allowing me to publish excerpts from the *Castorland Journal.* An earlier version of chapter 1 appeared in *Utopian Studies* 7 (1996) and was reprinted in *Female Communities,* edited by Rebecca D'Monté and Nicole Pohl (London: Macmillan, 2000). Part of chapter 6 was published in *Postmodernism and the Enlightenment,* edited by Daniel Gordon (New York: Routledge, 2001), which was reprinted from *Historical Reflections* 25 (1999). A segment of chapter 5 appeared in *English Language Notes* 31 (1994).

This book would never have appeared without the help of countless friends, colleagues, doctors, nurses, emergency personnel, and good samaritans who saw me through the aftermath of a ruptured brain aneurysm and supported me in countless ways during my recovery. I am thankful for their kindness, concern, and professionalism. I am forever grateful to those who directly saved my life: Emily Albu, Dr. Richard L. Kravitz, and Dr. Dachling Pang of the University of California, Davis Medical Center, and my gifted neurosurgeon, Dr. Michael T. Lawton of the University of California, San Francisco, who was assisted by Dr. G. Edward Vates and Lisa T. Hannegan, RN, MS, CNRN. I am also indebted to Alan Taylor, who stepped in and proofed as well as supervised the indexing of my edited volume, *Dreadful Visitations: Confronting Natural Catastrophe in the Age of Enlightenment*—in a strange twist of fate the proofs of the disaster book had arrived just before my own calamity—so that the volume was published on schedule.

I could never have completed this work without the steadfast and loving encouragement of my family. I am grateful to my parents, Jorun and Donald Johns, for inspiring me all my life with their enthusiasm for ideas, languages, history, and the arts. My older brother, Karl, lent his expertise at bibliography, while my younger brother, Andreas, could be counted on for adroit advice on translations. My in-laws have been a second family to me: my mother-in-law, Mary Lee Reynolds, and my late father-in-law, William H. Reynolds, have offered constant love and nurture over many years; Susan Reynolds, Anne Marie Reynolds, Ellen Reynolds Hall, Martha Reynolds, Joel Reynolds, and their families have supplied laughter and rallied round when I despaired.

My husband, Christopher Reynolds, has been an astute editor of my work, a compassionate caregiver, and a thoughtful, kind, and good-humored partner; our wonderful son Gabriel has cheered and inspired us. I could not have survived my disaster without them, and seeing their faces each day fills me with a sense of how happy I am to be alive. I dedicate this book to them.

Women's Utopias of the Eighteenth Century

Introduction

Utopia sits uneasily with postmodernism. Its universalism contradicts post-modern pluralism; its totalizing runs counter to emphases on heterogeneity and difference. Yet, for all of the commentators arguing that we live in a post-utopian age, there are others, notably Jürgen Habermas, who have insisted on utopia's continuing relevance.[1] Seyla Benhabib, a student of Habermas's work, has addressed the question of feminism, taking account of postmodernist critiques to insist that feminism needs Enlightenment ideas if it is to remain viable. Utopia in particular, she argues, is a concept that must be embraced: "Postmodernism can teach us the theoretical and political traps of why utopias and foundational thinking can go wrong, but it should not lead to a retreat from utopia altogether. For we, as women, have much to lose by giving up the utopian hope in the wholly other."[2] With a look at literary texts, Angelika Bammer observes that women's utopianism has indeed remained a viable political and intellectual force, even in a postmodern age. Feminist writing in the 1970s, she notes, was sustained by utopian thought even when utopia was declared dead. Female utopian authors figured their feminist challenge to the status quo in an unconventional way, not as "wholly other" but as a "partial vision," one that eschewed a comprehensive, totalizing plan, insisting on its partiality by being both fragmentary and overtly partisan, by refusing to obscure its political intentions. Even though Bammer's work focuses on the 1970s, her concept of the "partial vision" is nonetheless helpful in considering eighteenth-century women's utopianism.[3]

Indeed, female authors, recognizing their subordination and consequent limitations, articulated plans for sociopolitical change by advocating just such a partial vision. Although their view was fragmentary, however, it simultaneously harbored ambitious goals, for the authors generated a reproductive utopian model; their program began locally and incrementally but was intended to have global repercussions. Mary Astell, Sarah Fielding, Sarah Scott, and Mary Hamilton inspired and influenced each other, and the work of two Continental utopists, French author Jeanne Marie Leprince de Beaumont and German writer Sophie von La Roche, was in turn informed by the British paradigm. The women's shared vision was based on contemporary political and economic theories, on theology and practical reformism; they grappled with evolving discourses of contract, psychology, education, charity, and human reproduction.

In rewriting these discourses, feminist utopists portrayed ideal communities that would offer equitable ways of life, especially for women, the poor, and the sick. The women became what Michel de Certeau has called "*bricoleuses*," cultural consumers embedded in social and discursive systems who employ the tools at hand to make space for resistance. Responding to Michel Foucault, de Certeau argues that "the goal is not to make clearer how the violence of order is transmuted into a disciplinary technology, but rather to bring to light the clandestine forms taken by the dispersed, tactical, and makeshift creativity of groups or individuals already caught in the nets of 'discipline'." Engaged in nearly hidden attempts to adapt "the dominant cultural economy . . . to their own interests," female utopian authors imagined how small subterranean movements might reverberate intercontinentally.[4]

The partial vision thus implied a gradual utopian process rather than the sudden imposition of an ideal state along the lines of Thomas More's *Utopia.* Bammer points out that women's utopian visions during the 1970s transformed the very notions of "revolution" and "utopia": "Revolution was defined in terms of process. And the concept of utopia became concrete."[5] Substitutional revolutionary values gave way to a pragmatic, reformist model, while "abstract utopia," a term coined by Ernst Bloch denoting the immaterial, fairy-tale quality of escapist utopian visions, was overtaken by the material realities of "concrete utopia."[6]

Women's utopias of the eighteenth century anticipated this transformation. They figured the globalization of utopia through a process of reproduction, or a kind of self-perpetuating replication. I therefore use "reproduction" in its broadest sense, encompassing not only the birth and education of children in order to expand and multiply utopias but also the propagation of utopian ways of life and behavior through imitation and circulation, moral conversion, transcription and duplication (even to the point of plagiarism), and literary mitosis. One member of a utopia modeled behavior that inspired imitation and utopian converts; another gave birth to and educated followers; one ideal community formed another; one text called forth a sequel. By means of utopian duplication, itself modeled on a Christian paradigm, these writers proffered local solutions designed to ripple out and alter global conditions.

Because this pattern allowed reformers to adapt to particular circumstances even as they advanced a general ideal, it would stimulate feminists today who feel that the movement lacks direction. At the millennium, journals invited scholars to take stock of feminism, and articles such as "The Impossibility of Women's Studies" and "Do We Need a New Feminism?" conveyed the prevalent sense of uncertainty and conflict among feminists.[7] Recognizing that the movement is at a crossroads, Liz Faue has encouraged women "to take time out to dream, imaginatively construct alternative futures, and creatively sketch out paths to reach them."[8] Because such dreaming has largely been discouraged in the postmodern, post-utopian era, however, we have a dearth of models. Consequently, it is important to study earlier thinkers and, among them, eighteenth-century feminists. They anticipated nineteenth-century experimental communities as well as postmodernist critiques even as they leaned on Enlightenment concepts. That dynamic combination offers compelling images of ideal societies that can inspire the search for more profitable academic, socioeconomic, and political arrangements.

Women's Utopias aims to further several other arguments. First, I demonstrate that female utopists' political plans revealed a theoretical sophistication that has yet to be sufficiently acknowledged. These women writers were extremely well informed and highly opinionated. If they did not address moral philosophers in their own idiom, they nonetheless articulated their views in the most eligible literary forms: letters, fictions, and histories. Authors such as Astell and Scott, it is true, have begun to receive serious attention, but Leprince de Beaumont and La Roche are only gradually enjoying recognition. Indeed, the works of theirs discussed here—Leprince de Beaumont's *The New Clarissa* and La Roche's *Events at Lake Oneida*—have been bypassed by critics in favor of better-known but less reformist contributions: *Beauty and the Beast* and *Fräulein von Sternheim.*

Such selection leads to a second argument: The choices of texts made by critics, such as Leprince de Beaumont's fables and La Roche's novels of manners, have lent undue weight to a thesis about the ways narratives advance privatizing ideological forces of the eighteenth century. Commentators have maintained that early women writers were caught up in the vogue for sentiment and proved active collaborators in generating a cult of domesticity. Jane Spencer, for instance, describes the stultifying impact of conduct literature and the severe "terms of acceptance" female authors faced in their depictions of female heroines—terms that dictated a loss of freedom and narrowing range of action for both author and characters—despite women's increasing access to print culture.[9] Nancy Armstrong has contended that domestic fiction "actively sought to disentangle the language of sexual relations from the language of politics" as a way of obscuring its ideological function.[10] And, to be sure, the novels most frequently chosen for discussion by critics can be read to support such a thesis. Mary Davys's *Reform'd Coquet,* Eliza Haywood's *Betsy Thoughtless,* Charlotte Lennox's *The Female Quixote,* Frances Sheridan's *Sidney Bidulph,* Frances Burney's *Evelina,* and Elizabeth Inchbald's *A Simple Story* have all come to form a women's canon because they model the socialization of a central protagonist and can be viewed conveniently as forerunners of Jane Austen. More recent research and attention to other writings and genres, however, have complicated the domesticity idea and questioned the concept of strictly separate private and public spheres in the eighteenth century.[11]

I wish to contribute to such revisionist discussions. Female utopists challenged the privatizing effects of conduct literature and much domestic fiction as they created a communitarian model. In their novels, the development of a group of main characters took the place of individual *Bildung,* and unusual plot elements were introduced, including the organization of schools; the mathematical calculation of wages, savings, and populations; the building of public institutions; and the development of agricultural cooperatives. Literary innovations occurred as a way of enhancing a political message rather than of heightening aesthetic appeal or of advocating politeness. As a result, these texts cannot be assimilated easily into the established paradigm. They are generic hybrids with overt didactic intentions, works that hitherto have not defined the rise of the novel in criticism but have nonetheless influenced it.[12]

Third, I demonstrate how English Bluestockings attracted Continental writers and gave shape to a European community of female authorship. Today's scholarly focus on nationalism obscures drives toward internationalism, but female utopists, despite their pronounced patriotism, foregrounded cooperation at all levels. Leprince de Beaumont and La Roche made international community a central theme of their novels—La Roche went beyond European questions to introduce the issue of race and ethnicity in America—and it is clear that the writers sought out intellectual and, where possible, social contact with each other. My book therefore attempts to raise to an international and political level the discussions begun by scholars such as Sylvia Myers, Betty Rizzo, and Betty Schellenberg about the circles created by British women, and it extends the project of Gary Kelly, first by identifying women's utopianism as a compelling facet of Bluestocking feminism and then by revealing its ongoing impact on the Continent.[13]

Finally, I hope *Women's Utopias* will contribute to efforts to refine current critiques of Enlightenment ideas. Keith Michael Baker and Peter Hanns Reill note that "the many varieties of thinking commonly grouped together under the rubric of 'postmodernism' share at least one salient characteristic: they all depend upon a stereotyped, even caricatural, account of the Enlightenment." Such scholars as Dena Goodman, Lawrence Klein, and Daniel Gordon have attempted to expose the cliches that have led scholars to see the Enlightenment as "the other of postmodernism" (Gordon) and to call for a more nuanced understanding of eighteenth-century thought. Goodman, for instance, suggests that the discourse of difference was as prevalent as universalism in the Enlightenment, and she points to the importance of civility "as the very constitution of a society defined by difference." Also interested in Enlightenment sociability, Klein directs attention away from metaphors of light and sight and toward sound and conversation to characterize the eighteenth century as dialogic rather than scientistic. Such a move, he insists, should not be seen reductively as a defense of the Enlightenment but as "a defense of historical thinking against the unhistorical propensity to offer treatments of the Enlightenment in the tone of either accusation or defense." Gordon, also concerned with historical thinking, concludes, "Instead of defining the 'dialectic' of the Enlightenment as an absolute belief in history that led to a disenchantment in the late nineteenth and early twentieth centuries, we should see this dialectic as a process internal to the Enlightenment," a process that moved between historical optimism and doubt.[14]

Eighteenth-century female utopists were among the writers grappling with such a play between optimism and doubt. Their unenviable political position—extensive obligation without commensurate rights—led them to question some emerging ideological orientations even as they reinforced others. Their work, therefore, has implications beyond literary study to cultural and intellectual history. Taking women's views into account broadens our picture of Enlightenment thought, and confirms that current representations of "Enlightenment" bear further investigation.

Classifying Feminist Utopianism

Utopianism is a capacious concept; it includes broad descriptions of states of mind as well as narrow ideas about strictly Morean fictions. Commentators in one breath discuss literary works, experimental communities, and political programs. Even the simplest distinctions, for example, between fiction and nonfiction or between utopia and utopian, prove contestable, so that it requires broad reading and some courage to venture categorizations.

In fact, Frank Manuel and Fritzie Manuel, authors of the monumental *Utopian Thought in the Western World,* discourage scholars from "polluting utopia's natural environment with an excess of clarity and definition."[15] Nevertheless, works attempting to classify utopianism have offered critical conceptual frameworks; readers must only keep in mind that categories are flexible and boundaries porous.[16]

Historical classifications have offered valuable distinctions based on the content of narratives. Writing on utopian literature of the early modern period, J. C. Davis has defined five "modes" by considering the content of utopias and determining how the texts portray the distribution of resources in order to satisfy human desires.[17] The arcadia, for instance, posits a benevolent nature that easily supplies human appetites, which are moderate. In dreams like the medieval "Land of Cockaygne," by contrast, appetites are enormous and sensual satisfactions correspondingly opulent. The millennial vision offers a deus-ex-machina who satisfies a group's desire for salvation; the perfect moral commonwealth, however, accepts real-world social and political arrangements and imagines a society becoming harmonized through the moral reformation of individuals. All these differ from utopia proper, argues Davis, which is more "realistic" in acknowledging the human problem of "limited satisfactions exposed to unlimited wants." The utopia offers a plan of "a total social environment" that will contain the resulting social discord.[18]

Eighteenth-century utopias might also be viewed in terms of human desires and the means to satisfy them, although the change of times brings about a change in the perception of human needs. By the mid-eighteenth century, Britain had achieved greater political stability and was emerging as a formidable economic and colonial power. Until recently that was a reason for ignoring the period's utopian texts; scholars generally concurred with A. L. Morton that "utopian literature reached its lowest level in England during the eighteenth century," largely because the significance of utopian thought was seen to depend on its ties to political revolution and social upheaval. Commentators instead focused on texts surrounding the English Civil War and the French Revolution. Gregory Claeys, however, has shown the profit of studying British Enlightenment utopias, which often reveal views more radical than those expressed in political pamphlets. He argues that the expansion of commercial society led utopian writers to seek a "moral, religious and political order based upon rational social control."[19] Christine Rees concurs, suggesting that the period's utopian texts are united by "the dream of an environment under creative control, programmed to produce not only wonders, but also practical analysis of the working of society in eighteenth-century Britain."[20] An increase both in luxury and the desire for wealth led to a national debate about how to return to virtue and simplicity, and many utopian texts offered comprehensive depictions of more modest, less chaotic societies. For this purpose many utopian authors employed the traditional plot of utopian fiction: A voyager happens upon a distant land, is shown the customs and organization of the country, and then comes home to tell his people about it.

That common plot has generally been interpreted as a mode of critique, a way of viewing political and social systems from the outside and opening readers' minds to change. But scholars have also pointed to the ways in which such a plot can actually have a less radical function. Amy Boesky considers early modern utopias to be "founding fictions," stories that may represent various political perspectives but work to institute Englishness and the English nation. Lucy Sargisson goes so far as to claim that classical utopias are "profoundly conservative and repressive of difference and change."[21] Eighteenth-century feminist utopian writers did not read the tradition in such a revisionist manner, yet they altered the common plot because they saw in their changing social world opportunities for improving the lot of subalterns. As a result, their utopian visions seem unusual; they foreground themes that are subordinated in the mainstream tradition, such as love and friendship, education, and cooperation.

Because critics have sometimes casually used the terms *utopia* and *utopian* with regard to many eighteenth-century women writers, I will propose four categories to clarify how I see the field and to explain why, in *Women's Utopias,* I discuss certain texts and omit others. My study will emphasize the most comprehensive utopian visions by women, what I call "invented societies."[22] These represent something of a cross between Davis's "perfect moral commonwealth" and his "utopia" as they tackle real-world issues and depict a "total social environment," governed by law and custom, in order to figure a thriving community. Significantly, they draw on the energies of what Daniel Defoe called the "Projecting Age" to issue practical proposals for social reform.[23] Before I turn to invented societies, however, I will outline the other categories. As Davis's scheme suggests, other literary types possess utopian characteristics, but they do not represent full ideal communities. Claeys has used the term *subgenres* to describe robinsonades, dystopias, and so forth, which is a reasonable way of indicating kinship and at the same time distinguishing related genres from utopia proper.[24]

First, writings focusing on love and friendship fall into a subgenre I label "intimate utopia." That category includes the "feminotopia" identified by Mary Louise Pratt, who coined the term in order to describe women travelers' pictures of "idealized worlds of female autonomy, empowerment, and pleasure" that were inspired by the Turkish harem descriptions of Mary Wortley Montagu and evoked "an atmosphere of paganism, female erotics, and mysterious sisterhood."[25] Felicity Nussbaum brings the same term to her analysis of eighteenth-century British women's writing as she discusses travelers to the Orient, suggesting that their "utopian sites, forbidden to men's view, evoke heightened libidinal desire with homoerotic overtones." Nussbaum finds that Sarah Scott's *Millenium Hall,* with its focus on the deformed and disabled as figures for women "deformed" by patriarchal society, offers a British counterpart to the Turkish seraglio's inclusion of mutes, eunuchs, and slaves and that Scott's female community possesses an "undercurrent of homoerotic bonding," countering "conventional modes of marriage, maternity, and heterosexuality."[26]

Other intimate utopias have been identified by Moira Ferguson. She discusses the "personal polemic, or polemic of the heart" to describe a widespread feminist discourse that rejected familiar rhetorical strategies and instead sought to "subvert patriarchal domination . . . through affirming women in their support and love for one another."[27] Writings associated with this group include Delarivier Manley's description of the New Cabal in *The New Atalantis* (1709) and Eliza Haywood's *The British Recluse; or, The Secret History of Cleomira* (1722), which concludes with two women living together "in a perfect Tranquility, happy in the real Friendship of each other."[28] Still others are Jane Barker's writings on friendship in *Poetical Recreations* (1688), from which poems appear in the later *A Patch-Work Screen for the Ladies* (1723) and also *The Lining of the Patch-Work Screen* (1726); Aphra Behn's love poetry; Sarah Fyge Egerton's friendship poems (1703) and those by Anne Finch (1710s); friendship letters between Bluestockings; and Eleanor Butler's journals from Llangollen Vale (1785–1821), which describe her love for and life with her partner, Sarah Ponsonby, in Wales.[29]

These intimate utopias differ in significant ways from the societies I will discuss. For one thing, they often focus on a single instance of female friendship, and even though that loving relationship is viewed as an idealized representation of women's desire and satisfaction in general, the representation does not go on to suggest modes of restructuring community, of coordinating social economy in order to allow for female bonding, thereby to undermine patriarchy. Even Cavendish's *Convent of Pleasure* and Manley's *New Atalantis,* which contain representations of groups of women rather than single partnerships, emphasize the erotic to the exclusion of socioeconomic and organizational elements (and in any case the texts call into question the extent to which women can succeed at cohabiting). Instead, I will consider visions such as that described by Mary Astell (chapter 1). She expresses love for her friend, Lady Catherine Jones, comparable to that found in intimate utopias, yet that love is intended to be multiplied in the monastery of her *Serious Proposal,* a project that suggests ways women's feelings for one another, joined with the need for education and spiritual development, might be converted into a working plan for community and mutual empowerment. The single instance becomes the pattern for an integrated whole.[30]

Second, in addition to intimate utopias are educational utopias that offer plans for systematizing women's learning. Mary Astell's *Serious Proposal* has been suggested as the most salient example of this type, although many women harbored utopian hopes well before her, as Anna Maria van Schurman in *De Ingenii Muliebris* (1641), translated in 1659 as *The Learned Maid; or, Whether a Maid May Be a Scholar;* Bathsua Makin's *An Essay to Revive the Antient Education of Gentlewomen* (1673); and Hannah Woolley's *The Gentlewomans Companion* (1673).[31] The charity school movement elicited many plans for educating poor girls, and the increasing number of boarding schools for the middle classes inspired Sarah Fielding's *The Governess; or, Little Female Academy* (1749). All of Sarah Scott's writings concern education, which gives form to her utopian communities and guarantees their perpetuation. That is especially true of *Millenium Hall* (1762) and *Sir George Ellison* (1766) but appears in milder versions in *The History of Cornelia* (1751), *A Journey through Every Stage of Life* (1754), and *The Test of Filial Duty* (1772) as well. The centerpiece of Mary Hamilton's *Munster Village* (1778) is an artists' colony. I will discuss the texts by Scott and Hamilton as invented societies; education forms a central part of their plans, but it is not the only focus.

By contrast, Clara Reeve's *Plans of Education; with Remarks on the Systems of Other Writers* (1792) epitomizes the educational utopia because it concentrates on that single theme. The central correspondent, Mrs. Darnford, describes how educational institutions—seminaries, schools of industry, and girls' academies—will help Britain approach the ideal of "Utopia," which is envisioned as "a well regulated state" characterized by "a right and true subordination . . . where every order is kept in its proper state, and none is allowed to encroach upon, or oppress another."[32] Mrs. Darnford worries that history will prove cyclical and British civilization will "return to ignorance and barbarism" unless education staves off regression (27–28). She describes, for example, how a women's community runs a female seminary. The job of each member is listed, costs are calculated, uniforms will vary according to social rank, penalties and rewards will be offered, mail will be inspected, and the steering committee will meet every Monday at 10 A.M. (130). Her plans may represent "windmill schemes," Mrs. Darnford muses with reference to Don Quixote; nonetheless, she cites with energetic approval the projects of

Sarah Trimmer and Mrs. Scriven, successful institutions in Shrewsbury and Essex, as well as Madame de Maintenon's earlier school at St. Cyr (63, 100, 198). Although at one point a friend of Mrs. Darnford's expresses the desire to "build myself a neighborhood" along the lines of the utopian novel *Shenstone Green* (128), Reeve's text never fully represents such a plan of community. Her educational utopia is instead limited to schemes that will strengthen the nation by teaching morality and citizenship to its future subjects.[33]

A third type of women's utopian expression in the period is anti-utopian satire, a significant subgenre of traditional utopias as well. Delarivier Manley's *New Atalantis* (1709), Eliza Haywood's *Memoirs of a Certain Island Adjacent to the Kingdom of Utopia* (1725), and her *Adventures of Eovaai, Princess of Ijaveo* (1736) fit into this category. To be sure, these texts consider larger social questions—unlike most of the utopias of intimacy and education—and, as Claeys points out, the distance between satire and program can be "curiously close."[34] They concentrate on ridicule and scandal, however, over the society-building impulse. Haywood's *Eovaai* may contain a favorable representation of a republic, the land of Oozoff, and it suggests that a monarch should respond directly to the people, showing the dystopian results of government by an evil prince. Although these moments are significant and interesting, they are overwhelmed by the larger satirical and fantastical elements of the work, more concerned to criticize existing conditions and individual political figures than to imagine new possibilities.

Fourth, invented societies foreground the establishment of a viable mode of group life involving family, friends, neighborhood, and community. Plans for such complete societies are the visions that are central to my investigation. They take into account the full range of human needs—material, economic, emotional, intellectual, and spiritual; they construct environments, beautiful and efficient, that are to foster happiness and convenience; they posit social, economic, and emotional systems that are to offer fulfilling human ties; and they establish means to perpetuate the society. Even though these communities are concerned with education and emotional relationships, and even though the texts sometimes contain satirical passages, as in the other subgenres, their authors seek first and foremost to represent a world that offers satisfactions in many areas and for whole groups of people, and they delineate how that world can be instituted within their own. Invented societies are, therefore, the most comprehensive women's utopian type and at the same time restricted in number by the very compass of their vision. I will show how Sarah Fielding, Sarah Scott, and Mary Hamilton adapted the vision of Mary Astell to retheorize the position of women in profound ways, in particular reconceiving contractual relations in both economic and political terms to create a place for women as subjects (chapters 3, 4, and 5). I also consider the writings of Jeanne Marie Leprince de Beaumont and Sophie von La Roche, who imitated the British models and also brought an international emphasis to their societies (chapter 6). This all-encompassing form of utopia is initially to be seen in British texts because it depended for its articulation on new commercial relationships and corresponding political, legal, and social ideas, and those developments took place earlier in Britain than elsewhere (chapter 2).

Challenging the Traditional Utopian Pattern

Female utopists responded to the profound political, economic, and social shifts of the eighteenth century: the rise of parliamentary politics, the expansion of commerce and international trade, corresponding shifts in ideas about human psychology, education, and the family, along with related changes in notions of fiction. Pressed by economic necessity and feminist ideas, women writers exploited the openings offered by such changes to create their reproductive or replicative utopian model. In the process, they veered from the classical pattern of utopian narrative established by Thomas More's *Utopia* and perpetuated in eighteenth-century novels such as Simon Berington's *Signior Gaudentio di Lucca,* Robert Paltock's *Peter Wilkins,* and Francis Gentleman's *Trip to the Moon.* It is worth noting that I contrast the innovative utopias of some female authors with traditional utopias rather than create a general opposition between male and female-authored texts. Such a distinction would be unjustifiable because classical utopias were largely written by men, but not all men wrote strictly traditional utopias.[35] Even the works of Berington, Paltock, and Gentleman show responses to social changes; they repeatedly fell back on the patriarchal character of the traditional model, however, because it served their purposes. The feminist utopists discussed here could not make headway through the traditional form and therefore more readily registered socioeconomic changes in their narratives than did their colleagues. Consequently, the differences between classical utopias and the innovations of the female authors in Part 2 express not only the degree to which women are attuned to their environment but also women's ideological distance from their predecessors. Such differences, which can be read in representations of geography, history, ritual, institutions, psychology, and mapping, are easily enumerated.

Alterations in geography are at first sight the most substantial discrepancy. The stories of feminist utopian authors take place right at home, whether in Cornwall, the "pleasantest part of Lincolnshire," or Bordeaux. Even upstate New York—certainly exotic to European readers—was a real place as opposed to a fanciful no place such as Mezorania or Noibla.[36] At a time when travel and tourism were becoming more common, women's familiar terrain, physically and mentally accessible to average readers, demonstrated the extent to which women writers were determined to embed their stories in the political and social environment, to contribute to contemporary debate. The distance to utopia, these authors suggest, need not be far, and social change is within the power of individuals, even those of modest means.

The creation of utopia implies individuals' cooperative effort; it depends upon the participation of a number of people over a period of time. Sarah Scott, for example, shows how inhabitants appear at Millenium Hall one by one, presenting their individual biographies and explaining how they complete one project after another, thereby bringing society gradually to the "now" of the novel. They also make plans for the future, and when they reappear in the sequel, *Sir George Ellison,* it is made clear that gradual growth and accommodation to circumstances express their attitude toward time and change. Similarly, Sarah Fielding's David Simple wanders around London and slowly gathers people who will form his little society, the girls in *The Governess* take turns documenting their moral and physical arrival at Mrs. Teachum's academy, and Mary Hamilton's Munster Village is created and inhabited.[37]

By contrast, ancient tomes, perennial institutions, and repeated rituals ground authority in classical utopias. History is enshrined; it need not be rewritten but only celebrated. In Henry Neville's *Isle of Pines,* the Prince produces the sacred historical tome itself. Written by the founder and passed down from one ruler to the next, it describes the beginnings of the island's civilization.[38] Before Signior Gaudentio arrives in Mezorania he is told the ancient origins of its special traditions and customs. In Robert Paltock's *Peter Wilkins,* the old priest's prophecy is pronounced "twelve times in the Year, on particular Days, in the Moucherat [assembly], that the People might learn it by heart."[39] This holy revelation predicts the coming of a savior, one who turns out to be none other than Peter Wilkins, the narrator himself. Myths of origin are acknowledged through ritual; symbolic practices lend a sense of timelessness to the state.

Traditional utopias dwell on symbols and signs. Clothing, gestures, and symbols legitimate the disciplinary power of the state; they regiment the society by identifying people, by molding behavior and regulating desire, and by distinguishing those who hold power from those who do not.[40] Wearing these signs and participating in these practices, the individual is a walking manifestation of the power of the country, a state at once ideal and immutable. Mezoranians in Berington's *Signior Gaudentio,* for example, abide by severe sumptuary laws that prove especially strict for women. Female inhabitants must sew moons onto their robes not only to indicate instability but also to represent their stage of life. A new moon signals youth, a full moon midlife, and a waning moon old age. Women in the line of succession must wear a mark "to shew they were never to succeed to the *Popharship* or Regency, till there should be no Male Issue of the others at Age to govern."[41] Further, they must wear flowers to represent their association with men. Virgins being courted receive tight buds, women considering marriage sport more open flowers, and those engaged to marry present flowers that are fully bloomed out. Once they have appeared in public with a flower in full bloom women cannot change their minds: "If any dislike should happen after that, they are to be shut up, never to have any Husband" (244).

Women must quite literally bear the weight of these symbolic practices. In Gentleman's Noibla, an immigrant countess persuades a fashion-minded young girl to alter her standard-issue robe and is sentenced, "without Hope of Redemption, to the Valley of Weeping." When a woman meets a man she must participate in a prescribed ceremony: "the Man holds his Hand over the Female's Head, without touching, and says, *May Virtue and Constancy ever flourish:*—To which she replies, her Right Hand pointing to her Left Breast, *With Love and Obedience.*"[42] Such eighteenth-century reinscriptions of the traditional utopian pattern demonstrate nostalgia for the ideals of patriarchal order, whether they form part of a straightfaced representation, as in the case of Berington, or one containing satirical elements, such as Gentleman's.

Traditional utopias thus rely on the pressure of infrastructure to fashion ideal citizens; they feed skepticism about human nature and assume the need to curb its excesses through institutions. Courts of justice and other forms of discipline encourage certain kinds of behavior while discouraging others. In Berington's Mezorania, "a Company of young Men together" cannot travel alone "without grave Men and Persons in Authority along with them, who are a Guard to them in all their Actions: Nay, they are never suffer'd to lye together, each lying in a single Bed, tho' in a publick Room, with some grave Person in the same Room with them. Their Women are kept much in the same manner" (219–20). Berington fears that adolescent sexuality will bring on the decline of the state.

One might be inclined to attribute Berington's concern for strict surveillance to his vocation as Catholic priest, but it proves an equally important characteristic in playwright Francis Gentleman's Noibla. There a theater is designed so that "every Person is partitioned from his Neighbour, and so situated as to be in full View of the Namredal [magistrate], whose superintending Eye always commands strict Decorum" (94). (This plan appeared a full two decades before Jeremy Bentham's Panopticon or Claude Ledoux's utopian architectural drawings—all projects that sought efficient systems of surveillance and behavior control.)[43] Further, this magisterial Namredal presides at hearings where his authority is similarly theatrically supported. Like a priest in a confessional, he remains invisible behind a silk screen, and from there his disembodied judicial voice pronounces punishment or pardon. Infractions of the law in Paltock's Doorpt Swangeanti result in "slitting," that is, cutting people's wings so they are unable to fly. Such careful regulation thus prevents or punishes undesirable behavior as patriarchal figures, both literally and metaphorically above their people, ensure that some activities take place and others do not. Human actions are to be directed institutionally, from the outside.

In feminist utopias, human behavior is guided not by external forces but from within. Women writers invoke new psychological and educational theories, like those of John Locke, and use fiction, conversation, and play for behavior modification.[44] Such an approach suggests not only new ideas about subjectivity and individual responsibility but also attention to what the occasion demands rather than rigid adherence to a determined system. It is an attitude equally evident in these women's ideas about organizing their utopian communities. Form follows function in *Millenium Hall* and in other female-authored utopias. The purpose and growth of the community spur how structures are built, gardens laid out, and schools created. Mrs. Bilson, in Sarah Fielding's *Countess of Dellwyn,* considers how she can help the community and how the people can then help each other.[45] In *Millenium Hall,* when one community does not suffice for the women who desire to join, they start another; when their numbers grow too large, the women purchase another house in the area.[46] No master plan governs in *Millenium Hall;* instead, the women tackle each problem or project according to the needs and circumstances of the moment.[47]

Traditional utopias—with fully mapped towns characterized by geometry, balance, and repetition—could hardly be more different. Like the cities in More's *Utopia,* Mezoranian towns are all constructed on the same design ("in Imitation of the Sun and its Rays") with the advantage that the seat of power, located at the center, remains consistently in view of the populace and affords the sovereign a central surveillance point (168–73). In Francis Gentleman's *Trip to the Moon,* we are to admire "the extremely neat Regularity of the Streets, and the uniform Compactness of the Houses" (1:103), and in Paltock's Doorpt Swangeanti "the Figure of the City is a direct Square" that has two main avenues running perpendicularly through it and a circle at its center. Gentleman even supplies a diagram (315). Traditional utopias in eighteenth-century England provide total pictures of thoroughly systematized cities.

In classical utopias a leader must initiate social change by decree. That reflects the patriarchal politics dominating the traditional model, where power moves from God to the divine right sovereign. Women's utopias, however, reinforce new concepts of power and identity and thus foreground concerns about the relationship of individuals to each other, to the family, and to the state. Eighteenth-century female authors emphasize Lockean theories of authority, education, and human personality while they embrace Scottish enlightenment notions of morality and economics. By participating in commerce, both social and economic, the utopian subject will increase the domain of virtue. Individuals begin by reforming their own households and estates and can then move out into their neighborhoods, counties, and realms. Female utopists thus challenge the traditional pattern with representations that contain a rationale of process. Their communities have an ongoing history. They come into being and change through time, work with the personalities in the group, and spell out the continuing financial and psychic costs of their creation.

The impact of the evolving literary marketplace can be read in feminist utopian texts as well. One factor that allowed for the expression of feminist utopianism was a new understanding of fiction that recognized the uneasy position it occupied between the poles of lying and truth-telling. Catherine Gallagher has traced this development, explaining that although the identifying mark of the eighteenth-century novel (following Watt) was its "formal realism," this verisimilitude "was not a way of trying to hide or disguise fictionality; realism was, rather, understood to be fiction's formal sign. Eighteenth-century readers identified with the characters in novels *because* of the characters' fictiveness and not in spite of it."[48] Gallagher links the new understanding of fiction and the eagerness to embrace novelistic narratives to the developments I have mentioned in eighteenth-century life: the far-reaching effects of the financial revolution, new ideas of sovereignty, and the expansion of middle-class interests as well as the appearance of women writers as an important force in the literary marketplace. As did the general public with its growing faith in paper money and other forms of credit, women writers recognized the power that might be harnessed by invoking fictionality.

Utopian authors in particular were able to exploit this new understanding of the seemingly real for what appeared liberatory rather than purely conformist ends. They assumed that readers would comprehend an apparent reality, and yet, within its parameters, they would revel in fashioning a new one. As a variation on the domestic novel, utopia readjusted a familiar world according to women's desires for greater self-possession. As Gallagher points out, learning to read novels as fiction allowed for the creation of "new emotional dispositions," different modes of fantasizing. These could, of course, be called forth to construct wives and mothers as bourgeois subjects. But as Bridget Hill argues, women could now just as well "conceive of alternatives to their constricted existences. A fantasy world of independence, from their husbands and from the role allotted to them, began to open up."[49] The new understanding of fiction thus made space not only for creating domestic women but also for representing utopia.

Such a new perception of fictionality, and the new mental landscapes enabled by it, explains why women set their utopian novels in Britain rather than on some faraway island. Quick to exploit the possibilities of formal realism, feminist utopian authors freed their world of its modes; far from constraining their imaginations, realism allowed them to describe a society that might be. They thus innovated and offered new types of narrative utopias, whereas more conventional utopian writers until the end of the century remained tied to the traditional mechanism of the imaginary voyage. On the surface, the changes the women proposed seem minimal, perhaps insignificant compared to apparently radical dislocations such as those of Thomas More. Yet feminist utopists wished to modify socioeconomic life to include women as subjects, to retheorize toward reform rather than revolution; the modifications they imagined worked at the deep structures of everyday life. They sought a reorientation, not of political figures, ceremonies, and governments but of the places where emotional and material life met—those profound places of human interaction that scholars have only more recently begun to explore, such as love, sexuality, family life, and domestic economy.[50]

Hence a study of feminist utopias implies a redefinition of utopia in the eighteenth century, for these innovative visions were not linked to political upheaval, subversion, and radical ideology. Nor did they anticipate or describe thoroughgoing rearrangements in institutions of government, politics, or religion. Instead, they employed the new fictionality in order to anticipate deep reforms in the microeconomy of personal relationships and everyday community interaction. In that sense they redrew the horizon of the public sphere.

Utopia and the Public Sphere

Jürgen Habermas is so closely associated with the defense of utopia, the Enlightenment project, and the transformation of the public sphere that any study of eighteenth-century utopianism must take account of his ideas. While Max Horkheimer and Theodor Adorno point to the disastrous consequences of Enlightenment concepts, Habermas counters their skepticism by insisting that certain Enlightenment ideals remain worthwhile if the goal is a democratic society.[51] In *The Structural Transformation of the Public Sphere* Habermas suggests that, in fact, mid-eighteenth-century England offered a kind of golden moment in which places like coffee houses offered a space for private citizens to gain information, form opinions, and persuade others. Coffee houses represented a forum for rational-critical discourse where an overall equality held sway, where birth or status mattered less than understanding the issues of the day, issues that were debated in the press, the theater, and literature of all kinds. The free exchange of private citizens' ideas, Habermas concludes, directly influenced public policy and the workings of public authority.

Habermas's view has led to extensive critique, especially among feminists who emphasize that the realm of discussion was generally limited to propertied men.[52] But Habermas insists that the Enlightenment ideals expressed in this cultural moment—the belief in reason and rational argument, the (comparative) freedom of the press from censorship, the importance of an educated and informed public, and the right of citizens to gather and express themselves as equals—retain value, even if, as critics have underscored, historically the Enlightenment led to organized capitalism, the military-industrial state, and, ultimately, to the wars, genocide, and environmental degradation of the twentieth century. To Habermas, the Enlightenment project was not faulty, merely incomplete. Implied in his argument, therefore, and distinguishing him from many postmodernist thinkers, is affirmation of normative ideals and the role of philosophy as a critical discipline that—like the eighteenth-century coffee house—can bring together ever more specialized and disparate social discourses.[53]

Benhabib supports Habermas's model even as she adjusts it to include women and other marginalized groups—nonwhite people and the poor, for example. She argues that Enlightenment ideas about equal individuals and a free society are utopian visions to be embraced, because accepting these values will help to overcome the current sense of political alienation and bring everyone closer to real participation in a democratic community. She observes:

> The project of modernity can only be reformed from within the intellectual, moral and political resources made possible and available to us by the development of modernity on a global scale since the sixteenth century. Among the legacies of modernity which today need reconstructing but not wholesale dismantling are moral and political universalism, committed to the now seemingly "old-fashioned" and suspect ideals of universal respect for each person in virtue of their humanity; the moral autonomy of the individual; economic and social justice and equality; democratic participation; the most extensive civil and political liberties compatible with principles of justice; and the formation of solidaristic human associations.[54]

Postmodernist theory, although in many respects invigorating and refreshing for feminists, is debilitating in its strong versions, Benhabib notes. It has been salutary to reveal the coercion and illusions in Enlightenment views of the individual as a self-reflective male subject, of the grand narratives of history as progress, and of a metaphysical Archimedean point beyond contingency from which human beings can achieve objectivity. Benhabib, however, points to the dangers for feminists of taking these positions to extremes. First, disclaiming individual autonomy and agency altogether leaves feminists without the possibility of effecting social change. Second, viewing history merely as narratives collected chronologically renders meaningless the relevance of women's continuing history of real oppression. And, third, denying the possibility of critique leaves women no position from which to articulate new and fairer ways of living. Hence ideals of what Benhabib calls an "interactive universalism"—modified from Enlightenment values—are essential to feminists and cannot be discarded; namely, notions of the autonomous individual (tempered by ideas of mutual recognition like those discussed by Jessica Benjamin) and a belief in the capacity for critique (not from an Archimedean point or "nowhere" but from the perspective of an other or from geographically outside).[55] These are central, Benhabib insists, to feminist efforts to achieve social, political, and economic equality.[56]

Long before Benhabib, Enlightenment women utopists promoted what would later be termed a liberal-critical perspective, even as liberal ideology was coming into being in the eighteenth century. They proceeded from a belief that aspects of Enlightenment universalism derived from natural law offered women emancipatory possibilities. Hence their feminist goals prompted them to advocate corresponding economic notions of the autonomous commercial individual, of a free market in labor and goods, of free choices of marriage partners, and of certain types of equality and self-direction, all of which I will discuss in subsequent chapters. They endorsed Benhabib's "interactive universalism" as they sought a balance between individual autonomy and recognition, expressed ideas about how history might be written, and created utopias that were not—seen from the perspective of a person at the margin—"nowhere" but somewhere.

Eighteenth-century women could not have foreseen what would be the unhappy consequences of systematic capitalist development. Instead, they directed their focus on the plight of women and other subalterns and sought ways to use emerging socioeconomic ideas, along with Christian beliefs, to propose a fairer society. It is for these reasons that women's utopias of the mid-eighteenth century appeared very different from the highly regulated cities of traditional utopists. Their ideal societies corresponded to a developing model of a constitutional monarchy and commercial economy rather than reverted to a political ideology that rested on ideas of divine right and patriarchal authority. Although women writers of the eighteenth century brought liberal-critical Enlightenment ideas to British utopian literature, that type of feminism was soon overtaken by Romantic notions of transcendence after the French Revolution. Feminism was expressed most powerfully in forms altogether nonfictional, such as those of Mary Hays's *An Appeal to the Men of Great Britain in Behalf of Women* (1798), Priscilla Wakefield's *Reflections upon the Present Condition of the Female Sex* (1798), Mary Ann Radcliffe's *The Female Advocate* (1799), and William Thompson and Anna Wheeler's *An Appeal of One Half the Human Race* (1825).[57]

Developing a Reproductive Model

The invented societies I will describe in this book propose a reproductive utopian model, reproductive not in essential biological terms but because it contains within itself the power to proliferate and replicate itself. Female authors in the eighteenth century, constrained by subaltern status, offered partial visions that multiplied into universal ones. Each writer, however, approached the idea of reproduction differently, depending upon her social position, polemical aims, Christian convictions, and nationality. Mary Astell, a serious student of philosophy and theology, theorized her plan for a female monastery in *Letters Concerning the Love of God* by linking ideas about the imitation of Christ with emerging scientific ideas of circulation (chapter 1). Although her *Serious Proposal to the Ladies* drew on profound personal love, she struggled with ways of making that love serve devout Christian purposes, both meditative and active. Her model, which sought reproduction through imitation and transcription, succeeded in influencing the feminist utopian writers of the eighteenth century.

She was followed by Sarah Fielding, Sarah Scott, and the others who wrote in a time of fundamental social change. Chapter 2 is devoted to analyzing how these writers approached dominant ideologies. I take up the work of J. G. A. Pocock, Istvan Hont, and Michael Ignatieff to show how women utopists endorsed and adjusted civic humanist and jurisprudential discourses; they also echoed notions of Thomas Hobbes, John Locke, the Earl of Shaftesbury, and the Scottish moral sense philosophers (especially Francis Hutcheson and Adam Smith). They drew simultaneously on ideas of contractual reciprocity and the language of Christian charity and responsibility. In the process, they rerouted the conceptions of social contract, laissez-faire, and the division of labor to turn trade into benevolent exchange, individualism into community, and nationalism into internationalism.

In the second half of the book I will turn to specific authors in order to demonstrate how their novels reproduced utopias, both in the sense of imitating earlier women's models and of modeling the reproduction of utopian subjects and ideas within their texts. In chapter 3, on Sarah Fielding's work, I discuss how reproduction occurs, ideally, through the education of readers. Characters gather to live in community; they hear and interpret stories as they are alternately sheltered from and exposed to a money-driven world. Occasionally, a deft female protagonist, Astell-like, finds ways of traveling between the languages of utopian and non-utopian worlds and manages to replicate her discourse. Fielding thus reveals the utopian hope behind her view of female authorship.

If reproduction is not always successful in Fielding, however, it fares better in Sarah Scott (chapter 4). Like Fielding, a friend and houseguest who greatly influenced her, Scott combined the literary and the economic, positing an ideal contractualism that set in motion an endless sequence of reformative transactions. She reconceived the contract and depicted a self-replicating and ever-expanding utopia.

Mary Hamilton (chapter 5) reproduced utopia by plagiarizing. Her theft from Daniel Defoe's *Political History of the Devil* points up the double quality of feminist utopian writing. It reinscribes received language and revises it in order to reorient readers' perceptions. Copying, to Hamilton, promoted a proliferation of morality, civility, taste, and, ultimately, democratization. She made a feminist contribution to contemporary disputes on intellectual property and populism.

I look beyond Britain in chapter 6 to discuss Jeanne Marie Leprince de Beaumont and Sophie von La Roche, assessing the extent to which they imitated the English model and furthered reproductive utopianism. Leprince de Beaumont's *The New Clarissa* rewrote Richardson's *Clarissa* and Rousseau's *New Heloise* and at the same time represented an original contribution to French debates about depopulation. Sexual reproduction gave way to textual duplication as protagonists moved from promoting women's maternal role in increasing France's population to arguing the instrumentality of women in discourses of national reform. La Roche, for her part, depicted the construction of an ideal society on Lake Oneida in upstate New York. She reproduced an ideal reader and writer: Alexis de Tocqueville, who read her story as a boy and then sought out Lake Oneida as he traveled and conducted the research that lead to *Democracy in America*. La Roche's *Events at Lake Oneida,* an all-but-forgotten work about America written by a German woman writer influenced by the liberal sentiments of British women before her, became part of a French tome that has been hailed since its publication as a classic. Tocqueville's journey to Oneida confirmed the compelling power of utopian dreaming; argued the need to study the earlier, eighteenth-century women who engaged in it; and suggested that the influence of eighteenth-century feminist utopias reverberates in unexpected places.

By establishing the various ways in which women's utopian visions evolve into the nineteenth century, I will attempt to write women back into the history of utopian thought. Benhabib has encouraged precisely such an enquiry: "The traditional view of gender differences is the discourse of those who have won out and who have codified history as we know it. But what would the history of ideas look like from the standpoint of the victims? What ideals, aspirations and utopias of the past ran into a dead-end? Can we recapture their memory from the battleground of history?"[58] *Women's Utopias* is a contribution to this larger revision of history. By incorporating women's utopian writing within the group of texts through which we have traditionally surveyed the history of Europe, we must inevitably alter our understanding of that history.

PART 1

Defining Feminist Utopianism

1. Mary Astell's "Excited Needles": Imitation, Circulation, and a Theory of Feminist Utopia

All true Lovers of GOD being like excited Needles, which cleave not only to him their *Magnet,* but even to one another.
—Mary Astell, *Letters Concerning the Love of God*

This passage reveals Mary Astell in the manner of a metaphysical poet, bringing together ideas of a soul's heavenly and earthly attachments through a surprising scientific conceit, the figure of charged pins, compass needles, or perhaps magnetized iron filings clinging to each other. Astell's inclination to look to the past for literary models, as well as her conservative social outlook, patriarchal politics, and profound piety, may suggest that she is an unlikely starting place for a book on Enlightenment women's utopias. Her magnetic metaphor, however, reveals contradictory tendencies in her thought, and these tensions opened a space for her followers to adjust her theory of feminist utopia to further their own sociopolitical ends.

Astell was a High Tory who had Jacobite leanings and wrote political pamphlets that reinforced notions of divine right and complete obedience to the monarch.[1] After expressing some interest in Locke's epistemology early on, she later came to attack him on all levels, disagreeing not only with his notions of human understanding but also with his views on religion, education, and social contract. By the time she wrote *The Christian Religion, as Professed by a Daughter of the Church of England* (1705) she had fully embraced the theocentrism of John Norris; God was the sole source of the immutable truths that people with their God-given rational powers must seek to discern. Nonetheless, her influence on eighteenth-century feminists, whose political and philosophical views departed significantly from hers, was profound.

Ruth Perry, in her groundbreaking biography *The Celebrated Mary Astell,* suggests that this influence can be traced across generations of eighteenth-century female intellectuals. She points out, for instance, how Astell cultivated a friendship with the young Lady Mary Wortley Montagu, whose Whig politics and elevated rank placed her on the opposite end of the social spectrum but whose lively intellect, vast knowledge, and literary talents attracted Astell. Astell in effect chose Montagu as her successor in "female wit." She insisted on writing a preface to Montagu's *Turkish Letters* even though Montagu would only arrange to have the travel correspondence published posthumously, decades later in the 1760s. Moreover, the many links between Astell and the later Bluestockings, Perry argues, "substantiate the claim that they were carrying forward a tradition she began."[2] I wish to reinforce that claim by delineating a pattern of utopian thought among a group of women writers associated with the Bluestocking circle. They articulated feminist aims through visions of ideal societies, echoing Astell and, at the same time motivated by changing political, economic, and social pressures and circumstances, composing variations on her model.

Astell's pivotal contribution was *A Serious Proposal to the Ladies, for the Advancement of Their True and Greatest Interest* (1694), which gave Englishwomen a vision of a female monastery that, Astell hoped, would not only "amend the present and improve the future Age" but also recreate a "*Paradise* as your Mother *Eve* forfeited."[3] Astell's imagination, colorful language, and forceful arguments inspired readers to action. "A great lady," perhaps Princess Anne of Denmark herself, was prepared to sponsor the plan, and Bishop Gilbert Burnet initially expressed approval.[4] Daniel Defoe responded with his own outline for a women's academy, and Mary Wortley Montagu wrote later that Astell's monastery "was a favorite Scheme of mine when I was fiveteen, and had I then been mistriss of an Independant fortune, would certainly have executed it and elected my selfe Lady Abbess." The idea found its way into fiction as well. In *Sir Charles Grandison,* Samuel Richardson's protagonist argues in favor of a Protestant nunnery; in Samuel Johnson's *Rasselas,* the Princess Nekayah wishes to "found a college of learned women"; and in *Millenium Hall* and *Sir George Ellison,* Sarah Scott offers the fullest fictional realizations of Astell's dream.[5]

Perry calls *Millenium Hall* "an imaginative fulfillment of Mary Astell's first book." Moira Ferguson concurs, adding that Sarah Scott's communal life with her friend Lady Barbara Montagu represented "one of the most successful, practical implementations of Astell's educational proposal." Betty Rizzo has also detailed the Hitcham Community experiment planned by Sarah Scott and Sarah Fielding and later put in practice by Scott, Elizabeth Cutts, Mrs. Arnold, and Grace Freind.[6]

In 1770 a contribution to the *Public Ledger* "by a Lady . . . who wishes to see the sex become more useful members of the community" called for "an unexceptionable Female Coterie." The author described a learned society for "ladies in every situation of life," married or single, headed by a governess and financed by subscription but "not intended to be so expensive, as to exclude the middling class." The meetings would include lectures "on religious subjects, morals, history, or manners," and each member would "provide books, globes, musical instruments, or painting utensils" with the aim of "improving the mind, and mending the heart" to achieve a "universal philanthropy."[7] Astell's vision thus retained its allure and inspired new projects throughout the eighteenth century.

As she composed the *Serious Proposal to the Ladies,* Astell exchanged letters with the Rev. John Norris, and their correspondence was later published as *Letters Concerning the Love of God* (1695). The exchange offers important clues to the sources of Astell's renowned project; indeed, her letters reveal how she reconciled her love of God and women to create a theory of women's community. She melded diverse ideas about the imitation of Christ with scientific notions of circulation, and her female utopia consequently posited a system of emulation that pervaded her writing. Astell's interest in primitive Christianity and early devotional practice led to her theoretical links among imitation, transcription, and community, ideas which, in turn, laid the groundwork for the reproductive model that characterized eighteenth-century women's utopianism.

Astell was, of course, not original in tying her educative project to notions of imitation; not only Christian but also classical authors had treated the subject extensively. Imitation pervaded ethical and rhetorical discourses, appearing in Plato and Aristotle, reemerging in medieval and early modern rhetorical treatises, and entering the realm of women's conduct and education, notably through Christine de Pizan's *The Book of the City of Ladies* (1404).[8] Astell would have been inspired by Christine's call for edification (*aedificare,* to build), the summons to "take the trowel of your pen" and erect a city filled with all of history's good women by writing a legendary, thereby creating a place where a mother sets "a good example of integrity and learnedness" for her daughter and all are encouraged "to cultivate virtue, to flee vice, to increase and multiply our City, and to rejoice and act well."[9] Encouragement to learn from and imitate virtuous female models was furthered in the seventeenth century by Thomas Heywood in *The Generall History of Women* (1657), which asked "what properer object can there be of women's emulation than the deeds of other famous women."[10] And, like Christine, Heywood created a catalog that is simultaneously a descriptive history as well as an instructive project.

Commentators from the beginning, however, recognized the potential pitfalls of imitation.[11] Viewed from the ethical angle, the transformative power of imitation depended entirely on the quality of the model; a bad example could only produce an undesirable outcome. J. C. Davis has argued that Thomas More actually penned *Utopia* in order to curtail imitation because that would combat the sin of pride in an increasingly competitive sociopolitical environment. More thus became a forerunner of Hobbes, seeing in Henry's court and in Tudor society in general a growing self-interest among people who attempt to outvie each other through emulation. "In More's hands, the utopian exercise was one in the construction of an alternative milieu—one which blocks emulation and forces pride to wither."[12]

Emulation of prideful, self-interested subjects would thus only expand the force and grip of deadly sin. Considered from the rhetorical perspective, imitation inevitably raised the question of plagiarism. Although most thinkers felt that, for purposes of education, copying illustrious models was crucial, they were also compelled to justify doing so because it smacked of another sin—theft. In his influential *On the Sublime,* for example, Longinus encouraged authors to imitate "the great prose writers and poets of antiquity" and yet protested that "such a proceeding is not theft; it is like obtaining a pattern from beautiful forms or images or other works of art."[13] In the eighteenth century, Samuel Johnson took his cue from thinkers like Longinus to express a widely supported view: Emulation was necessary for writers to improve, and many poetic ideas had become commonplaces, so accusations of plagiarism were often unfounded. "No writer can be fully convicted of imitation, except there is a concurrence of more resemblances than can be imagined to have happened by chance; as where the same ideas are conjoined without any natural series or necessary coherence, or where not only the thought but the words are copied."[14] Questions of plagiarism and imitation were debated more vigorously in the eighteenth century as the controversy over copyright and proto-Romantic ideas about originality gained ground.[15]

Astell recognized the problems associated with the bad examples that secular life offers; she shunned worthless husbands as unsatisfactory models, and she attacked the emulation of French "Fashions and Fopperies."[16] Determined to perfect a religious project that would make an irreproachable Christian paragon available to women, she focused on the power of spiritual instruction that imitation can afford. In contrast to More and others, Astell the feminist did not worry, in the context of the female monastery, about the undue assertion of self or the charge of stealing self-expression. She concerned herself with allowing what she deemed a true female self to emerge in the first place.

Later, in keeping with Astell's example, feminist utopists chose to view imitation not in a rhetorical or philosophical vein but in an encompassing Christian, charitable, educational, and communitarian context. While they adapted questions of imitation to a changing economy that involved women in new ways, they conceived narratives that doubled as their own serious proposals articulated by Astell-like paragons who used Astellian language and displayed Astellian verve as a way of establishing communities that allow for the emergence of female subjectivity. Furthermore, Astell's turn to the genre of the project, which had Whiggish connotations, opened her discourse to the more progressive political uses to which her followers put it. In the female monastery she imagined nothing less than a reconfiguration of power, viewing power not only as directed vertically from an omnipotent God but also as mutually and horizontally exchanged among women. In effect, her feminism compromised her absolutism. Astell's ideal society thus paved the way for women writers to posit a new and liberal utopia even as it answered their desire to return to primitive Christianity in an increasingly secular society.

Scholars have noted the utopian quality of Astell's female monastery, but they have not recognized the extent to which she was a self-conscious utopian thinker. Astell's was a deeply conceived utopianism that constituted the core of her feminism: Women achieve subjectivity and independence in the context of an ideal society in which they do not assert identity but model themselves after each other, transcribing the copies of heavenly originals they experience around them. In the process, metaphysical and physical realms are joined; Astell conceived a system that integrated emotional impulses and the needs of the mind. In the *Letters Concerning the Love of God,* she asked John Norris searching questions on passion and charity, questions that show her generating the theory behind her female monastery. In the end, Astell, a fierce advocate of platonic love, magnified that passion with the power conveyed through the figure of the absolute; the perfect love of God issued in power, love, and subjectivity for women of the utopian community.

Historians and literary critics have noted Astell's interest in passion and power, but they have paid less attention to the interaction of the two in her thought. Instead, they have concentrated on only one of these issues at a time, as though they were regarding a picture of a duck-rabbit and, seeing the one, would not distinguish the other although it was made up of the same lines. For instance, Astell's love of women is said to fuel her proposal for a female monastery and animate her writing on marriage and its discontents. Perry concludes that "the energy of her feminism" lies in Astell's feelings about women's "*sensible* Beauty," which, as Astell said in Letter III of the *Letters Concerning the Love of God,* "does too often press upon my Heart, whilst *in-*

telligible is disregarded." Perry suggests that Astell, in projects and writings on women's education, reshaped her love "into a more benevolent, serviceable, and universal form."[17]

Hilda Smith also refers to "the bases in personal affection of her feminist concerns."[18] She writes that Astell's love, combined with her other enthusiasms, sparked her notion for a women's college. Smith refers in particular to one passage from the preface of *Letters Concerning the Love of God,* in which Astell expressed admiration for Lady Catherine Jones. She described the state of excitement that praying near Jones brought on:

> I myself have observed in her so much Sweetness and Modesty, so free from the least Tincture of Vanity, so insensible of that Worth which all the World admires; such a constant and regular Attendance on the publick Worship of GOD, Prayers and Sacraments; such a serious, reverent and unaffected Devotion, so fervent and so prudent, so equally composed of Heat and Light, so removed from all Formality, and the Extremes of Coldness and Enthusiasme, as gave me a lively Idea of Apostolical Piety, and made me every Time I prayed by her, fancy my self in the Neighbourhood of Seraphick Flames! But—my Expressions are too flat, my Colours too dead to draw such a lovely Piece![19]

Considering this passage, Smith concludes that "the image of the two women praying together was not wholly spiritual. There was emotional excitement welding together Astell's love for her friend, her sex, her religion, and the newly discovered wonders of scholarship that does much to explain her early feminist thought and plans. A female college would combine all these things. . . . Such study in such company would more than adequately substitute for all other satisfactions that people sought in life."[20] "Emotional excitement" connects Astell's various passions and interests. Both Smith's and Perry's responses to her writings therefore suggest that emotional energy, love, represents the sustaining element of her feminism and feminist project.[21]

By contrast, Catherine Gallagher has pointed to mind rather than emotion, and to the absolutist imagination in particular, as the key to Astell's feminism. As a staunch Tory with Jacobite leanings, Astell looks to the figure of the absolute monarch for a representation of female subjectivity.[22] Women are Cartesian selves subjected to but simultaneously mentally coextensive with a divine-right monarch deriving his powers from God: "The mind for Astell becomes the real self. . . . The figure of the monarch is not called upon to unify or subdue a potentially anarchic assemblage of parts of the self, but is rather the earthly representative of the absolute that underlies all self-consistency. . . . the absolute (both God and monarch) is the necessary foundation for each individual subjectivity. Rational subjectivity, and hence individuality, comes into being only by subjection to the absolute Supreme Being."[23] Gallagher rightly points to rationality as the locus for women's identity in Astell, who argued that reason infuses human beings with divinity. Thus she emphasized attention to education and the development of women's rational faculties. Such education would make women the absolute selves imagined and created by God. With a similar focus Patricia Springborg locates the *Serious Proposal* in a context of works on women's academies and, focusing on the *Serious Proposal, Part II,* on philosophical debates about cognition.[24] Perry observes that "the starting place for Astell's feminism" was "a belief in an immaterial intellect which had no gender but was an essential feature of all human nature."[25]

Hence Mary Astell's feminism sprang from reason, according to one view, or from passion, according to another. I do not propose to argue against either—both have compelling aspects—but want to demonstrate the constant, complex interaction between emotion and rationality in Astell's feminism and how she integrated desire into her largely platonic view. I will consider questions of love and power in her writings and suggest that a careful reading of *Letters Concerning the Love of God* shows how Astell theorized her well-known *Serious Proposal to the Ladies,* her plan for a female monastery, and the impact that had on *A Serious Proposal, Part II.* In these works Astell arrived at a means of achieving simultaneously her mental, spiritual, and romantic ambitions. It was a utopian resolution.

* * *

When John Norris asked permission to publish their correspondence as *Letters Concerning the Love of God,* Astell agreed but on two conditions: first, that her name be withheld, and, second, that the work be dedicated to her friend, Lady Catherine Jones. The *Letters* discuss the love owed to God and the love that can rightly be given others. Astell had read Norris's *Discourses* and, perceiving an inconsistency in his argument, she wrote to him in 1693. Norris, impressed with her astute thinking, encouraged further correspondence that continued for most of the next year. He sought to publish the letters for a number of reasons. Their subject interested him and would, he thought, certainly interest others; they were written, surprisingly, by a woman; and, most of all, he felt they demonstrated the progress of a soul from uncertainty to a sure and undivided love of God. There was something novel as well as instructive in them, and they might help others come to a realization he considered of paramount importance: They owed all love to their Creator. This was Norris's main point, and he reiterated it throughout the *Letters.*

Historians, however, have focused on the *Letters* less for their theological and philosophical content than for the forthright manner in which Astell expressed love for another woman.[26] She asked Norris's advice about it, saying she was experiencing a "disorder." What she perceived as problematical, though, was not the fact that she loved a *woman* but that she *loved* a woman. In other words, Astell worried not about sexual orientation but about her inability to carry out Norris's injunction to love God only. And while Norris presumably published the letters because he felt Astell had come to an acceptable resolution to her crisis, and while Astell felt comfortable with the outcome, it is worth considering the dynamic of the resolution and the way it exposed the connections among Astell's philosophical ideas, the love she had for her friend, and her hope for women's empowerment. Her utopian conclusions took her far beyond Norris's instruction.

One of Norris's primary concerns in publishing the *Letters* was to encourage rather than discourage passionate feelings. Although love should not be divided between God and any earthly creation or "creature," that does not mean one ought to stifle desire or thwart passion. Instead, one must reroute it in God's direction. Norris felt that publishing the correspondence would stir readers to do just that. So, with another letter to Astell, he persuaded her to agree to publication. He sought to use not only the compelling nature of her arguments but also the warmth of her language to incite the ardor of readers toward God:

> For (as many Discourses as there are upon the Subject) to my Knowledge I never met with any that have so inlightened my Mind, inlarged my Heart, so entered and took Possession of my Spirit, and have had such a general and commanding Influence over my whole Soul as these of yours. And I question not but that they would have the same Effect upon other Readers if they were but exposed to their View, and would help to fan and blow up that divine Fire which our Saviour came to kindle upon Earth, but which the Neglect of careless Men has let almost go out. And indeed never was there more need of such warm quickning Discourses than in this cold frozen Age of ours, wherein the Flame of divine Love seems not only to burn with a blue expiring Light, but to hang loose and hovering, just ready to fly away and be extinct. (a6v–a7)

Norris's concern, then, was to circulate Astell's overabundant passion, warm others with the heat of Catherine Jones's "Seraphick Flames," and ensure that the fire was then directed toward God.

Astell agreed to the publication and argued that she had understood Norris's point, that she had learned her desire could not be directed "towards her I love" (50). Seeing the correspondence as a way of making "Progress towards a Cure" (51), she asks readers to believe that she has achieved it in the end, but the personal testimony to her newfound knowledge in Letter V suggests that what Norris demanded was not easy. She explained how one must stifle desire in order to concentrate on God: "Indeed if we allow the Creature to be in any degree our good, 'tis hard to keep our selves from desiring it, and if we permit Desire, we can never be secure from irregular [i.e., excessive] Love, that Shame and Misery of Mankind, it being easier not to desire at all than to desire with Moderation. For Love is an insinuating Passion, and where-ever 'tis admitted, will spread and make its Way" (95–96). In Letter VII Astell further complicated the issue by raising the question of loving one's neighbor. Because the commandment says that one must love one's neighbor as oneself, she reasoned, and because the love one has for oneself is benevolent, "love of Benevolence" can be directed toward a neighbor or fellow human beings, whereas all "love of Desire" must be directed toward God, the only being capable of satisfying it.

That was Norris's position, but Astell's discussion reveals the diligence and mental exertion necessary to put the theory into practice. Can it be put into practice at all? Can we interpret the ardent language Astell used toward Catherine Jones in the preface as purely platonic and the love of benevolence rather than desire? What are we to make of the excitement at the "Seraphick Flames" and at the "lovely Piece" represented by Jones, particularly when we know that Astell searched all her life for a special friend? For Norris, love became "Seraphic" precisely because it transcends the body; for Astell, the heat of Jones's seraphic flames was physically palpable.[27]

Indeed, scholars have identified Astell's embrace of the physical as the place where she departs most emphatically, in the *Letters,* from Norris's doctrine. Perry observes, "Despite her basic agreement with Norris that God is the only efficient cause of all sensation, Astell continued to be uneasy with the way Norris dismissed the world." Astell conveyed something approaching a Lockean epistemology as she attempted to give "the senses and objects of the world their due" without "giving up a belief in the ultimate causality of God." E. Derek Taylor agrees that in this period "Astell pursued her attempt to carve out a position somewhere between Norris and Locke," even though by the time she wrote *The Christian Religion, as Professed by a Daughter of the Church of England* (1705) she came to embrace fully Norris's theocentrism, realizing that "to merge soul and body via a 'Sensible Congruity' amounted to taking the first step down a slippery slope that led to Lockean conclusions."[28] It was something that, given Locke's politics, had become especially unacceptable to her. Perry and Taylor thus maintain that Astell's *Letters,* by veering toward Locke, are less representative than her later work. Her discomfort with Norris during this period emerged from the significance she attached to her own sensations.

As Perry has pointed out, Astell generalized her love, reshaping "the urge into a more benevolent, serviceable, and universal form."[29] Moreover, she came to see love as godlike and original, so her "love of desire" was transformed into love of what she termed "unmixed benevolence" that must no longer seek satisfaction because it fuels itself. Astell imagined this self-fueling love occurring with a process of imitation and replication in the context of a female monastery, a process that hinted that "something of desire," despite arguments to the contrary, remained even after Norris's lessons ended. Astell was creating a system in which, on one level at least, her desire could be satisfied.

The system began with the imitation of the divine. Astell explains her feelings for Jones in the preface by saying that "out of the Regard I owe to the glorious Author of all Perfection, I cannot but pay a very great Respect to one who so nearly resembles him" (b5v). Astell could love Jones because Jones was so close an imitation—indeed, a replication—of the divine being. In loving Jones, she was loving God. And, according to Astell, Jones's love of God was what brought about her resemblance to the divinity, for such love results in emulation and union:

> The End of Love is to unite its self to its Object, every Motion it makes is in order to that End, and since Heterogeneous Substances can never cordially unite, since without Similitude of Disposition there can be no Union, therefore Love does ever endeavour after Likeness; it would if it were possible have an Identity of Essence, and, as far as the Nature of things will admit, incorporate with the beloved Object. Hence nothing is so excellent at Imitation as Love, nothing does so easily assimilate, which by the way, is one reason why we ought not to love the World, because of the Danger of being conformed to it. If then we love GOD intirely we shall with all the Powers of our Soul endeavour to be like him, and according to the Degree of our Love, so will be the Nearness of our Resemblance. For we cannot make GOD like our selves, if therefore we desire a Union we must *be conformed to the Divine Nature.* (185–86)

Catherine Jones's great love for God created the resemblance she bore to the divinity. If Jones was a manifestation of God on earth, then Astell's love and imitation of her allowed for union even as they meant being "conformed to the Divine Nature."

Astell drew on Norris to articulate her idea of love's power to bring about resemblance and unity, but in his version love's power is a largely metaphysical force that operates in a solitary way. Although he took notice of the things of this world, they are divorced from the heavenly; Astell, however, always found links between the realms of the metaphysical and the physical. According to Norris:

> Likeness is the greatest indearment of Love, and the most natural Foundation of Delight and Complacency. We see this in all the Orders of Being, and in all the Degrees of Life. In the Sympathetic Associations of Vegetables, in the Voluntary Consortings of Animals, and in the chosen Friendships of Men. But most of all may this be seen in God himself. What is it but the most perfect Likeness and Conformity of Essences, Understandings and Wills that renders the Sacred Persons of the mysterious and adorable Trinity so infinitely lovely and agreeable to each other! . . . That therefore which makes the Persons of the Holy Trinity delight in one another, must needs make the pure Soul delight in the Holy Trinity. . . . It remains therefore, that having this excellent Hope [of joys of heaven], we study to purifie ourselves even as God is pure, and so endeavour to resemble and transcribe the Divine Perfections here, that we may contemplate them with the greater Complacency and Delight hereafter.[30]

Divine love and human love were an analogy in Norris; one could only attempt self-purification in the hope of achieving divine unity in the hereafter. For Astell, however, the relationship was synecdochic and continuous.

* * *

Astell's preoccupation with the idea of imitation and transcription may well have been prodded by Norris, but the goal of resembling Christ was central to Christianity from the beginning. The first Christians were urged to put off themselves and follow Christ. After Christ's death, believers were to live in him, which involved keeping his commandments and following his example.[31] These injunctions led directly to the development of monasteries, both for men and for women. The first eremitical monks withdrew from the world to the desert to lead more holy lives. With the institutionalization of monasticism following the Rule of St. Benedict in Italy and the monasteries established in northern Europe, cenobitical monasteries emerged in which divided groups of men and women would live in community. These necessarily always faced the challenge of existing simultaneously within and outside of society. According to C. H. Lawrence, "There was always a dialectic between monasticism and the world the monk had abandoned. The forms taken by religious institutions at different periods were conditioned by the demands and expectations of the society that supported them." Consequently, monasteries were not immune from demographic and economic shifts that precipitated crises, especially monasteries of the late Middle Ages: "The great social and economic changes that overtook Western society after the middle of the thirteenth century, especially the growth of urban populations and the wider dissemination of literacy among the laity, produced a new kind of religious sentiment, which experienced the ascetical vocation as primarily a search for individual fulfilment."[32] Western monasticism itself, then, experienced tensions in its attempts to be in the world but not of it and to integrate the individual spiritual journey within the life of a group.

The most noteworthy reform movement coming directly out of the late medieval crisis was *Devotio Moderna* (the Modern Devotion) led by Geert Groote in the Netherlands during the late fourteenth century. It sought through a revival of primitive Christianity to amend religious practice for both women and men.[33] Groote encouraged practical asceticism; he taught "a simple affective piety, based upon devout reading of the Scriptures, a regular meditation upon the human life of Christ. It was a plain man's version of the spiritual life. . . . What mattered was interior conversion, the renunciation of personal wealth and ambition, and a humble perseverance in everyday tasks. The main road to perfection lay through voluntary poverty, both material and spiritual."[34] That program, Groote felt, did not require individuals to take orders. Doctrine mattered less than virtuous behavior, and the intricate arguments of scholastics paled beside useful instruction. Groote instituted houses for women, and men's communities were eventually established after his death in 1384. Groote's followers formed a semimonastic order called the Brotherhood of the Common Life by uniting their resources and building a house. Groote's Brothers of the Common Life focused on educating poor boys, transcribing and writing books, and preaching. As boys were educated according to Groote's ideas, the movement expanded, and Deventer in the Netherlands became a regional center of learning that attracted young students.

Out of the movement emerged a classic text, the *Imitation of Christ*, thought to have been composed by Thomas à Kempis, one of Groote's adherents. It first served as a meditation manual for the Brothers and for other monastics affiliated with Groote's movement.[35] "Be watchful and diligent in the service of God, and meditate frequently on why you came hither," it advised. It became second only to the Bible in the extent of its readership, articulating for Christians a practical means to follow Christ and offering guidance for meditation and self-scrutiny. For Giles Constable, the *Imitation* "summed up and handed on to later generations much of the spiritual teaching of the twelfth and early thirteenth centuries," distilling a tradition on the imitation of Christ, a movement that, generally speaking, shifted from an emphasis on the imitation of the *divinity* of Christ to—in the late Middle Ages—an imitation of his *humanity*. Later, the *Imitation* inspired Protestants as well as Catholics and was read well after the Reformation into the seventeenth century.[36] Even in the late seventeenth century Norris was still deeply influenced by the text; his writings echoed the *Imitation*, which he cited in his preface to the *Letters Concerning the Love of God.* The other most popular works in the period—*Holy Living, Holy Dying,* and *The Whole Duty of Man*—also found inspiration in the *Imitation.* As an educated and devout woman, Astell was intimately acquainted with all these texts.[37]

Astell's arguments in the *Letters* demonstrate that she was familiar with the practical kinds of ideas on the imitation of Christ that emerged in the reform movements of the late Middle Ages and the sorts crystalized by *Devotio Moderna* and the *Imitation.* The language of familiar devotional practice supplied her ways of explaining her passion to herself and to Norris as she moved between "the need to strive, struggle, and fight" and the need to develop "an inner spiritual life."[38]

Indeed, Astell did not arrive at the justification of passion without struggle or sacrifice. She recognized that she had a problem, because, according to Norris, the active love that people should direct toward God ought to differ from the benevolence they show to human beings. And while Jones's extraordinary capacity to imitate and resemble God would appear to confuse her status as an object of love, she nonetheless remained a human being or creature. How could Astell love God in Jones without loving Jones? Astell meditated on and worried about her tendencies to wish for union, reasoning that people must be wary of their love, must always be taking their pulses as it were, to be certain of desiring God rather than the creature. The surest way of knowing what people love most is determining what they think about most often: "What we love will be uppermost in our Minds; there is no better Diagnostick to discover our Love than by observing what is the most frequent Subject of our Thoughts." She added an analysis that sounds familiar and modern: "For Thought seems to me to be nothing else but the Determination of the Soul to some certain Object which she desires either to contemplate or enjoy, a forming in her self the Images and Representations of what she delights in, or contriving how she may obtain it, and remove what stands betwixt her and it: And therefore where-ever the Weight of our Desire rests, the Stream of our Thoughts will follow; 'tis to no Purpose to drive them away, for though we may for a while put a Force on them, they will insensibly steal back again" (189–90). Therefore, in order to direct love to the proper object, which is God, one must constantly scrutinize one's thoughts. Astell struggled to overcome the habit or custom of envisioning the beloved creature, which brought her back to her feelings for Jones: "Custom . . . is no small matter: It is the most difficult thing imaginable to recall our Thoughts and withdraw the Stream of our Affections from that Channel in which they were used to flow. Which is a further proof of the great Necessity that lies upon us betimes to cut off all Desire from the Creature, to shut up all the

Avenues of our Souls from created good, even from those dearest Idols that bear the nearest Resemblance to our Maker, to whom our Benevolence is due, though they ought not to usurp our Desire" (213–14, misnumbered 213).[39]

If Catherine Jones was Astell's "dearest Idol" bearing "the nearest Resemblance" to God, then it was she for whom Astell had to "cut off all Desire" and "shut up all the Avenues" of her soul. Astell finally convinced herself to do so by saying that even though "a Sister Soul may give somewhat better Entertainment to our Love than other Creatures can," that soul was no purer than her own, so "how can it supply our Wants, or consequently be the proper Object of our Desires?" (133–134). Norris's lessons cost Astell considerable mental anguish; they were assimilated with pain and tremendous effort of will. But over the course of her struggle, evident in the *Letters,* she came to the creative solution of the *Serious Proposal:* her plan for a female monastery. The "Religious Retirement" emerged as the place where Astell's desire, and women's desire in general, could find expression and receive satisfaction.[40]

How did this plan relate to Astell's belief in the power of imitation and the love that seeks resemblance and unity? In her outpouring of affection for Jones, Astell had lamented that "my Expressions are too flat, my Colours too dead to draw such a lovely Piece!" Regretting her incapacity as a writer to reproduce such beauty, Astell introduced the language of transcription: "Would to GOD we would all transcribe, not this imperfect Copy, but that incomparable Original she daily gives us" (b6v). Catherine Jones defied Astell's attempts to create a copy of her, for, to Astell, she was an emanation, an incarnation of the Maker; she became the "Original" that all women must "transcribe" for themselves because Astell's copy could never be a perfect enough substitute.

Such language of transcription formed part of an expanding and shifting metaphorical realm given the rise of publication, but in this context it emanated from the preoccupations characteristic of *Devotio Moderna,* either directly or filtered through Norris. Norris on occasion turned to such a metaphor, as when he told readers to "endeavour to resemble and transcribe the Divine Perfections here."[41] It is perhaps unsurprising, then, to find that such language appeared prominently in the best-known late-seventeenth-century edition of the *Imitation of Christ* compiled by John Worthington, a divine linked to the Cambridge Platonists, a group that included Norris himself ("the last of the Cambridge Platonists").[42]

Worthington's 1654 translation was entitled *The Christians Pattern; or, A Divine Treatise of the Imitation of Christ.* It went through many editions, and the 1677 impression later became the basis for John Wesley's popular version. Of particular interest, the 1677 edition contained a revised preface that emphasized the transcriptive and reproductive method of à Kempis's book: "Though the general scope and drift of the Book be the transcribing of so glorious a Pattern as is the *Life of Christ,* God manifest in the flesh . . . yet all along in this Treatise there are to be found the seeds & principles of the most necessary and Practical Truths, together with many inward and experimental discoveries of the *Kingdom of God in us,* and the Process of Regeneration" (a3v).[43] Worthington explained how à Kempis was an active transcriber as he sat in a scriptorium, copying and disseminating the Bible and "good Books" (c).

The transcriptions of à Kempis and Worthington would sow the seeds that grow into a reader's recognition of the Kingdom of God within and initiate an inner "process of regeneration." Worthington's text thus underscored how the discourse of transcription, copying, and reproduction evoked an idea of monasticism, piety, and meticulous devotional practice. Interested in a nonconventual return to early Christian asceticism and "Apostolical Piety," Astell, in keeping with the aims of *Devotio Moderna,* encouraged the transcription of Christ in Jones, whose faith expanded so rapidly that she would "quickly outstrip our Theory, and oblige the World with what was never more wanted than now, an exact and living Transcript of Primitive Christianity."[44] Women who had access to Jones in the female monastery would become as apostles and members of the early church, enjoying proximity to the Word and undertaking the work of transcription.

In order to transcribe the original—Christ in Catherine Jones—women would live in the monastery of the *Serious Proposal,* where, by "a generous Emulation to excel in the best things," they could develop their minds for "a much sweeter and more durable delight" so that "the Souls of Women may no longer be the only unadorn'd and neglected things."[45] As Astell put it in the *Letters,* "Ladies may be at last convinced that the Beauty of the Mind is the most charming Amiableness, because most lasting and most divine, and that no Ornaments are so becoming to a Lady as the Robe of Righteousness and the Jewels of Piety" (b6v). By being near each other in the monastery and partaking of the divine presence of an "original" like Catherine Jones, all women could, through loving imitation and union, become direct resemblances of the divine mind. As seraphic emanations they would turn into "originals," ornamented and attractive, and be imitated themselves. Thus the *Serious Proposal* imagined women's empowerment through each other with the force of the divine.

It is with this method of empowerment in mind that we should also read the *Serious Proposal, Part II,* published three years after the first project. In this work, Astell complained with some impatience that admirers of the *Serious Proposal* had not yet established the female monastery. If women perceive something as a good idea, then they should have "the Vertue and Courage to Act accordingly." She continued:

> Why won't you begin to think, and no longer dream away your Time in a wretched incogitancy? Why does not a generous Emulation fire your hearts and inspire you with Noble and Becoming Resentments? . . . Imitation is the heartiest Praise you can give, and is a Debt which Justice requires to be paid to every worthy Action. . . . the best Commendation you can bestow on a Book is immediately to put it in Practice. . . . If you *approve,* Why don't you *follow?* And if you *Wish,* Why shou'd you not *Endeavour?* especially since that wou'd reduce your Wishes to Act, and make you of Wellwishers to Vertue and Good sense, become glorious Examples of them.[46]

From a very practical standpoint, Astell argued that women should imitate a good model so they could become "Glorious Examples" and be imitated themselves. She thus showed how love is translated into the political sphere, how desire is turned into action.

In addition, Astell's impatience suggests just how her personal feelings could provide the fuel for her project; when one wishes for something, one must pursue it. The pattern of loving imitation let her locate that pursuit in ambition for women in general. Astell could never accept that her sisters might not want the good and might not seek to imitate what they saw, admired, and desired; of course, that was their wish. Her aim was to show that the seed of the Kingdom of God was within them. In an early poem, "Ambition," Astell revealed just how she imagined that other women must share her goals for divine glory. After describing her feeling of ambition, she says that the stirring in her spirit proves that women in fact have souls:

> What's this that with such vigour fills my brest?
> Like the first mover finds no rest,
> And with it's force dos all things draw,
> Makes all submit to its imperial Law!
> Sure 'tis a spark 'bove what Prometheus stole,
> Kindled by a heav'nly coal,
> Their sophistry I can controul,
> Who falsely say that women have no Soul.[47]

These thoughts found an echo in the *Serious Proposal:* "Let such therefore as deny us the improvement of our Intellectuals, either take up *his* Paradox, who said *That Women have no Souls;* which at this time a day, when they are allow'd to Brutes, wou'd be as unphilosophical as it is unmannerly; or else let them permit us to cultivate and improve them."[48]

Astell's ideas about ambition combined with her absolutist imagination. In the same poem she said that her ambition was to be the monarch of herself: "may I but reign / And Empire o're my self obtain."[49] Those already adorned with crowns should be no less concerned to achieve this blessed state. Astell dedicated the *Serious Proposal, Part II* to Princess Anne, who, she hoped, would be the patron of the monastery. With such virtuous, generous support, Astell said, a prince can "become truly Godlike . . . for the Service of GOD, and the Resembling Him, being its only Aim, His Approbation in a soft and inward Whisper, is more than the loud *Huzza*'s and Plaudits of ten thousand Worlds."[50] Just as the aim of the community consists in becoming godlike through transcription, so, too, can the sovereign achieve a divine state by following the model Astell suggests, a model resulting from her attempt to imitate Catherine Jones in "Resembling Him."

In her next book, *Some Reflections upon Marriage* (1700), Astell repeated her ideas about loving imitation, this time pointing to the absurdity of marrying a man and thereby accepting him as sovereign lord when he can in no way become an imitable figure for a woman:

> Indeed, your fine Gentleman's Actions are now a-days such, that did not Custom and the Dignity of his Sex give Weight and Authority to them, a Woman that thinks twice might bless her self, and say, Is this the Lord and Master to whom I am to promise Love, Honour and Obedience? What can be the Object of Love but amiable Qualities, the Image of the Deity impress'd upon a generous and godlike Mind, a Mind that is above this World, to be sure above all the Vices, the Tricks and Baseness of it; a Mind that is not full of it self, nor contracted to little private Interests, but which, in Imitation of that glorious Pattern it endeavours to copy after, expands and diffuses it self to its utmost Capacity in doing Good.[51]

There was no difference, in Astell's estimation, between the kind of partner one ought to choose in marriage and the kind of companion with whom one should establish a friendship. In each case one must search for the imitable "Image of the Deity impress'd upon a generous and godlike Mind." Astell thus matter-of-factly translated ideas of mystical devotion derived from the late Middle Ages into a contemporary context as a way of critiquing gender roles and marriage.

The same devotional tradition allowed her to shape the main argument of her early works: By mustering the ambition to imitate each other imitating God, women can become divinely empowered. They can attain a perfect love of God and each other, "A Love that rewards itself, a Fire that is its own Fuel."[52] If Astell had to give up the exclusive love of Jones, she would trade it, in effect, for a godlike love that is original, a love she called "unmixed benevolence" rather than "love of desire."

Rather than consisting in benevolence alone, however, this love combined two types of love—the benevolent and the desirous, the one seeking no return and the other needing satisfaction—because Astell imagined that this love *circulates.* It exists dynamically among a group of people who constantly exchange it. Astell described this mutually reinforcing divine energy with a vivid metaphor. Her love for Catherine Jones—now set to the correct "Measures" by Norris's teaching—became transformed into a love that was more general and imitative but every bit as powerful. Jones was a person "whom now we have duly stated the Measures, I may venture to say, I love with the greatest Tenderness, for all must love her who have any Esteem for unfeigned Goodness, who value an early Piety and eminent Vertue. All true Lovers of GOD being like excited Needles, which cleave not only to him their *Magnet,* but even to one another" (b5v).

Merely one of many "excited Needles," Astell in this passage cleaves, as does Jones, to others whose magnetic charge derives from God. Passionate energy has thus been diffused and given "proper measure" with the aid of a scientific metaphor confirming God as source while simultaneously allowing mutual attraction. Love is shared and circulates, magnetism moves in all directions, and the friend by whom Astell had been rebuffed has become a member of the magnetic community, participating in reciprocal, mutually emulative, and energizing love. Astell thus set up a community that answered her needs perfectly. The monastery imagined in the *Serious Proposal* represents the exact place where the kind of love theorized in the *Letters* is supposed to circulate. Moreover, "This happy Society will be but one Body, whose Soul is love, animating and informing it, and perpetually breathing forth it self in flames of holy desires after GOD, and acts of Benevolence to each other."[53]

In employing a magnetic metaphor, Astell again drew on sentiments of Norris and reworked them to satisfy her own needs. She grasped his idea that "God is the true great *Magnet* of our Souls," and, as with the ideas of imitation and transcription, she explored the implications of the comparison.[54] Magnetism, she decided, does not work in only one direction, from her soul to God. Astell took the metaphor to its logical conclusion to argue for a magnetic space of mutual female friendship where all "excited Needles" become magnetic.

This space, Astell's "Religious Retreat," had many antecedents. Perry points to earlier nunneries, small communities at Great Lumley and Little Gidding, and discusses the plans of seventeenth-century female educationalists. Patricia Springborg also locates Astell's proposal in a line of women's academies, emphasizing Madame de Maintenon's school at Saint-Cyr (founded in 1686) and the Port Royal School, founded by a woman during the thirteenth century.[55] In its modern incarnation the Port Royal School was apparently influenced by Geert Groote's Modern Devotion.[56] Although the movement spawned the Brothers of the Common Life and the *Imitation of Christ,* it was actually based on a women's community, the Sisters of the Common Life. Because that group combined many qualities Astell had proposed for her female monastery, it must be considered as one of the potential inspirations for the *Serious Proposal.*

Groote developed the ideas for the Modern Devotion as he established the Sisters of the Common Life. It was a nonconventual women's society instituted in 1374, a decade before the Brothers of the Common Life came into being. The sisters were originally a group of poor women to whom Groote gave the use of his house in Deventer. We can date their formal institution from the constitution that he drew up for their society five years later. He eschewed vows, and the women remained members of the local parish church. They wore regular but simple dress and were to avoid familiarity with men. The women could move freely, although travel was restricted to a distance of ten miles and visits could last at most eight days. Two matrons acted as treasurers and assigned tasks. Manual labor was required, and Groote denounced begging because the women were capable of earning their bread. Although the sisters were not required to give up their property to the group, they shared income and expenses and willed property to the house upon their death.[57] They developed facility in agriculture, oversaw a successful dairy business, and earned money by sewing, knitting, spinning, and weaving.[58]

By 1400 more than twenty houses of sisters were established in the area of the Netherlands that surrounded Deventer; there were, in fact, more sister houses than brother houses.[59] The extent to which the houses were educational institutions is not clear, although the brothers eventually took spiritual responsibility for the sisters. The similarities to Astell's plan are therefore notable: combination of the active and contemplative life; rejection of vows; adoption of modest clothing; belief in useful education but not elevated learning; insistence on productive work; freedom to come and go and, at the same time, disapproval of unnecessary visits; absence of men; and emphasis on charity, worship, and inner devotion.[60]

* * *

We may never know precisely which models inspired Astell, but it is clear that the plan she wished to create for other women would approximate the practices of the early Christians and allow a women's community to grow and female friendship to thrive.[61] Women's mutual love, energized by the magnetic love of God, would sustain and empower them. Such an image culminated

Astell's lifelong deliberations about the purposes of friendship, which again appeared influenced by medieval and monastic ideas. In the *Serious Proposal* she explained that there should be no reason why the women of the monastery should not pair up and certain couples find they have a special bond:

> as in Heav'n that region of perfect Love, the happy Souls . . . now and then step aside from more general Conversations, to entertain themselves with a peculiar Friend; so, in this little emblem of this blessed place, what shou'd hinder, but that two Persons of a sympathizing disposition, the *make* and *frame* of whose Souls bears an exact conformity to each other, and therefore one wou'd think were purposely design'd by Heaven to unite and mix; what shou'd hinder them from entring into an holy combination to watch over each other for Good, to advise, encourage and direct, and to observe the minutest fault in order to its amendment. The truest effect of Love being to endeavour the bettering the beloved Person.[62]

With the emphasis on bettering one's partner, Astell was solving a problem she had outlined in her early poems when she lamented that she had no friend ("Why shou'd it be, / Friendship shou'd only be forbid to me?").[63] Such a relationship was one of the few things she might wish for, but she nonetheless thanked God for seeing fit to deny her such a blessing. He obviously wanted all her love for himself. In 1689 she wrote:

> I thank thee Lord that I am Friendless too,
> Tho that alas be hard to do!
> . . . .
> Yet humbly I submit,
> To that most perfect will of thine,
> And thank thee cause thou hast denied me it.
> Thrice blessed be thy Jealousie,
> Which would not part
> With one smal corner of my heart,
> But has engross'd it all to Thee![64]

Even before Norris's instruction, then, Astell pondered the love of God and the degree to which her desire must belong to the Creator.

"Enemies" presents a different look at friendship. Astell observed that a friend is sometimes blind to one's faults or reluctant to apply "sharp Wine" to a "secret ulcer," whereas, paradoxically, enemies were her "truest Friends":

> Kind Monitors you tell me of my faults,
> Your spurs correct & mend my halts,
> With cleansing Physick purge my mind,
> That no crude humours may remain behind.[65]

The correspondence with Norris brought Astell to a refinement of this argument. He convinced her that God uses pain as medicine, as therapy, for the good of the person. If someone she loved caused pain—in a poem she pointed out that nothing hurts so much "as the unkindness of a darling Friend"—then the pain was given her as a remedy from God.[66] Her enemies, then, her "truest Friends" who point out her faults, and thereby make her better, are conflated with the "darling Friend" whose unkindness is no longer seen as painful but as God-directed for Astell's own good.

Thus what Astell had meant to point out as a paradox—enemies were her friends because they made her better—became the basis for the platonic friendship she so wished for in her early poetry. These types of friends blend together, finally issuing in the desirable friends of the *Serious Proposal,* those whose "true Friendship" can be measured by a capacity "to endeavour the bettering the beloved Person."[67] Indeed, this is how a friendship becomes truly divine. It is not that the two souls resemble each other and are meant to mingle and unite, or that one person's interest gives way to that of the friend, or that the two "watch over each other for Good" or "advise, encourage and direct" each other, but that they make each other more and more perfect for God's sake, more glorious and ever-better examples. In Astell's vocabulary, that makes them increasingly powerful because they become more magnetic, more godlike, and more attractive.

To Astell, that is the ideal friendship, one she argues is shared rather than possessive.[68] In her "Amicable Society" there will be "no Rivalling but for the Love of GOD, no Ambition but to procure his Favour, to which nothing will more effectually recommend you, than a great and dear affection to each other." Twice Astell pointed out that particular friendships should not "prejudice the general Amity." And yet, while she called the friendship in the monastery "a Noble Vertuous and Disinteress'd Friendship" and a "refin'd and disinteress'd Benevolence" she stressed that before "contracting so important a Relation" women should "look into the very Soul of the beloved Person, to discover what resemblance it bears to our own."[69] The capacity for loving union appears to *precede* the striving to resemble Christ. Hence, becoming more like Christ is a mission a couple undertakes together to deepen and prolong their union. What is more, this friendship, despite Astell's arguments to the contrary, includes the idea of possession:

> besides that holy emulation which a continual view of the brightest and most exemplary Lives will excite in us; we shall have opportunity of contracting the purest and noblest Friendship; a Blessing, the purchase of which were richly worth all the World besides! For she who *possesses* a worthy Person, has certainly obtain'd the richest Treasure. A Blessing that Monarchs may envy, and she who

> enjoys is happier than she who fills a Throne! A Blessing, which next to the love of GOD, is the choicest Jewel in our Caelestial Diadem, which, were it duly practic'd wou'd both fit us for heav'n, and bring it down into our hearts whilst we tarry here. . . . [I]f we . . . cannot spare a hearty Good-will to one or two choice Persons, how can it ever be thought, that we shou'd well acquit our selves of that Charity which is due to all Mankind? For Friendship is nothing else but Charity contracted; it is (in the words of an admired Author) a kind of revenging our selves on the narrowness of our Faculties, by exemplifying that extraordinary Charity on one or two, which we are willing, but not able to exercise towards all.[70]

This important passage reveals the links among Astell's ideas about emulation, power, and love. Both admiring monarchy and seeking to be monarch of herself, Astell found a way to such power that was even surer than ruling a kingdom. It involved attaining the power of God through emulating divine love, which she achieved by detecting, imitating, and uniting with the divine in her beloved objects. As long as all women in the female monastery had such a "great and dear affection" for one or two people, and as long as Astell's feeling for Catherine Jones was shared and replicated—with love moving toward God through its loving and imitated objects in the manner of "excited Needles"—then the love remained, for Astell, charitable rather than excessive, general rather than exclusive.[71] It was a love of benevolence rather than desire. Joining the world and the beyond, it prepared women for heaven and let them experience bliss "whilst we tarry here."

This was Astell's way of reconciling her love of God, longing for friendship, personal ambition, and desire for women's empowerment. Instructed by Norris, she had struggled and absorbed his lesson, but she transformed his teaching into a doctrine that suited her emotional needs and empowered the women she cared so much about by making them godlike. This, then, was the way Astell theorized for herself both the "absolute" and the "emotional excitement" historians have described as the foundation of her feminist project. She simultaneously bridged the gap between metaphysical and physical worlds, stretched her platonism, and envisaged a utopia of "excited Needles."

* * *

Astell believed so thoroughly in the possibilities of emulation that she complied with Norris's wish to publish their correspondence about the love of God. Rather than accede to his arguments for doing so, she decided it was worthwhile to replicate her productions because they might catch women's attention and inspire transcription. As she observed, "I cannot imagine to what Purpose [my letters] will serve, unless it be to decoy those to a Perusal of them, who wanting Piety to read a Book for its Usefulness, may probably have the Curiosity to inquire what can be the Product of a Woman's Pen, and to excite a generous Emulation in my Sex, persuade them to leave their insignificant Pursuits for Employments worthy of them" (b5).

Astell's wish "to excite a generous Emulation" had important implications. The latent love in this initial curiosity can, once activated into emulation, form part of a mutually reinforcing magnetic power that finally participates in divine love. Publishing her letters might make "excited Needles" of other women whose desire to emulate could bring them and keep them within God's magnetic field. But publication also provided a chance to be emulated—imitated, transcribed, and therefore loved. Astell could take on the power of an "original" and become for other women what Jones had been for her. She thus justified taking up the pen and creating a community of female readers and writers. To the extent that she was replicated in others (through their reading and transcription) and concomitantly reflected the divinity, she achieved her ambition—power of a kind that mattered to her—and simultaneously set in place a strategy for passing it on.

Astell's instruction at Norris's hands resulted in personal loss to be sure, but she nonetheless profited. She may have generalized her love and therefore missed a personal union, but in her writing-in-order-to-be-transcribed, and in her imitation of her friend emulating God, she set up a system in which she could give and receive love as well as power. Although the *Letters* show the emotional source of Astell's feminism, and her politics and theory reveal a deep concern to achieve female power and selfhood through reason and the absolutist imagination, the two forces are inseparable.

Astell's personal conflict could only be resolved, and her ambition achieved, by replicating her feelings in a community of women where such loving aspiration circulated, via the power of God's magnetism, through mutual emulation. This, I believe, is why Astell figured her feminism as utopianism and why the method of attaining female subjectivity involved not an isolated striving for power or a perpetual solitary retreat to meditation and prayer but a process of imitation and transcription in a group context. It also explains the force behind Astell's lifelong practical attempts to create a women's community in the *Serious Proposal*, the *Serious Proposal, Part II*, and her later, unfailing efforts to establish and maintain the Chelsea girls' school. Astell succeeded in outstripping Norris's philosophy even as she convinced herself that she had largely assimilated his argument. Her writings therefore show Astell taking what could be confining doctrine and molding it to suit her emotional needs as well as her practical desires to empower women.

That conclusion thus foregrounds an inconsistency in Astell's thought. Despite her patriarchal politics, she looked not only to the figure of the absolute in God and monarch for an image of female subjectivity but also to an exchange of love and education through emulation in women's community. The circulation she theorized hinted at the nascent liberal implications of her thinking and reinforced Perry's and Taylor's conclusions that the *Letters* are unrepresentative of Astell in that they betray materialist Lockean tendencies. Even the magnetic distribution of emotion, education, and power began to seem more like an efficient exchange in the marketplace than unidirectional gifts sent down from an all-powerful deity.

Moreover, Astell, instead of looking to the past for a literary model, relied on the emerging modern form of the project, not a "modest" Swiftian satire in this case but a *Serious Proposal*—a form associated with Whiggish trade interests. Jean-Michel Racault has included projects as "utopie-programmes" in *L'Utopie narrative en France et en Angleterre, 1675–1761.* Although he distinguishes between "utopies-programmes" and "utopies-narratives," he acknowledges that the two have a tendency to slide together, and he draws conclusions about national differences on the basis of these utopian modes. Racault speculates that the project became a far more popular form in England than in France because the Glorious Revolution of 1688 impelled people to try to implement changes dreamed up during the English Revolution, resulting in countless practical proposals of myriad sorts. The political stasis in France, by contrast, encouraged writers to set down their wishes in elaborate fictions far removed from reality and entirely impracticable.[72] According to Daniel Defoe, who had responded to Astell's *Serious Proposal* with "An Academy for Women," the "True-bred Merchant" is the one "the most capable, when urg'd by Necessity, to Contrive New Ways to live. And from hence, I humbly conceive, may very properly be deriv'd the *Projects,* so much the Subject of the present Discourse. And to this sort of men 'tis easy to trace the Original of Banks, Stocks, Stock-jobbing, Assurances, Friendly Societies, Lotteries, and the like," because their proposals "tend to Improvement of Trade, and Employment of the Poor, and the Circulation and Increase of the publick Stock of the Kingdom."[73]

Astell may have been a staunch Tory supporter of the landed interests, but the *Serious Proposal* associated her with reformers and entrepreneurs. The interpersonal economy she invented in her women's community, combined with the change-oriented form she selected for doing so, meshed easily with the ideas of contract and consideration that formed such important parts of her followers' mental landscapes. It explains, in part, how later female utopists were able consistently to ally themselves with Whig rather than Tory interests even as they embraced Astell's vision. Astell's theory of utopia stimulated their conceptions of community even though it failed to inspire the foundation of a women's monastery in Astell's own time.

2. Feminist Utopia and the New Commercialism

Mary Astell's desire for a return to primitive Christianity and a space for female friendship found dedicated advocates among eighteenth-century female authors who had utopian inclinations. They adhered to the pattern she established for spiritual growth in women's community. But they also grappled with material life and the ways in which the distribution of resources intersected with other forms of social exchange. It has been argued that the expansion of capitalism elicited the rise of the novel as a domesticating force.[1] Female utopian authors, however, used the novel to challenge the separation of private and public spheres and the consequent limitations on women's freedom of action and expression. They reconceived contractualism even as a modern commercial system was in its infancy. Their utopianism, unlike the traditional form, involved a developing approach to economy in its broadest sense, encompassing not only financial transactions but also emotional exchanges.

Like the moral philosophers of the time who articulated systems of human interaction based on contractual models, feminist utopists of the eighteenth century imagined a world of exchange that was reconfigured to include women as subjects. It was a world of *benevolent* exchange in which money counted but Christian charity determined value. What emerged was an ideal state where women could value themselves, were esteemed for their contributions to society, controlled their money as well as their affections, and had a hand in determining the shape of their communities. Women writers therefore offered a variation on the "most serious" Enlightenment utopias, which, according to Gregory Claeys, "preserve . . . a mixture of radical republicanism and Christian primitivism" in order to provide "an alternate ideal of sociability, moral economy and community against the growing individualism of the wider society."[2]

In this chapter I will explain how feminist utopians pursued emerging liberal notions of exchange and the individual yet sought to incorporate community standards of virtue. By imagining the utopian reconciliation of virtue and commerce, they countered increasing pressures to separate the public realm from the private, economy from domesticity, and justice from benevolence. Although their view never became dominant, their utopianism offered a way of characterizing one type of mid-century British feminism. My argument, therefore, responds to commentators who have questioned the existence of feminism at mid-century, as in, for example, Valerie Bryson's denial: "In many ways, the middle years of the eighteenth century seem to represent a retreat from feminism. . . . there is no *direct* line between [late-eighteenth-century feminists] and the writers of Mary Astell's day." Jane Spencer maintains, "Despite occasional publications like the pseudonymous 'Sophia's' *Woman Not Inferior to Man* (1739), and the intermittent feminism of Lady Mary Wortley Montagu's periodical, *The Nonsense of Common Sense* (1737–38), the tradition of feminist polemic was, on the whole, submerged during the eighteenth century." And Hilda L. Smith asserts, "There is no clear chain of thought from the seventeenth-century feminists to the modern movement." Historians have generally been inclined to date feminism from the publication of Mary Wollstonecraft's *Vindication of the Rights of Woman*, but there was a multifaceted feminist tradition before her time. Utopianism was one notable form of feminist expression in the middle of the eighteenth century.[3]

The economic outlook of feminist utopian authors placed them between contending contemporary ideologies, civic humanism on the one hand and the jurisprudential tradition on the other.[4] Both ideologies reacted to the expanding wealth and luxury that increasingly efficient production and global trade was bringing to Britain. More specifically, J. G. A. Pocock has argued that civic humanism, based on classical and Florentine republican models, was revived in the mid-seventeenth century in order to counter the image of the new commercial personality. Civic humanism posited "the unspecialised agrarian ideal of the patriot" who pursued not self-interest and capital but public good.

> [It] affirmed that the human personality was that of a *zōon politikon* and was fully expressed only in the practice of citizenship as an active virtue; man (the male bias of this ideal bordered on the absolute) was by nature a public being, and his public action was less that of a magistrate exercising authority than that of a citizen exercising equality. . . . To qualify for equality and citizenship, the individual must be master of his own household, proprietor along with his

> equals of the only arms permitted to be borne in wars which must be publicly undertaken, and possessor of property whose function was to bring him not profit and luxury, but independence and leisure. Without property he must be a servant; without a public and civic monopoly of arms, his citizenship must be corrupted.[5]

Women are servants in this model. They carry the burden of reproductive labor along with the rest of the household and are unqualified to bear arms, incapable of becoming citizens, and unable to achieve "human personality."

Strangely enough, the focus of civic humanism on virtue and the public good nonetheless attracted women who had political ideals. Sarah Scott created Sir George Ellison, a character who represents a virtuous landowner fulfilling the duties of his station, and her histories lauded the related image of Bolingbroke's patriot king. Scott's Gustavus Ericson acts the perfect warrior prince who can fight bravely but prefers to set an example of peace and prosperity and civilize his people, and Theodore Agrippa D'Aubigné also turns from fighting for the Protestant cause to writing poetry and improving manners.[6] Jeanne Marie Leprince de Beaumont's heroine Clarissa explains that in their ideal community her husband "shall imitate the ancient Romans, who, at one time bore arms, and at another, disdained not to cultivate their little estate, the inheritance of their ancestors."[7]

Ancient and Florentine types of friendship also affected feminist utopians strongly. Sarah Fielding translated Xenophon's *Memorabilia,* which contains discussions of friendship. The issue, a major theme in all her work, is particularly evident in the full title of her first novel: *The Adventures of David Simple, Containing an Account of His Travels through the Cities of London and Westminster in the Search of a Real Friend.* David Simple tests various people of diverse philosophical convictions, and they disappoint. He then finally meets the sensitive soulmates with whom he can form a community of perfect friendship, involving the classical—and also Christian—ideals of sharing goods, promoting the happiness of the others, and mutual protection and advancement. Friendship in this conception is linked directly with politics because it forms the basis of the state. A state cannot exist without the concord of friendship at its core, nor can friendship survive in a disorderly and contentious state.[8] The two are mutually constitutive. The extensive discourse on sociability and politeness that developed during the eighteenth century extended and changed the ancient models to accommodate new socioeconomic and political realities.[9]

But if civic humanism and the idea of the patriot offered models for male characters, they proved insufficient for envisioning a sociopolitical place for female subjects. Jurisprudential discourse and the market society it supported, although far from perfect, offered opportunities for conceiving of a female civic personality to complement that of the male citizen. The jurisprudential tradition, as the name suggests, relies on notions of natural law and follows the work of natural law philosophers Hugo Grotius and Samuel Pufendorf.[10] In England, their ideas were taken up by John Locke and to a good extent by Scottish Enlightenment philosophers, Francis Hutcheson, David Hume, and Adam Smith among them.[11]

While civic humanism is centrally concerned with virtue, natural jurisprudence focuses on justice; property is protected by the power of the sovereign and the law. The citizen in this model, according to Pocock, "appear[s] a fluid, historical and transactional vision of *homo faber et mercator*, shaping himself through the stages of history by means of the division and specialization of labour, the diversification and refinement of the passions. The political image of man [is] replaced by a social and transactional image of man and politics."[12] The Financial Revolution of the late seventeenth century, with its expansion of credit and investment, raised the issue of citizenship. Given the changes in types of property and wealth, what was the relationship of identity to government? What grounded political being? For women, whose civil existence remained a mystery, those questions were pivotal.

Although postmodernist commentators have focused lately on the antifeminist aspects of liberal ideology, feminist utopists of the eighteenth century seized on nascent liberal ideology to devise a creative and empowering response to the uncertainties, the flux and novelty, of the commercial system of the period. As Pocock observes, "A case might be made for the view that women could expect more mobility, and even active agency, from a commercially conceived society than from the alternative model of the masculine and self-contained classical patriots."[13] Indeed, feminist utopists saw several critical benefits for women in the new discourse because it promoted:

1. the doctrine of equivalent exchange;
2. the opposition to slavery, a condition on which civic humanism depended;
3. the flow of cash and credit, which they believed critical to maintaining benevolent and emotional ties; and
4. the idea of an original social contract.

Although the jurisprudential paradigm and the discourse to which it gave rise failed to offer a complete solution, sometimes reinscribing women's subordination, female utopists nonetheless found in it critical arguments that served their purposes.

Each of these points must be considered individually. First, women saw opportunity in an ideology that based identity and promoted fairness in equivalent exchanges. Where a civic humanist gained a sense of unified personality from citizenship and patriotism, a new, "specialized" commercial individual—specialized through participation in the division of labor—maintained a sense of self by contractual exchanges, receiving as much value as he or she gave. As Sarah Scott's George Ellison proudly points out, Britain was a place where "all live in a state of reciprocal services, the great and the poor are linked in compact; each side has its obligations to perform; and if I make use of another man's labour, it is on condition that I shall pay him such a price for it, as will enable him to purchase all the comforts of life" (16–17). Scott would agree that new contractual links among autonomous individuals can promote justice and civilize society, because commerce depends upon expanding trust among people who can count on receiving value for their expenditure.

J. G. A. Pocock has discussed this increased cultivation in society as part of a growing feminization of new commercial individuals and marked by greater politeness. The eighteenth century, he remarks, "saw women in the role of cultural entrepreneurs, encouraging the exchange of politeness and refinement in a variety of forms."[14] Catherine Gallagher suggests that for these reasons women writers in the early eighteenth century had a window of opportunity to participate in public discourse, and she points especially to the careers of Delarivier Manley and Susannah Centlivre in this context. She notes, however, that contradictions abounded in the new representations of the feminine. Pocock, for instance, cites Gibbon's anxiety that women might "grow less chaste" with an increased political-commercial role. At the same time, then, that positive images of women's discourse were circulating, counterimages of woman as temptress, corruptor, and effeminizer of men remained.[15] John Millar, author of *The Distinction of Ranks* and student of Adam Smith, harbored fears similar to Gibbon's. He measured the progress of society by its treatment of women. After women experienced continual improvement from hunter-gatherer to commercial societies, their situation would deteriorate as men, with passions liberated by commercial society, behaved toward them with ever-decreasing dignity.[16]

Writers such as Scott and Fielding were well aware of contemporary representations. On the one hand, they benefited from a culture in which new images of the feminine were circulating. They were associated with the Bluestocking circle, whose social activities and literary productions were well known and publicly lauded and which helped fashion their authorial identity.[17] On the other hand, that achievement gave them leave to follow the example of Mary Astell in entering political discourse and expressing feminist convictions that tested ideas of the feminine. Their writing often sought to confound feminine and masculine traits in fictional characters in order to obviate easy equations of actual women with the "feminine" and men with the "masculine." Instead, they proffered a vision of the admirable Christian, whose commerce is benevolent and whose charity designates worth.

Therefore, while profiting from new discourses of femininity created by commercial society, women utopists were inclined to look further into the political possibilities of the emerging order. They were attracted to contractualism because it based personality not on the ownership of land or the achievement of leisure but on participation in equivalent exchanges; exchange value in whatever form allowed individuals to engage in transactions. This does not mean female utopists advocated a thoroughly egalitarian society; indeed, a doctrine of equivalent exchange can reinforce a rigid class hierarchy. Rather, they sought fairness for themselves and relief for the indigent. Thus Fielding suggested that conversation is a commodity that women should be able to trade. Characters' stories are possessions shared with other individuals and deserve consideration (both in ethical and legal terms); fictions penned by women should earn compensation.

In this they were raising an issue that concerned moral philosophers and political economists. Even Adam Smith's *Wealth of Nations* (1776) sought to explain how commercial society could accommodate the poor. As Istvan Hont and Michael Ignatieff conclude, "The *Wealth of Nations* was centrally concerned with the issue of justice, with finding a market mechanism capable of reconciling inequality of property with adequate provision for the excluded. Smith was simply transposing into the language of markets an ancient jurisprudential discourse, carried into modernity by Grotius, Pufendorf and Locke, about how to ensure that private individuation of God's dominion would not deny the propertyless the means of satisfying their needs." Smith's answer, "a system of competitive markets in food and labour," was to offer a higher standard of living for the poor in commercial society. He considered a competitive system to be more just and desirable than an economy based on civic-humanist principles, which involved enslaving productive workers. Commercial society thus had the advantage over a civic-humanist model in that "however unequal men might be, in property and citizenship, they could be equal in access to the means to satisfy basic need." Smith would justify the commercial system on the grounds that a common laborer in England enjoyed a higher standard of living than even the most lavish African prince.[18]

A decade before the appearance of the *Wealth of Nations,* Sarah Scott endorsed a commercial society that did not level class distinctions but advanced workers' independence and raised their standards of living. Laborers in the rug factory managed by the Millenium Hall ladies receive high wages, and girls in their school system are taught saleable skills. Fielding not only suggested that women's conversation be viewed as a commodity to be exchanged for money but also published her books with that view in mind. Hamilton and Leprince de Beaumont depicted women as entrepreneurs. The ideal of feminist utopists was a state of "reciprocal services" where even the poorest laborer could "purchase all the comforts of life."[19]

Consequently, the second reason women embraced the jurisprudential tradition is that productive labor does not rest on the backs of slaves or uncompensated workers. A civic humanist, by contrast, depends for his leisure entirely on the productivity of his household; women, unable to act independently, must produce, reproduce, and follow the will of their master. That undesirable status was familiar to female authors from their own experiences under a "male policy" they were eager to dislodge via the new economic discourses. As Fielding argued, women suffer "double slavery" because they must pay the debt of gratitude in addition to paying with their labor. Scott engaged the analogy of marriage and slavery directly in *Sir George Ellison*, but with calculated irony she made the slave-owning husband the one enslaved by his wife rather than vice versa. Scott upset gender expectations in this way precisely in order to surprise readers into understanding and agreement. Ellison becomes so disillusioned with the slave system that he returns to England, where he believes contractualism will further fairness and justice.

Third, women adopted the jurisprudential model because it frees the cash and credit necessary to sustain the web of human connection. Fielding indicated that women need capital if they are to attain a place in the social web—if they are to support themselves and maintain the relationships that in turn sustain them. Emotional ties, she argued, cannot endure without some financial ground of support. David Simple's family disintegrates as poverty and disease sever bonds that love alone cannot preserve; Sarah Scott's couples ensure their affective ties by sound financial management. These authors' lives and letters reinforced the preoccupation with cash and credit. People of comparable social rank, they believed, should be on an equal footing, whatever their sex; they should be able to develop the emotional bonds they desire. Yet the gentlewomen they especially set out to defend often end in a state of dependence and, unable to command cash or credit, are exploited by others. Fielding in particular analyzed the position of the "toadeater" whose poverty and consequent subjection forestall the possibility of true friendship: "It is a Metaphor taken from a Mountebank's Boy's eating Toads, in order to shew his Master's Skill in expelling Poison: It is built on a Supposition, (which I am afraid is too generally true) that People who are so unhappy as to be in a State of Dependance, are forced to do the most nauseous things that can be thought on, to please and humour their Patrons."[20]

If a "state of dependance" led to abuse by the powerful, it was emotionally wrenching for underlings who took seriously the deferential obligations of the debt of gratitude. Although this social expectation was theorized by male philosophers of the period as a source of human connection and friendship, feminist utopists exposed how it left dependents without control over their feelings. Because benefits accrue to the donor as much as to the receiver, they suggested that benevolence is a bargain like any other; it should not prolong a receiver's state of dependence. Female utopists were centrally concerned with charity, but that capacity for benevolence depended upon possessing resources—both financial and emotional—that could be given and exchanged. Money, the central component of an autonomous public sphere, was revealed as simultaneously enabling private attachments. Hence female utopians recognized and insisted on the interplay between the so-called public and private spheres at the same time that competing discourses worked to bifurcate those realms.[21]

Finally, women embraced the jurisprudential model because its idea of origin—a foundational social contract—posited a historical moment when they were the equals of men. Human beings, born free in a state of nature, with identical access to land and resources, decide for reasons of security or efficiency mutually to consent to a government that will apply laws and dispense justice. In their novels, feminist utopists reenacted moments at this social ground zero where characters came together to create a community, mutually setting the emotional and financial terms upon which the society would be structured.[22]

In civic-humanist discourse, by contrast, there was no need for a social contract arising out of a state of nature because individuals "are naturally political, having been created by God in his image as capable of intelligent self-rule . . . Property brings power: the power of masters over servants, the power of masters over themselves. . . . in instituting [authority] among themselves, they enter upon the world of political relations and begin to act as the images of God which they are."[23] Women are always already excluded. They possess neither property nor power, nor are they argued to be innately political or capable of self-rule. Contrarily, the jurisprudential model allows for an originary moment when the state of nature gives way to political life. Women's current subordination is thus the product of history rather than essence, and as such it can be undone.

* * *

Despite these four grounds for feminist endorsement of the jurisprudential model, the ways the model was interpreted by prominent Enlightenment thinkers suggest that it failed on some fronts to address a number of women's central needs. It is all too evident that most noted philosophers in the tradition did not fully consider women's place and their contributions. John Locke, unusual in his insistence that discussions of family politics include the issue of mothers, nonetheless concluded that authority should ultimately reside in fathers because they are "the abler and the stronger." If, surprisingly, women are thought fit to acquiesce to marriages or own property, they are still not examined as political beings or subjects consenting to government via the social contract. According to Francis Hutcheson, who followed Locke in taking women as wives and mothers seriously, women should have the right to consent to marriage, and they should possess equal power over children. But he, too, insisted that parental power is different from political power and that the "method of constituting or continuing . . . civil power" involves not women but "some deed or convention of men." Adam Smith's political economy barely mentioned women or mothers; their availability for marriage and childbearing as well as their labor was taken for granted in his calculations.[24]

Indeed, jurisprudential discourse assumes the fact of women's unpaid work. Although all the theorists agreed that the nation's wealth depends upon population, for example, not one of them calculated the worth of women's reproductive labor. Smith argued that higher wages will result in higher population and that poverty undermines it, so he advocated high wages. Men must be the breadwinners of the family (although he failed to explain why). Their productive labor, which results in a desirable exchange value, has priority over any unproductive labor resulting in mere use value. As Diana Coole concludes:

> Although he does not mention women among those "frivolous" persons whose professions are unproductive, the derogation of activities which yield nothing to the market could only promote the idea that a domestic labour productive only of use-values, was actually unproductive and unimportant, a separate sphere to be ignored by the bourgeois science of production. . . . Women would count, then, only in so far as they produced commodities, and when they reproduced new generations, it would be at the behest of the market. Liberal economics thus desexualized productive and reproductive activity into impersonal components of the market, excluding women *qua* women from consideration yet taking for granted the structural disadvantages they suffer.[25]

Given the tremendous disadvantages for women of marriage and reproduction, it is not surprising that feminist utopians proposed numerous ways of avoiding them. Astell forthrightly cautioned against them, substituting instead a vision of a female monastery; Fielding depicted unmarried women who devise alternative domestic arrangements; Scott created an entire community of single women; Hamilton's heroine puts off marriage so she can control her resources and create the artists' colony she desires; and Leprince de Beaumont's most active protagonist is a widow.

Jurisprudential philosophers further assumed that, despite women's political nonidentity, they remain under political obligation. In return for being fed and clothed, instructed and defended, women must pay the debt of gratitude and subject themselves to the state as well as to their masters. Hence female utopists routinely represented a woman's situation as one of a debtor, a position analyzed by Thomas Hobbes, who reasoned that "benefits oblige; and obligation is thraldome; and unrequitable obligation, perpetuall thraldome." Although Hobbes did not have women in mind, their position is precisely that of his "desperate debtor" who, because of benefits received, remains in "perpetuall thraldome."[26] Nothing women do or achieve will ever pay their debt, no matter how hard they work or how much they try to please. According to Sarah Fielding, the impecunious in general and women in particular are thus slaves, wearing themselves out for unworthy masters in order to pay unpayable obligations.[27] Therefore, although jurisprudential philosophers opposed a civic-humanist system that placed the burden of productive labor on the shoulders of uncompensated domestics, their endorsement of the debt of gratitude obliquely reinscribed just such slavery. Women and toadeaters in the jurisprudential model supplied the place of domestic slaves in the civic model.

Similarly, philosophical theories of benevolence, which are equally tied to custom and ideas of gratitude, only reinforced a gendered hierarchy of values, as justice became the masculine counterpart to a feminine benevolence. Adam Smith may have concurred with feminist utopians that in an ideal society "all the different members of it are bound together by the agreeable bands of love and affection, and are, as it were, drawn to one common centre of mutual good offices." He insisted, however, that such a state can never be achieved in this world. People can be persuaded to act in the interest of another only if they receive material consideration. "Society may subsist among different men, as among different merchants, from a sense of its utility, without any mutual love or affection; and though no man in it should owe any obligation, or be bound in gratitude to any other, it may still be upheld by a mercenary exchange of good offices according to an agreed valuation."[28] Smith's famous example is that of the butcher and the baker, who give food not from a sense of benevolence but from self-interest. Smith reasons that because society can exist at a common-denominator level without ties of benevolence, gratitude, and consequent obligation, those "social virtues" are inessential. Fellow-feeling, "mutual love," and friendship are equally inessential because they follow from benevolence and gratitude. By contrast, justice is critical. Smith concludes:

> We feel ourselves to be under a stricter obligation to act according to justice, than agreeably to friendship, charity, or generosity; that the practise of these last mentioned virtues seems to be left in some measure to our own choice, but that, somehow or other, we feel ourselves to be in a peculiar manner tied, bound, and obliged to the observation of justice. We feel, that is to say, that force may, with the utmost propriety, and with the approbation of all mankind, be made use of to constrain us to observe the rules of the one, but not to follow the precepts of the other. (80)[29]

For Smith, justice is essential to society, whereas benevolence is not. He speaks from the perspective of an enfranchised male who can practice benevolence whenever he feels like doing so and by his "own choice." In another passage Smith details the psychic benefits reaped by the charitable male yet nonetheless offers a telling metaphor to argue how inessential benevolence is to society:

> Though Nature, therefore, exhorts mankind to acts of beneficence, by the pleasing consciousness of deserved reward, she has not thought it necessary to guard and enforce the practice of it by the terrors of merited punishment in case it should be neglected. It is the ornament which embellishes, not the foundation which supports the building, and which it was, therefore, sufficient to recommend, but by no means necessary to impose. Justice, on the contrary, is the main pillar that upholds the whole edifice. If it is removed, the great, the immense fabric of human society, that fabric which to raise and support seems in this world, if I may say so, to have been the peculiar and darling care of Nature, must in a moment crumble into atoms. (86)

Benevolence becomes the noncritical feminine "ornament," whereas justice is the critical masculine "pillar." Smith reinforces a cultural view of these qualities as gendered and differently valued. Speaking from the perspective of a male giver rather than a subjected receiver, he imagines the satisfying sensation of "deserved reward" for purposefully dallying in the feminine realm of beneficence.

Smith undermines his argument, however, by discussing standards of behavior in the same way he does justice. Although justice may appear more essential because without it society would "crumble into atoms," standards of behavior prove equally important; society "would *crumble into nothing* if mankind were not generally impressed with a reverence for those important rules of conduct" (163, emphasis added). Although "*Nature*" may have brought forth the fabric of society, it failed to secure the texture; *cultural* norms must be reintroduced as the critical custodians of the fabric. Not surprisingly, among these "important rules of conduct" is the observance of the duty of gratitude. A breach constitutes one of the "blackest" wrongs, even if it cannot be called illegal, and "the heart of every impartial spectator rejects all fellow-feeling with the selfishness" of the wrong-doer (78).

Women were forced into domestic slavery by the custom of the duty of gratitude rather than any legal or religious sanction, and they risked social ostracizing for failing to be grateful, for presuming or expecting to be supported. Moreover, they had no legal redress if support was denied, because it was the result of beneficence. Susan Staves has shown how common-law rights of dower were replaced in this period by contractual agreements for jointure and pin money. These came to be seen—even among legal thinkers—as private gifts of husbands rather than as rights of women. Although a woman could sue for arrears in pin money, she could only do so for up to a year. Further, as Staves concludes, how many would put their husbands in jail for failing to give them pin money? Hence even money to which women had legal right was viewed in practice as largesse on the part of husbands.[30]

If jurisprudential thinking, as interpreted by prominent eighteenth-century commentators, had been carried to its logical conclusion, cultural norms would have negated the natural rights with which women were born. To combat that inconsistency, feminist utopists insisted that benevolence become part of the system of equivalent exchanges so everyone might be supplied and no one left a perpetual debtor. Rather than do away with natural law and cultural norms in their imagined societies as a means of protesting inequalities—something one might expect—feminist utopists instead strive to apply them consistently. In their communities, men cannot avoid the duty of gratitude toward women, and women cannot avoid it toward men. Obligation moves in all directions on the model of equivalent exchange. Thus feminist utopists champion societies like Adam Smith's utopia, where mutual good offices came from friendship, love, and affection. The ways they portray such communities suggest that all members possess equally the resources necessary to achieve and sustain friendship. Obligation, in their scheme, does not create debt and a sense of desperation, because good offices are reciprocal and can be counted on. It can, then, become a means of binding people together rather than oppressing them. Gratitude is valued, as in Smith, but like obligation it goes both ways, from the underling to the charitable, enfranchised male and back again.

Feminist utopian authors therefore urged that obligation for benefits be a part of the general economy. In these benevolent contracts, an equivalent return could be expected, leaving no one the loser. Hence the feminists advocated a system that reimported ideas of benevolence without returning to a patriarchal model or fully advocating a civic one. Although civic humanism's emphasis on virtue and valuing of friendship were strongly endorsed, they were incorporated into a jurisprudential model that allowed women to imagine themselves as full participants via equivalent exchange.

Female utopian writers further achieved that vision by drawing on the concept of Christian charity and love. Indeed, they revised the heroism of the patriot ideal to incorporate Christian rather than pagan virtues. By contrast, both civic humanists and jurisprudential philosophers downplayed the significance of religion. Pocock explains the disjunctions between civic humanism and Christianity by pointing out that a civic humanist would practice the virtue of *ataraxia* (tranquility) rather than *agape* (love) and embrace a morality that was "neo-Stoic, and more likely to lead to a deist than a Christian religious expression." Moreover, Pocock sees "anti-Christian possibilities latent in the civic ideal."[31]

The jurisprudential tradition less thoroughly rejected Christian morality. Francis Hutcheson clearly sought to reconcile liberal ideology and a Christian outlook. Yet some of the best-known philosophers of the Scottish school were either famously atheistic, like David Hume, or rumored to be skeptics, like Adam Smith. Sarah Fielding took such thinkers to task and satirized skeptics, stoics, and free-thinkers in *David Simple* and *Volume the Last.* Mary Astell reconciled benevolence and desire as she imagined a community fueled by divine love. And Sarah Scott turned to Christian charity as a reason for women not to accept but to avoid exploitation. She disparaged the "suffering virtues" and called instead on abused married women "to act thro' Love":

> I admire a Woman who chuses to avoid Injuries rather than indolently to grieve under them, and to work for a Support instead of weeping for want of one. A Person long used to act thro' Love, could not easily give up the Reins of Government to Fear; and when People practise that Excess of Christian Meekness, which is now thought only a female Virtue, of turning the other Cheek to him who has smote the one; and to him who has taken Part of her Right and Property, giving the rest also, only from want of Courage to resist, she may be a greater Coward than others, and perhaps a better Wife in the Opinion of some Men, but not a better Christian.[32]

Here Scott brings her interpretation of Christian duty—"to act thro' Love"—as a defense against those who would argue that married women lack both legal and religious reasons for resistance. She transforms the Christian call for charity into a justification of women taking up the "Reins of Government" of the self and overcoming the fear that enslaves them as "desperate debtors." Husbands have taken "Right and Property" from wives, and women should expect something in return.

The political language in which Scott articulates women's position demonstrates her view of their role as citizens. If natural and civil law fail to confirm this role, then one can appeal to a higher law, Christianity. Moreover, Christian charity, for Scott, requires that one actively give of one's self. If wives and daughters possess so little, if they cannot control even their own bodies, then what can they possibly give? From Scott's perspective, Christian doctrine fully supports the natural law tenet of self-ownership for women as well as men.

In addition, models of ancient Christian communism and monasticism continued to influence feminist utopists as they did Thomas More and Mary Astell, who lauded the piety of ancient Christians. The New Testament record of primitive Christian community comes from Acts 4:32–35: "And the multitude of them that believed were of one heart and of one soul: neither said any of them that ought of the things which he possessed was his own; but they had all things common. And with great power gave the apostles witness of the resurrection of the Lord Jesus: and great grace was upon them all. Neither was there any among them that lacked: for as many as were possessors of lands or houses sold them, and brought the prices of the things that were sold, And laid them down at the apostles' feet: and distribution was made unto every man according as he had need."

Fielding repeatedly endorsed the communal sharing of property, Scott described a communist society in *The History of Cornelia,* and Leprince de Beaumont fully outlined an "*Union Chrétienne*" in the *New Clarissa* (2:76). Scott's most elaborate community is called "*Millenium* Hall," invoking the era of peace that the Second Coming will introduce. Perhaps Scott was purposefully drawing on the words of Mary Astell, who imagined the "*Millenium* Days" of women's liberty "in which the Wolf and the Lamb shall feed together, and a Tyrannous Domination, which Nature never meant, shall no longer render useless, if not hurtful, the Industry and Understandings of half Mankind."[33] Scott's narrator, however, gives the community that name provisionally and casually as a way of maintaining the collective's anonymity; it is as though Scott were reluctant to make a grand claim. Similarly, the communal sharing of property is approached and avoided simultaneously, a desirable but perhaps unachievable vision. Its extremism sets in relief and lends credibility to the more moderate communities advanced in the novels, as if to suggest that, utopian as those societies may be, they are viable rather than visionary, feasible rather than fantastic. The retreat from communism demonstrates the thoroughly pragmatic quality of the authors' visions and the seriousness with which the representations were offered; communism mattered less than an equalizing benevolence.

Feminist utopian authors thus worked within the discourses available to them yet rewrote them from the position of female subject to advocate a consistent application of ethical principles and offer visions of self-possession and independence. Hence their work avoided radical solutions, something characteristic of eighteenth-century feminist utopianism that was coextensive with its expression via the new form of narrative fiction, the novel, and that allowed them to dodge the patriarchal representations of traditional utopias.

PART 2

Women's Utopian Visions

3. Sarah Fielding: Ideal Readers and Utopian Commerce

Sarah Fielding offered the first example of a feminist approach toward what I have called a liberal utopia. Although the expression "liberal" was not coined until the early nineteenth century, it is commonly used by political theorists in discussing the eighteenth century and is helpful to describe how Fielding departed from the traditional conception of utopia as she employed narratives to analyze the extent of the individual's freedom and economic range, and of the individual woman in particular. She sought a viable place between benevolism and realism, even as she distinguished between true friendship, which fosters utopian conditions, and false friendship, which breeds domination and subjection. Betty Rizzo has pointed to Fielding's astute analysis of power dynamics and the ways education is to "abolish tyranny and encourage benevolence," and Gillian Skinner has suggested that tyranny and benevolence are articulated in the languages of economic theory and sensibility, concluding that Fielding's novels "explore the compatibility (or otherwise) of the commercial world and more idealistic principles" and that "the problem . . . is one with which their female characters can most readily engage."[1]

I will extend these discussions and deepen the links between Astell and eighteenth-century feminist utopists by concentrating on Fielding's deployment of the fictional figure of an Astell-like female paragon who is at once teacher and negotiator. Through lessons in reading and interpretation this ideal woman—who appears in *David Simple, Volume the Last,* and throughout Fielding's works—instructs individuals in fathoming tyranny, becoming utopian subjects, and perpetuating sensitivity and understanding. Through an unflinching look at economic realities she exposes the dystopian consequences of counterfeit charity even as she is committed to the idea of a society in which friendship might survive. The paragon thus undertakes two projects, creating ideal readers and positing a model of utopian commerce. Like her female paragon, Fielding ventured social critique and repeatedly registered utopian dreams even as she despaired about the extent to which woman, whether teacher or trader, would be credited in mid-eighteenth-century England.

* * *

Fielding's novels, published between 1744 and 1760, reflect the familiar binarisms characteristic of Augustan satire and sentimental literature. Her characters often fall into opposing camps. Portia is set against The Cry; David Simple and his friends must, yet cannot, protect themselves from the attentions of Ratcliffe and the Orgueils; and Cleopatra and Octavia embody antithetical notions of the feminine.[2] Some characters are models of human intractability. As cruel people with hardened hearts, they consciously or unknowingly do all they can to hurt the weak. Other characters are sensitive individuals who suffer at the hands of the unsympathetic and powerful ogres. Fielding split readers into two camps as well in a move common to the satirical writing that so influenced her. Pope and Swift both depended on forming readers into an exclusive club of like-minded individuals who could feel superior to and ridicule mercilessly those left out.

In *David Simple,* Fielding used the method differently from her Augustan forebears. She oversaw the sentimental creation of a club of tenderhearted, childlike adults who scorn brutality and insensitivity. These are her utopian subjects, capable of true friendship and benevolence. Worthy readers are encouraged to join the club of initiates as they experience tender sensations and are moved by the events of her tale: "The Raptures *David* felt at that Moment . . . are not to be expressed; and can only be imagined by those People who are capable of the same Actions" (133).[3] Like Astell, who wished to "decoy" female readers into joining a community of magnetized devotees, Fielding drew readers by appealing to their hearts and sympathies.

Such emotional understanding and the inability to communicate feelings in words has been identified as a hallmark of sentimental literature, and Fielding's *David Simple* represents one of the first books in the genre.[4] What has received less attention, as George Starr has pointed out, is the religious association of sentimentalism: "Stigmatized as 'zeal' or 'enthusiasm' during the Restoration, the ardor associated with Puritanism had become suspect. Sentimentalism arises in the eighteenth century partly as a reaction against this taboo, and represents a kind of return of the repressed, a reopening of channels through which a broad range of human emotion, from passionate intensity to exquisite delicacy, might once again find expression."[5]

Fielding exploited the discursive strategies of an established devotional tradition in hopes of invigorating readers' sympathy and generosity, although she harbored profound doubts about her chances of success. To what extent were readers educable? The writers of Christian devotional literature grappled with whether readers could only understand sensations with which they are familiar or whether new feelings can be learned, using metaphors of transcription and the soul-as-text. John Worthington noted, "The great practical Truths of Religion, the Mysteries of the inward Kingdom of God, are best discerned by such Readers as are sincerely religious, such as have in some measure read the same things in their own souls."[6] He suggested that reproducing desired readers requires a predisposition on their part to the wished-for behavior; they must already possess within themselves the seeds that the author will cultivate. Mary Astell agreed that it is a person's inborn, latent love of God that needs to be brought to consciousness through the magnetic power exerted by a friend's imitation of Christ. In the absence of such direct contact, her *Letters* must serve. Devotional literature thus points to a discursive means of activating sensation and creating a cohesive group of feeling individuals.

Fielding concurred. Her doubts about her ability to reproduce sympathetic readers are revealed in her tendency to polarize, and her satiric vein suggests that people are inevitably already part of a tenderhearted or an insensitive group. Nonetheless, she held out the dim hope that even a skeptical reader will be softened to benevolence through the educational impact of her text. Like Astell, she believed with Portia in *The Cry* that "the seeds of good-nature, benevolence, and every amiable quality are in almost every human breast" (2:217) and that cultivating these seeds is an author's function. In her translation of Xenophon, we read that "Socrates, without setting himself up for an Instructor, had full confidence, that all who attended to his Discourses, and embraced his Doctrines, would never fail in Point of Friendship, either to him, or to each other" (18).

That image would have appealed greatly to Fielding, who created learning environments in and of her fictions, schools that would become gardens for tending the growth of benevolent individuals. With such an education, women in particular could turn into self-possessed utopian subjects capable of engaging the interest of others by teaching, writing, and undertaking philanthropic activities. Michel de Certeau has argued that "the ideology of the Enlightenment claimed that the book was capable of reforming society, that educational popularization could transform manners and customs, that an elite's products could, if they were sufficiently widespread, remodel a whole nation."[7] Feminist utopists wished to further that effort, although Fielding, still impressed with the fallen nature of her world, was far from assuming that "assimilating" a text would necessarily result in "becoming similar to" it, even though she fantasized such powers of the book. By the end of her career in the late 1750s and early 1760s, however, Fielding entertained the thought of reform proliferating textually throughout an entire nation. That ambition was even stronger among the later writers she inspired, Sarah Scott and Mary Hamilton in particular, who wrote chiefly during the 1760s and 1770s (chapters 4 and 5).

To the older Fielding, teaching how to read was critical. Although Lettice Cary, Bathsua Makin, and Judith Drake had in the seventeenth century written in detail about the structure of women's education and the knowledge women should master, Fielding followed Astell's lead and considered the psychology of pedagogy.[8] Her concerns are most apparent in her children's book, *The Governess* (1749). Within the text, stories and interpretations of stories were to mold the minds and manners of Mrs. Teachum's pupils. Outside the text, Fielding's juvenile readers were simultaneously to absorb her didactic message to become ideal subjects in their own rights. Fielding had taken courage from the Lockean notion that an individual's experience influences development, and she relied on the malleability of children's minds. Young readers remain, unlike most of their hardened adult counterparts, capable of being moved and taught by stories, and the tales of *The Governess* often take the didactic forms of the fairy story, fable, or exemplum.[9] Children can identify with characters who are taught how power should be used, how envy and other vices should be stifled, how suffering should be endured with patience, and how property is best shared with others.

Fielding, however, apparently undermined her own best efforts because the ideal subjects for whom she hoped tended to recede into the half-light. In *The Governess*, for instance, the girls at Mrs. Teachum's academy are encouraged to love Jenny Peace, the oldest student and prefect, who has told them stories and instructed them in gleaning morals from those tales. The girls sob when Jenny must leave the school at the end of the book. As soon as she has departed, their sympathy for her quickly turns into a study of her traces in the letters she sends and in her history, which the girls are instructed to explicate and emulate:

> There was no Day thought to be better employed than that in which they received a Letter from their absent instructive Friend, whose Name was always mentioned with Gratitude and Honour. . . . All Quarrels and Contentions were banished . . . and if ever any such Thing was likely to arise, the Story of Miss *Jenny Peace*'s reconciling all her little Companions was told to them; so that Miss *Jenny*, tho' absent, still seemed (by the bright Example which she left behind her) to be the Cement of Union and Harmony in this well-regulated Society:

> And if any Girl was found to harbour in her Breast a rising Passion, which it was difficult to conquer, the Name and Story of Miss *Jenny Peace* soon gained her Attention, and left her without any other Desire than to emulate Miss *Jenny*'s Virtues. (125)

The "Name and Story" of Jenny Peace create a presence sufficient to construct the ideal atmosphere of friendship and calm as well as form the ideal young subject who will stifle her passions, "pay to her Governors the most exact Obedience, and . . . exert towards her Companions, all the good Effects of a Mind filled with Benevolence and Love" (126). As in Astell's vision, emulation of a model among the group results in a harmonious society. Jenny Peace becomes the imitator of Christ, whose physical disappearance had left his disciples and sympathizers to textual interpretation and imitation. Indeed, despite Jenny's centrality she disappears into a story like those read in class; the young girls are encouraged to strive for that fabular status and become transcriptions themselves.

Thus Fielding's ideal subject was simultaneously her ideal reader on the way to becoming her ideal fable. Unlike the judgmental Cry, for instance, an ideal reader possessed the capacity to interpret sympathetically, to be moved and therefore changed by what she read so that eventually others could read and transcribe her performances. The interaction with people and the interpretation of texts is all of a piece, with sympathy the critical element in being able to understand and connect.

Such an education in sympathy or friendship and its enfabling virtue is not true only of Fielding's book for children but her novels as well. In the preface to *The Countess of Dellwyn*, for instance, she makes her didactic intention explicit. People tend to read with a limited agenda, she complains. A seafarer might read Virgil merely to determine whether he knows geography rather than to consider the "beautiful Strokes" that will convey human truths. She therefore concludes, "Many Persons have endeavoured to teach Men to write; but none have taught them to read; as if Reading consisted only in distinguishing the Letters and Words from each other" (xxxiv). Later in the story Lord Dellwyn is made to suffer for not having been a reader earlier in life, in particular for not having read Shakespeare's plays. Had he done so, he would have recognized the Iagos around him (2:117).

Fielding's utopian subjects—David Simple, Camilla, Valentine, and Cynthia among them—are all ideal readers, innately trained and capable of sympathetic interpretation as they absorb the story of Isabelle or construe the city through which they ride, even as their own stories become the subjects of sympathetic interpretation by others in *David Simple*.[10] With the exception of Cynthia, these characters, too—following Jenny Peace—disappear.

In addition, Fielding's literary criticism elucidated the reproduction of her ideal individual as ideal reader/text. In the *Remarks on Clarissa,* she reinscribed the situation of Richardson's novel by creating characters paralleling those of his story, and she concluded with an epistolary exchange in order to rewrite the Richardsonian version. Miss Gibson succeeds in converting the initially dubious Bellario by interpreting Richardson's novel for the gathered group and then by writing letters. She is a new Clarissa who, unlike the old one, can demonstrate that reformation of a rake is possible by literary means after all. But that confidence founders as Miss Gibson identifies with Clarissa's self-effacement and expresses a desire "to pass through Life unnoted" (52) despite her assertive performance at the prior literary discussion.[11] Like Jenny Peace, Miss Gibson disappears, leaving only traces. In Fielding, recourse to the pen and the text points less to belief in the power of inscription and sway of the implied author—as it did in Astell, who felt her *Letters* might alert women to their spiritual needs—than to an uneasy relationship among self, agency, and interaction with others.

It cannot be assured, Fielding implied, that readers will read correctly. She set her hopes on training them, especially young ones, to interpret accurately so they would glean the proper moral and therefore act benevolently. In so doing they reproduce themselves as utopian subjects, eventually becoming texts to be read by others. But without Mrs. Teachum hovering in the background, ready to intervene and set interpretation straight, and without Miss Gibson at hand to draw the right conclusions from a text, chances are that the others will fail. Socrates, the most successful teacher of all, cannot escape the world's pressure toward self-elimination. By the time Fielding wrote *The Cry* even the goddess Una could only supervise rather than counter The Cry's responses, regardless of her strong support for Portia. Teaching someone to read is a difficult business: The chain of reproduction—teaching toward an eventual enfabling that will teach toward yet another—can easily come to a dead end in the face of an ineducable and unsupervised interpreter.

Fielding's texts thus represent a discussion with herself about what it is in her power to reform. Her vision of a world in which properly educated readers reproduce both themselves and a benevolent society survives, but only between profound despair and quiet hope. Despair emerges from characters who are grotesquely vicious, unschooled, and incapable of learning sympathy or friendship. Fielding implies that this represents the state of most people's minds. Hope arises from situations in which a young woman like Jenny Peace or Miss Gibson is able to teach onlookers to interpret by her method and, through force of presence alone, see the world through her text. Although that ought to fill readers, especially young female ones, with faith, very few utopian subjects emerge (subjects even the persuasive skills of Portia and Miss Cummyns cannot construct). Most of the few characters whom readers are encouraged to cheer on ultimately die, vanquished by the cruel characters who survive. Finally, even the energetic and vocal female advocates of benevolence dwindle into texts read by few—if not misread even then—to become the invisible mimics of Clarissa's wish "to pass through life unnoted" and find rewards in heaven. Children, seen but not heard, grow into adults who are to be perhaps read but not seen. Fielding's hope that the power of her texts would evoke her presence sufficiently to transform readers—despite her physical absence—was all but overcome by a lack of faith in the interpretive capacities of the untrained and untrainable readers who made up an uncongenial world.

* * *

Although Fielding supported Astell's vision of the paragon, she lacked Astell's confidence in the transcribability of the model. Nonetheless, in spite of the overpowering difficulty Fielding sensed in reproducing utopian subjects and ideal friends, such people exist in her fiction. Critics have emphasized the separatism of Fielding's utopian groups, especially because their analyses have focused on *David Simple* and *Volume the Last.*[12] Through the figure of the female paragon, however, Fielding attempted to blend competing discourses and thereby hoped to bridge the gap between ideal and real societies. Cynthia in *David Simple* and Mrs. Bilson in *The Countess of Dellwyn* in particular are mediators and teachers, and the latter succeeds in generating communities of mutuality in a commercial world. Despite Fielding's tendency to portray isolated and opposed camps, then, she hoped that an inventive woman could bring the two together.

A similar observation has been made by Gillian Skinner, who has noted how "sensibility and commercial instinct" is combined "within a female figure." Fielding created Mrs. Bilson in particular, she suggests, to show how "sentimental virtues are allowed to be compatible with economic sense." Skinner's discussion of the values of the texts proceeds in literary-generic terms to establish the sentimental parameters and in political-theoretical terms to outline the degree of adherence to a civic-humanist program. She concludes that Fielding wishes to defend the middle classes and expose the vices of the aristocracy.[13]

Although I largely agree with Skinner, I am concerned to reveal the epistemology that grounded Fielding's writing and linked it to Astell's conception of the possibilities, through discursively initiated reproduction, of the proliferation of utopian groups. This constitutes an important source of the hope we sense in Fielding's portrayal of Mrs. Bilson and contributes to its stunning novelty. Class remains significant, but Fielding's interest in the issue followed from her concerns about gender and religion. Indeed, she never lost sight of either, nor did she abandon belief in the centrality of education. Her concern was with the possibility of changing readers. That method of instruction was to alter economies on all levels—the circulation of words, feelings, and resources—in order to inscribe a reproductive model to perpetuate utopian transformations. Her "theory," as Rizzo has termed it, was then adopted by the Bath Community and absorbed by Mary Hamilton.[14]

Within Fielding's utopian groups polarization evaporated as true friendship, as in Astell, brought about likeness and unanimity. A divide as unbridgeable as sex and gender was rendered insignificant. David Simple sets out on his search for a friend, and it matters not whether this person should prove male or female. The same-sex relationships between Portia and Cordelia in *The Cry* and between the young Cynthia and Camilla in *David Simple* prove as significant as the later heterosexual links between Portia and Ferdinand, Camilla and David, or Cynthia and Valentine. As if to avoid affective exclusion, all of these characters create utopian living groups in which property is shared, labor is done cheerfully for the benefit of all, and children are cared for communally. Fielding's vision resembles classical and early Christian ideals, the most renowned being Plato's *Republic,* where partners and children are shared and it is "the sharing of feelings of pleasure and distress which binds a community together."[15] Friendship forms a central theme in Fielding's translation of Xenophon, which might have drawn her to that work in the first place.[16]

The example of the primitive Christians' communism is consistently echoed in her depictions, where community affections are circulated alongside resources. In the *Familiar Letters,* Harriott and Priscilla are perfect friends who fall in love with the same man. He marries Harriott, but all three nonetheless live together—albeit after Priscilla has conquered her passion for Harriott's husband—for the rest of their lives (1:322–27). True friendship inevitably trumps sexual desire in Fielding's work. Even if heterosexual pairing prevails, the overwhelming impression is of a diffused love capable of fulfilling individual desire and furthering the attachment of others. Fielding was thus able to portray coed communities, whereas Astell decried marriage and envisioned a women's monastery. Both used classical and early Christian models of friendship to question customary affective paradigms.[17]

Because Fielding was such an astute reader of social relations, the contact she allowed her utopian communities with the world forced members to see their affective diffusion in light of its singularity and compare it with a world that considers bodies in isolation and genders them, setting value on their sex as well as on the money that community members found so difficult to handle. Consequently, a utopian group like David Simple's is continually confounded. Wishing to determine value on its own, wanting to diffuse emotional and other forms of capital it possesses, it is constantly forced to confront the market's value-finding mechanism. *Volume the Last* becomes the story of how commercial society and its practices—supported by the avarice of Ratcliffe, the stoicism of Orgueil, or the jealousy of his wife—thwart the group's ability to determine worth and distribute value.

Fielding's utopians do not even speak the same language as those outside.[18] When, toward the end of *Volume the Last,* David Simple seeks to borrow money, he and the moneylender Nichols engage in a dialog that is at cross-purposes. David fails to understand Nichols's desire for a bond or security. If Valentine returns from Jamaica, then that is enough, for "Valentine is my Brother, my Wife's Brother, and that's the same thing" (289). Love and kinship ensure that Valentine will pay the debt. David can only conclude, "You don't talk our Language, Sir." "Not your Language, Sir?" Nichols responds. "I think I talk plain English; and only want to know what Security I should have, should I advance any Monies?" (290). David's utopian language represents an incommensurable discourse in *Volume the Last,* a system—economic, linguistic, and psychological—separate from the grasping, selfish world of bonds and obligations represented by Nichols, shared by The Cry, and characteristic of the adults outside Mrs. Teachum's school.

At the same time, the apparent incommensurability of Fielding's utopian discourse with "plain English" is not absolute. Although they may dislike modern commercial life, at least some of her utopian characters understand the language of exchange. Cynthia in *David Simple* acts as a bridge or translator between utopian and worldly discourses. A character who echoes sentiments of Mary Astell, especially on the question of marriage, she creates the strongest link between Fielding and her literary forebear.[19]

Cynthia also sets up a connection and contrast between her ideals and a reality corresponding with the much-debated theory of Bernard Mandeville as expressed in the notorious *Fable of the Bees.*[20] Mandeville argued that private vices generate economic activity that trickles down and brings about public benefits; such vices ought, therefore, not be discouraged. Cynthia, for her part,

> was considering, amongst the variety of Shops she saw, how very few of them dealt in Things which were really necessary to preserve Life or Health; and yet that those things which appeared most useless, contributed to the general Welfare: for whilst there was such a thing as Property in the World, unless it

> could be equally distributed, those People who have little or no share of it, must find out Methods of getting what they want, from those whose Lot it is to have more than is necessary for them; and, except all the World was so generous, as to be willing to part with what they think they have a right to, only for the pleasure of helping others; the way to obtain any thing from them is to apply to their Passions. (148)

Communitarianism may be the ideal, but Mandevillianism is the reality. Private vices may lead to public benefits. Fielding quite self-consciously juxtaposed two economic worlds: one of shared property and human generosity and the other of appeals to the passions of haves by have-nots. She bypassed consideration of an Edenic world without property to speak instead of the way property is distributed and benevolence, the voluntary redistribution of property. *Volume the Last* may illustrate an irreconcilable conflict between two systems and end in death for the idealists, but the bilingual Cynthia, who understands both languages and has reconciled the desirability of the one with the necessity of the other, survives.

Thus it is through the character of Cynthia in particular that Fielding tried in *David Simple* to find accommodation between discourses and transform the reader's interpretations of the economy of human interaction in order to achieve a bilingual state. As usual, her method revolved around the issue of friendship, the state of mind that would reorganize relations of value in the human economy. Fielding, however, brought the issue to the fore in discussions of dependence. Intending to teach readers, Fielding exposed the distance between abject dependence and a desirable, utopian condition of friendship. She began with the existential dilemma of the impoverished gentlewoman.[21] It was a fate Fielding knew well, and one her character Cynthia endures, Mrs. Teachum avoids, and Camilla bemoans:

> There is no Situation so deplorable, no Condition so much to be pitied, as that of a Gentlewoman in real Poverty. I mean by real Poverty, not having sufficient to procure us Necessaries; for good Sense will teach People to moderate their Desires, and lessen their way of living, and yet be content. . . . Men think our Circumstances give them a Liberty to shock our Ears with Proposals ever so dishonourable. . . . If we were to attempt getting our living by any Trade, People in that Station would think we were endeavouring to take their Bread out of their mouths, and combine together against us; saying, we must certainly deserve our Distress, or our great Relations would support us. Men in very high Life are taken up with such various Cares, that were they ever so good-natured, they cannot hearken to every body's Complaint, who applies to them for Relief. And the lower sort of People . . . will not suffer us to be equal with them, and get our Bread as they do; if we cannot be above them, they will have the

> pleasure of casting us down infinitely below them. In short, Persons who are so unfortunate as to be in this Situation, are in a World full of People, and yet are as solitary as if they were in the wildest Desart; no body will allow them to be of their Rank, nor admit them into their Community. (132–33)

The passage demonstrates the poverty-stricken gentlewoman's difficulty in finding employment and reveals her existential plight.[22] Without a social place, destitute gentlewomen hovered outside the web of human life. Neither the civic-humanist model, which emphasized the role of property in creating identity, nor the jurisprudential model, which based identity on transaction, offered a foothold. The fear of placelessness and isolation threatened as much as the fear of starvation.

Thus Fielding drew attention to a figure—the poor gentlewoman—who is left out of discussions of poverty among divines and moral philosophers but who, she insisted, must be included. Although she rarely mentioned specific thinkers, the language she employed made it clear that she was well aware of contemporary discussions. She considered sentimental ideas like those of Shaftesbury and his followers, the moral sense philosophers, who opposed Hobbes and Mandeville and imagined the natural inclination of human beings to be sociable rather than competitive and self-centered. With them Fielding conceived of the individual as part of a social web or "system" from which only "monsters" are excluded.[23] That explains the impoverished gentlewoman's horror at losing her place. She becomes a being—a forerunner of Frankenstein's creature—shunned by society, as alone as if "in the wildest Desart" and with friendship out of reach. As Shaftesbury put it, "Now if banishment from one's country, removal to a foreign place, or anything which looks like solitude or desertion, be so heavy to endure, what must it be to feel this inward banishment, this real estrangement from human commerce, and to be after this manner in a desert, and in the horridest of solitudes even when in the midst of society?" (1:335).

Although Fielding agreed with Shaftesbury about the significance of the exchange of "natural affections" (1:315), she also took a larger economy into account, which moved her from a purely benevolist toward a realist position. She anticipated Adam Smith, who proposed an individual at once emotionally linked to others and yet, prompted by physical needs, self-interestedly attached to economic life. As Fielding put it in *The Cry*, "As this world is at present constituted, what we call the lower part of mankind work for pay, and by that means support themselves and families; yet their assistance by the means of their labour, is as necessary to the rich, as the pay of the rich is to the labouring man" (1:140). Where Cynthia, in Fielding's earlier work, emphasized catering to the desires of the rich, in *The Cry* the focus is on reciprocal needs and compensation. Fielding imagined a seemingly benign, mutually beneficial, exchange. Her characterization "common subsistence" pointed to the dual springs—benevolist and realist—of her economic conception.

A number of thinkers sought such a middle way in the wake of Mandeville's shocking assertion that private vices foster public virtue. Donna T. Andrew, in *Philanthropy and Police,* explains how Mandeville helped reroute theories of benevolence and forced clerics and political arithmeticians to look again at human desires and needs and the social impact of commerce.[24] In the seventeenth and early eighteenth centuries, divines argued that benevolence was the central element in a Christian's life. "The act of giving was an affirmation, an imitation of the life of Christ," poverty was a part of God's providence, and benevolence allowed people "to win salvation in the exercise of their mutual ties of obligation and gratitude."[25] God had given people property to steward and distribute to those in need, and charity was seen as the inheritance or property of the poor, something rightfully theirs.

Gradually that view shifted. It became more common to see benevolence as a voluntary act of mercy bestowed on the poor rather than a duty required of just Christians. Donors were to discriminate carefully between worthy and unworthy objects of charity, and worthiness had to do with the extent to which a beggar would show moral improvement, proper subordination, and increased industry. Such views on the part of clergy were influenced by political economists who emphasized the importance of the supply of laborers and economic productivity. Population preoccupied them as an issue because it was regarded as the strength of the nation; the poor were to be relieved as a way of increasing the number of workers.[26]

Hence the undeserving poor, those who could work but would not, were not to be relieved because that was seen as a way of encouraging idleness and diminishing virtue. Mandeville reasoned that although true charity involved selflessness and an imitation of the poverty of Christ, such values could not sustain a prosperous mercantile nation. Moreover, true charity ran counter to the real desires of people to emulate not the life of Christ but that of wealthy neighbors. As one commentator put it, "Man being Naturally Ambitious, the Living Together, occasions Emulation which is seen in Outvying one Another in Apparel, Equipage and Furniture of the House."[27] Even charitable contributions, Mandeville felt, were largely given as a result of pride and vanity. *The Fable of the Bees* offended his contemporaries, but it had a profound impact on social analysts.

Even if such thinkers were forced to adjust their ideas about human motivation and take account of—and to that extent accept—the impact of commerce on human virtue, they rejected the extreme nature of Mandeville's characterization. Human beings possessed social affections as well as self-interest. If happiness was the greatest of human desires, then the impulse to achieve happiness would be expressed in the need to satisfy social passions as well as wishes for material objects. Furthermore, a moderate desire for material well-being was perfectly reasonable and promoted the social good; an immoderate desire—for example, the love of drink—was more likely to lead to destructive excess and end the public benefits of such behavior. The debate to refute Mandeville forced his critics to adopt some of his conclusions in a milder form and led to a more unified and revitalized outlook on benevolence among the clergy and political economists.[28]

* * *

Fielding reinforced this compromise position in her novels. On the one hand, her utopian groups oppose the covetousness of the world to speak a different language from that of the people surrounding them. For instance, Fielding repeatedly returned to the issue of communal property; it became the happy ending for a number of her stories, *David Simple* and *The Cry* among them. In the tale of "Caelia and Chloe" in *The Governess,* the guardian aunt writes a will settling her fortune equally on both her nieces, and "in her Life-time there was no Occasion of Settlements, or Deeds of Gift; for they lived all together, and separate Property was not so much as mentioned or thought on in this Family of Harmony and Peace" (52). On the other hand, however, a character such as Cynthia brings experience of real-world dependence into the group. She introduces a Mandevillian discourse based on a larger definition of need that includes physical subsistence and gender difference but, simultaneously, does not do away with ungendered affection, shared property, and the diffusion of value, seeing these as equally necessary. She thus blends the positions of David Simple and Nichols, moves between the ideal of Shaftesbury and the cynicism of Hobbes or Mandeville, and travels the middle way of the divines and political economists, who, in refuting Mandeville, also adopted some of his insights. It is from this position that a new sort of utopianism emerged.

Fielding began with a critique of women's socioeconomic dependence. For her, impecunious gentlewomen were left outside the social web and in the mentally anguishing position of being taken for granted even as they were kept on tenterhooks by society. She—as does Sarah Scott after her—described it as a "double slavery," and, characteristically, emphasized the psychological aspects of the predicament. Double slavery is most clearly depicted in Fielding's portrait of the companion, a job that often became the fate of poverty-stricken gentlewomen.[29] Without possibilities for work, as Camilla laments, women's best possibility of gaining bread is through marriage. As Astell had pointed out, however, and as Fielding concurs, marriage often was disguised prostitution and servitude in which women became sexual objects, childbearers, and upper servants for their husbands. Cynthia wittily rejects a marriage proposal with that observation in *David Simple* (85–88). She then becomes companion to a lady of fashion who treats her so badly that she is forced into a slavery similar to the marital kind she had successfully evaded:

> By that time I had remained with her two or three Months, she began to treat me as a Creature born to be her Slave: whenever I spoke, I was sure to offend her; if I was silent, I was out of humour; if I said any thing in the softest Terms, to complain of the Alteration of her Affection, I was whimsical and ungrateful. . . . At last, I reflected, it must be owing to a love of Tyranny, and as we are born in a Country where there is no such thing as public, legal Slavery, People lay Plots to draw in others to be their Slaves, with the pretence of having an Affection for them. . . . in my Opinion, those Persons who give up their Time, and sacrifice all their own Inclinations, to the Humours of others, cannot be over-paid by any thing they can do for them. Men never think a Slave obliged to them for giving him Bread, when he has performed his Task. And certainly it is a *double Slavery* to be made servile under the pretence of Friendship; for no labour of the Body could have been so painful to me, as the having my Mind thus teazed and tortured. (90–91, emphasis added)

Dependence on a patron or husband represented double slavery because it bound a person's mind (feelings of gratitude and affection) as well as body (time and physical inclination to act). Chattel slaves, by contrast, are at least able to eat and despise the cruelty of their owners. Fielding neatly described the psychology of tyranny, which continued in her analysis of toad-eating:

> It is a Metaphor taken from a Mountebank's Boy's eating Toads, in order to shew his Master's Skill in expelling Poison. . . . And the Metaphor may be carried on yet farther, for most People have so much the Art of tormenting, that every time they have made the poor Creatures they have in their power *swallow a Toad,* they give them something to expel it again, that they may be ready to swallow the next thing they think proper to prepare for them: that is, when they have abused and fooled them, as *Hamlet* says, to the top of their bent, they grow soft and good to them again, on purpose to have it in their power to *plague them the more.* (89)

Being under someone else's power is bad enough; worse still is the Sisyphian cycle of abuse and benevolence endlessly renewed.

Women were Fielding's focus, but her astute observations on power and tyranny did not leave men out. Cynthia befriends a "led Captain" in a comparable predicament (91). The Yorkshire gentleman in the *Familiar Letters* uses the metaphor of a pet squirrel to describe his circumstance: "When the poor Creature, impatient of his Chains, jumps and tears about, till he has almost loosen'd one of the Links, and is ready to get free, the Mistress kindly takes him up in such a manner, that the Chain is slackened, and he does not feel it; and whilst she is stroaking him with one hand, with the other she rivets his Chain so fast, that it is impossible for him to escape" (1:310–11). David Simple also takes this position in relation to Mr. Orgueil, and Sarah Scott's George Ellison experiences the same emotional manipulation by his first wife.[30]

Yet according to Fielding, it was generally only a man's feelings, and not his sex, that placed him in this position. The Yorkshire gentleman lacks "Resolution enough to break from" Philotas, the abusive object of his affections (1:316). His inability to act stems from (initially at least) chosen emotional attachments. Fielding's dependent women, poverty-stricken, suffer emotional turmoil without having chosen emotional attachment. The consideration of gender allowed Fielding to move from an understanding of individual psychological manipulation to an indictment of the economic system in general. A utopian group was the only place where the two predicaments, financial and emotional, could simultaneously be overcome.

Because financial dependence was understood to lead to emotional subjection, it reinforced how Fielding linked a critique of custom to her economic analysis. The linchpin of double slavery was the customary "duty of gratitude" for benefaction, as can best be illustrated by Cynthia's circumstance.[31] Cynthia regrets the alteration in her patron's affections, the loss of friendship that the difference in power between the two has occasioned. "The Lady . . . had something very amiable in her Manner, and at first behaved to me with so much Good-nature, that I loved her with the utmost Sincerity" (88). Soon, however, Cynthia laments, "She had raised my Love, by the Obligations she had confer'd on me, and yet continually provoked my Rage by her Ill-nature: I could not, for a great while, any way account for this Conduct . . . I was caught, like the poor Fish, by the Bait which was treacherously extended for me, and did not observe the Hook which was to pierce my Heart, and be my Destruction" (90, 91).

Cynthia, using Fielding's favored animal metaphors like those involving the pet squirrel and the toadeater to describe the innocent sufferer of a tyrant's abuse, points to the love her mistress had raised through obligations. In other words, Cynthia, a companion, is not doing a job for subsistence; she is receiving a benefit requiring thankfulness. Although, according to a rigorous moral philosophy, the mistress's support ought to have been offered as charity—giving without expectation of return—Fielding wished to show how far reality was from this ideal. To that end, she considered the duty of gratitude as an exchange of power.

Analyzing benevolence in a newly commercial world, Fielding took a position that mediated the extremes of divines who saw benevolence as essential to Christian life, of moral philosophers who cared most about the aesthetic value of this custom, and of Sarah Scott, who saw benevolence to poor women as a contractual arrangement, much like other bargains. Scott resuscitated the older perspective, more common in the seventeenth century, and pointed out that benevolence had rewards. Because a benefactor has been compensated emotionally and spiritually for his expenditure, a recipient ought not to be made a perpetually obliged physical and emotional repayer of an unpayable debt. Fielding intimated that view as she began to question the sway of custom. Most of all, she rewrote discourses on benevolence by pointing out how all discussions take place from the perspective of donors rather than receivers. Following Mandeville, she emphasized that givers generally want something in return for their charity.

Most of the major philosophers of the day expressed opinions on the duty of gratitude, and their ideas formed a facet of the debates on reconciling virtue and commerce and were energetically defended. One of the most comprehensive and influential discussions occurs in Samuel Pufendorf's *Law of Nature and Nations* (1672), a text John Locke recommended in his educational writing.[32] It had tremendous influence on the Scottish school of philosophy and became the basis for Gerschom Carmichael's lectures as well as Francis Hutcheson's *System.*[33] Pufendorf reviewed the literature on the subject, quoting, among others, Cicero, Pliny, Xenophon, Tacitus, Seneca, Aristotle, and Ambrose. Although he concluded that beneficence ought to be freely given, he also pointed out the longstanding debate about "whether ingratitude is actionable in a court of law." Pufendorf determined that "when a man exhibits mixed ingratitude, or when he not merely fails to be grateful, but even requites with injuries and evil deeds, then there is a cause for war and an action based on a real injury; and an ungrateful mind, added to this, showing the man's base blemish, gives reason for all the more haste in the prosecution of the injury, and all the more severe punishment of a person whose depravity cannot be lessened even by kindness" (377–78). Thus he agreed that favors ought to be given without expectation of return. Only when ingratitude develops significant dimensions, going on beyond the failure to be grateful to the point of vicious returns, does it justify attack and legal punishment. Beneficence and gratitude thus belong to the realm of unenforceable social custom unless ingratitude on the part of a recipient develops to an actionable extent.

Adam Smith picked up on Pufendorf's analysis in his separation of actionable and unactionable behavior, but not before he had incorporated the ideas of intervening philosophers such as Shaftesbury and Hutcheson. To Shaftesbury, benevolence was an object of beauty, a sign of the harmony of society and a sign of a mind that both loves and promotes this order: "The admiration and love of order, harmony, and proportion, in whatever kind, is naturally improving to the temper, advantageous to social affection, and highly assistant to virtue, which is itself no other than the love of order and beauty in society" (1:279). Prompted by an aesthetic impulse, the benevolist recreates in society the virtue—"order and beauty"—found within the self.[34]

Hutcheson took a more pragmatic, less aristocratic stance. He translated Shaftesbury's aesthetic value of order into appreciation for the balance and order in exchanges of benevolence and gratitude. There is no more beautiful vision, he said, than witnessing a benevolent act and the grateful response it evokes, hence the powerful effect of such a scene on people who witness it at the theater. "Thus strong Sentiments of *Gratitude*, and vigorous Returns of good Offices observed, raise in the Spectator the highest *Love* and *Esteem* toward both the *Benefactor*, and even the *Person obliged*, with *Security* and *Delight* in Virtue."[35] Spectators' sense of virtue—their "moral sense"—is reinvigorated by watching plays that have benevolent content (theatrical ideas expanded on by Adam Smith in discussions of the "impartial spectator").[36]

Hutcheson then transported those ideas from the theater to the theater of the world. In his later *Short Introduction to Moral Philosophy* and in his *System*, the concept of the aesthetic value of benevolence appeared consistently in close association with property rights (as in the *Short Introduction*) or contracts (in the *System*). Hence it is to be analyzed not only aesthetically and morally but also simultaneously in terms of rights and obligations. Hutcheson asserted that an exchange of benevolence and gratitude is beautiful because it has the balance and order of a contract—the symmetrical relation of right and obligation—and is therefore conducive to virtuous social interaction. An influential, practical theory of benevolence was therefore adapted to new socioeconomic circumstances.

Although these moral philosophers generally followed the modern idea that no duty of benevolence exists—it is seen instead as mercy—there is a corresponding debt of gratitude on the part of the recipient. The relationship becomes lopsided rather than mutual. Increasingly during the eighteenth century benefactors were encouraged to evaluate the moral character of a receiver before making a donation. Consequently, the receiver's values were required to pass strict scrutiny, whereas the giver's attitude remained unexamined. For Hutcheson, benevolence ought

> to be proportioned to the merits or claims of others. Among these claims we regard, first, the moral characters of the objects, and next their kind affections towards us, and thirdly the social intercourses we have had with them, and lastly the good offices we formerly received from them. None of these considerations are to be neglected, and least of all the last one; since there's no obligation more sacred than that of gratitude, none more useful in life; nor is any vice more odious than ingratitude, or more hurtful in society. When therefor in certain cases we cannot exercise all the beneficence we desire, offices of gratitude should take place of other offices of liberality.[37]

A giver, researching the character and affections of those in need and motivated by the duty of gratitude for past favors, thus donates to a receiver whose character assures a similar motivation to repay in future, if not through further gifts then through "offices of gratitude," because these are "useful" to society. If such offices are so useful, however, then why does the state not demand benevolence of people? Hutcheson argued that laws fixing a certain quantity or proportion to the wealth of a giver would be unreasonable and much abate the beauty of such actions. He followed Pufendorf, saying that liberality would then appear like paying a tax or discharging a legal debt.[38]

Rather than focus on poverty or the afflicted, Hutcheson was most concerned about givers and spectators. His comments echo the perspective of clerics giving charity sermons and addressing potential donors rather than recipients. He worried about the emotional, spectacular, and aesthetic effects that would be lost if the legal redistribution of income were enforced. Possibilities for the love and esteem of grateful people toward donors would be diminished, and those viewing this benevolent spectacle could no longer have their own moral sails filled by witnessing a "spontaneous" act of generosity. Moreover, people would no longer give because they recognized in receivers devotees of the "natural law" of gratitude such actions are intended to perpetuate: "The prevailing of gratitude encourages every generous disposition, and gives lovely impressions of mankind. The truly great mind does good to others as its natural work from its own sweet dispositions and natural impulse to exercise them, whatever returns are made. It has its main end when it acts its part well. But the lower virtues of others are discouraged by ingratitude: and the ungrateful are the common enemies of all the indigent, as they discourage liberality, and as far as they can, dry up the fountain whence the indigent are to be supplied."[39]

Adam Smith was greatly influenced by his teacher, Hutcheson, when he argued that ingratitude is the "blackest" of sins. Hutcheson conceded to Mandeville: Most people are not so benevolent after all, for it is not true generosity but the return, the gratitude of the dependent, that motivates their donations.

The customary debt of gratitude provides incentive for a potential donor. Those of "lower virtues" need to feel reinforced through giving; they must get back a sense of self and self-satisfaction from being approved by spectators and sensing the dependence of the other. In effect, the theatrical moment of benevolence lets them gain knowledge of their power over others. Hutcheson thereby emphasized the dramatic spectacle that reinscribes "lovely impressions of mankind" by giving selfhood and control to givers, with viewers as sentimental and legal witnesses to this psycho-social-contractual exchange.[40]

With this as background, we can now return to consider how Fielding adapted these views to her own purposes. Although Hutcheson clearly spoke from the position of giver, confidently blaming the ungrateful for discouraging the liberality of their superiors, Fielding pointed out the gentlewoman's position as recipient. She rejected Hutcheson's concern for a theater of "lovely impressions" to insist on the very real injustices that power imbalances bring about. Her impoverished gentlewoman's unending gratitude—indeed, her love—is demanded as a way of creating the donor's sense of self, of power and control, so that, oddly enough, the person can perpetuate such power on the body and mind of the dependent. Fielding focused on the figure of the impoverished gentlewoman, a figure that moral philosophers failed to see and clergy ignored. Where they assumed that proximity increased sympathy, Fielding showed that people who are the most closely connected might well be the most abused. She demonstrated how private relationships can challenge optimistic theories of benevolence by illustrating the injustice in toad-eating and in the feminine position of powerlessness created by financial and emotional need.

Fielding, having pointed out this "double slavery" so unwittingly reinforced by custom and theories of benevolence, still took the notion of gratitude seriously. She could not help but find it attractive as an ideal, and characters in her utopian state of "true friendship" constantly give and act out their thanks for favors. They are as ready to oblige as to be obliged. In an ideal society, the debt of gratitude is not obliterated but equally distributed; under such circumstances, Fielding implied, a sunny theory like Hutcheson's can hold sway.[41] Yet for the most part, Fielding's ideal characters, as ready to bear obligations as to oblige themselves, mistakenly misread the language and actions of individuals outside the group. They interpret benevolence as a sign of friendship, recognition, and good feeling rather than as the gratitude-demanding, obligation-creating, subjecting activity that it is. They remain monolingual. Their utopian discourse appears to remain incommensurable with the language, the "plain English," of the rest of the country.

As a result, most of Fielding's utopian groups must exist entirely apart from the worldly economy—as do, for example, the happy communities that conclude her novels—or they must disintegrate, as happens in *Volume the Last,* having been forced into unwanted patterns of valuation and subjection. These utopias represent ineffectual "abstract" visions, to invoke Ernst Bloch's terminology, and we must look elsewhere for Fielding's "concrete" utopian idea.[42] We must look to characters like Cynthia who will renegotiate benevolence to allow for a new sort of utopia, one in which friendship might survive. That renegotiation paradoxically depends on accepting certain commercial premises, like that of the jurisprudential subject who, owning the self, can therefore contract with others. Although I have focused on Cynthia of *David Simple* as a bilingual translator between Fielding's polarized worlds, she drops out of the picture for much of *Volume the Last* and entirely after it. To pursue Fielding's utopian concept requires consideration of later writing.

Fielding's hope remained dim in these final works, but she made a unique contribution in the development of eighteenth-century English utopianism with the "History of Mrs. Bilson," a story inserted into *The Countess of Dellwyn* (1759), where discourses of virtue and commerce are reconciled and the balance imagined by Finkielkraut is achieved.[43] In that tale, the young Mrs. Bilson's father leaves her, a child, "without having taken care to place his Daughter above the Danger of Dependance," nor can she rely on "that last, and too often poor Resource, the Kindness of Relations" (1:159). The trajectory of her life begins like that of Cynthia but becomes very different. Destitute, she is forced to marry Mr. Bilson, whose imprudence lands him in debtor's prison, and they are constrained to take up residence in The Fleet. There, rendered powerless and unable to act because of his debt, Bilson becomes a stay-at-home father, teaching their sons while Mrs. Bilson goes into business by setting up "a portable Shop in the Manner of some Milaners" (1:180). The gender tables have been turned.

Next, the parameters of women's employment are altered. Lady Dently, a relation-ex-machina, engages Mrs. Bilson as a companion, but "she would suffer her to have another kind of Traffick with her than the rest of her Customers had, and that, as they bought the Produce of her Time, she might purchase her Time alone; for that nothing she could make would be half so valuable to her as her Conversation" (1:193). Conversation becomes a respected, saleable commodity that will allow a woman a living sufficient to support not only herself but also her family.[44] Such an argument was vital to mid-century women writers because it legitimized female publication, both morally and economically, and argued against taking women's work for granted. Commercialization and commodification thus allowed for a new perspective on women's contributions. Fielding created Mrs. Bilson and let her land the job she found the most congenial, as a purveyor of conversation, a seller of words. Eventually, the Bilsons move in with Lady Dently, who takes care of Mr. Bilson's debt. In what would appear to be one of Fielding's typical positive endings, "This Family, equally happy in obliging and receiving Obligations, retired into the Country" (1:202). Consisting of self-possessing subjects, "this Family" can incur the debt of gratitude and also discharge it. The oppression of the debt of gratitude is lifted.

Unfortunately, Lady Dently dies, and, given Fielding's track record, one might expect the story to take another turn for the worse, along the lines of *Volume the Last.* Instead of being left penniless, however, the Bilsons inherit Lady Dently's estate. Finally possessing sufficient capital, they can create the new utopia. They immediately "set out to gratify the Wish that had been nearest their Hearts," that of freeing from debt all the prisoners of The Fleet "as deserved it" and those elsewhere whose characters "they could obtain any Insight into," furthermore setting "them up in their respective Callings" (1:202–3). They create "Seminaries" for young people and almshouses for the aged. They also provide stocked and furnished homes for newlyweds as well as medical care for the poor, whom they instruct in saving and managing money. Predictably, poor gentlewomen receive special attention:

> The Compassion of these worthy Persons was not confined to the lowest Poor; the Indigent of a higher Rank still more excited their Pity: Dependants on the Rich appeared to them more wretched Beings, than those who were brought up to Labour. They hired a large House as a Receptacle for Gentlewomen, who either had no Fortunes, or so little that it would not support them. For these they made the most comfortable Institution; every Convenience of Life was provided for them, and they were under no Restraints, but to the Rules of the House, which were regulated in the most exact and punctual Manner; and the wisest Regulations were to secure the Peace and Happiness of the Society, who were provided with all Conveniencies for rural Amusements, a Library, musical Instruments, and Implements for various Works. (1:207–8)

In these three sentences Fielding resolved the problem that had so perplexed Camilla and Cynthia. As Carolyn Woodward has pointed out, she drew on Mary Astell's monastic vision and foreshadowed Sarah Scott's in describing impoverished gentlewomen who gather together in mutual support.[45]

Fielding has the Bilsons handle all their projects with such economy that even people "of Birth" who have suffered accidents, sicknesses, or losses can count on their relief (one presumes that the formerly spendthrift husband leaves fiscal management to his wife). Their efficient organization ensures that no energy is expended uselessly, no talents are wasted, and no feelings misplaced: "The Old spun and knitted for the Young; and those who were not decrepid served for Nurses to the Sick; relieving each other by turns. They were all assistant to each other; every Institution had some Correspondence with the rest, which helped to lessen the Expence of all" (1:206). Reciprocal exchange creates not only the most efficient but also the most cost-effective application of people's efforts. We shall encounter a very similar utopia in Scott: the community as an economically run, efficient machine that takes particular consideration of impoverished gentlewomen and in which no one rests unhappy or idle.

In the virtuous economy created by Fielding (and imitated later by Scott) we see an accommodation that inscribes new altruistic theories and practices. Nascent forms of benevolence in the period have been called "associated philanthropy" because they depended on the involvement of a group of donors rather than on an individual's bequest.[46] Bequests at death had formerly played a large part in charitable activity, but in this period "associated philanthropy" was based on collecting money from subscribers who would then participate in the management of charities. Charity schools, like the Chelsea girls' school Astell created, were organized in this way. Other projects, many of which began during the 1740s and 1750s when Fielding was writing, included the foundling hospital established by Thomas Coram, the British and City of London lying-in hospitals, the Marine Society founded by Jonas Hanway, the Magdalen hospital for penitent prostitutes, and the Lambeth Asylum for orphaned girls. This new form of charity therefore favored the active involvement of donors, encouraged the moral reform of recipients, and, it was felt, brought about the improvement of the state. Scholars have commented on how these activities made space for women's participation and leadership.[47] Fielding recognized the utopian potential in such groups, which ideally linked the interests of donors and recipients. As a result, she not only endorsed but also plumbed the rationales of such efforts and queried their psychological and emotional effects as a way of marking a fair and useful path.

Yet Fielding never moved away from her focus on faith and devotion. She saw the story of Mrs. Bilson in religious terms as "a Proof of the Efficacy of religious Principles toward extracting the sharpest Sting from the highest Adversity" (1:215). Falling back on the devotional Christian tradition, she suggested that social innovations of the kind she described exist, not in the first place to increase justice or equality in the nation—although that appealed to her—but to cope with the pain of unhappiness, misunderstanding, and deceit in a fallen world. Mrs. Bilson's life is contrasted with that of the miserable Lady Dellwyn. The one exceptional woman is able to make something positive out of her difficult marriage, whereas the other, more typical one is not. Although the story contains a utopia, Fielding's profound pessimism and determinism framed a narrative expressing women's nearly impossible chance for escape to happiness and security. Like the Countess of Dellwyn, most women are forced into marriages that bring out the worst in them and leave them high and dry. Most often in Fielding the only vague possibility of finding peace in a hostile world comes through a Christian resignation that extends into the kind of self-erasure prescribed in the *Imitation of Christ.* Fielding consistently looked back toward Astell's world.

Yet she also looked forward to Sarah Scott's. Fielding's utopianism countered sadness and resignation throughout her career; it proved as persistent as it was dim. Mrs. Bilson's story ends with a young daughter, Miss Bilson, who marries Sir Harry Cleveland: "The Family changed its Persons, but not its Manners; and they continued a Blessing to the World from Generation to Generation" (2:291). Fielding thus could muster a fantasy of the success of reproductive utopianism, the proliferation of an ideal morality. Her utopian vision began as the oppositional discourse of incompatible worlds but ended in a picture of individual initiative and community productivity that set the stage for Sarah Scott and Adam Smith.

Given women's unenviable economic, social, and political position in mid-eighteenth-century England, it should be no surprise to find female authors challenging assumptions that "whatever is, is right" and articulating longings for a better world. Although most utopian authors of the time followed a traditional pattern involving a faraway island utopia and looked nostalgically to feudal and absolutist models, Fielding sought ways to work with the economy as it existed in order to make a place for women—gentlewomen in particular. Drawing on educational plans and projects from her seventeenth- and early-eighteenth-century predecessors and engaging contemporary debates about benevolence and economic individualism, she conceived of friendship, learning, and economic productivity all occurring in the same utopian space. Initially, the community comes together in *David Simple* as the happy conclusion of a novel about the search for friendship. True friendship, we learn, is divided and shared; it does not understand market valuations. However, Fielding's subsequent work, *Familiar Letters, The Governess,* and *Remarks on Clarissa,* began to display the fissures developing in her conception, and *Volume the Last* exploded it, demonstrating a thoroughgoing pessimism. Later, in *The Cry* and *The Countess of Dellwyn,* Fielding tried to salvage utopia. Her most optimistic picture, "The History of Mrs. Bilson," provides the counterpoint to a sad story of a woman's hopeless existence.

The shifts in Fielding's career suggest that she was "buoyed up" by her participation in the Bath Community of women in the late 1750s, when *The Count-*

ess of Dellwyn appeared. Rizzo calls Fielding "the theorist of the group" and explains how the women, Sarah Scott, Barbara Montagu, Elizabeth Cutts, Miss Arnold, Margaret Riggs, and Margaret Mary Ravaud, along with other frequent visitors, consciously set out to counter tyrannical aspects of patriarchy by practicing "an enlightened benevolence in the community" and providing "an example of an alternative way to live" based on "genuine Christianity."[48]

Unlike the elite or respectable purveyors of benevolence whose angle of vision led to notions of a theater of benevolence that consistently refueled a giver's sense of identity and power, Fielding, from a receiver's point of view, saw utopia as the place where benevolence no longer came at her expense. As much as their benefactors, Fielding's newly free gentlewomen were able to earn by their talents—the conversation Mrs. Bilson is able to sell, for example, or the novel Fielding is able to market—and could then, the profits of labor in hand, set about creating the world for which they hoped, an efficient and secure place that Fielding and Bilson conspired to establish.

Buttressed by the Bath Community, Fielding's utopianism thus developed from an "abstract" utopia to a vision that could include rather than erase herself and see women overcoming subordination through their own efforts. No longer subjected by the double slavery that comes of the duty of gratitude and of false friendship, she was able, by embracing evolving economic notions, to imagine a benevolent society that not only rejected common property but adopted the profit motive, that eliminated waste and sought a maximum return on individuals' labor. Divines and moral philosophers concerned with benevolence stopped short of evaluating the position of impoverished gentlewomen. It was left to women writers to supply that, to point out the necessity of educating girls in order to create benevolent subjects who might most efficiently garner profits and disperse benefits.

Fielding's works therefore demonstrate the beginnings of the liberal utopian vision in their yoking of realism and benevolism. She departed from convention to propose a utopia that would create a fairer and freer way of life for women, one that took up and extended rather than rejected new economic realities. Sadly, such utopian departures were the exception rather than the rule in Fielding's writing. Most often she enfabled her utopian subjects and true friends, leaving protagonists desperate and readers bereft. Yet if we focus on Fielding's hopeful moments, we can more easily discern the feminism of her social critique and are better able to view the writing of her successor, Sarah Scott.

4. Reconceiving the Contract: Sarah Scott's Self-Replicating Utopia

Sarah Fielding strongly influenced Sarah Scott, a younger member of the Bath circle who often took in and cared for Sarah Fielding in the last years of her life and wished to include Fielding in the Hitcham experiment, a scheme to implement the Bath circle's utopian ideas. Unluckily, Fielding, who took part in the planning and would have spent her last days most comfortably in those circumstances, was close to death and could not join the Hitcham group.[1] If Sarah Fielding's utopian ideas were always developing, Sarah Scott's visions of ideal communities were pervasive and vigorous; the implementation of utopia became her central project as she sought to realize Fielding's utopian economy.

Despite Scott's interest in economy and commercial culture, however, scholars have emphasized how the discourse of civic humanism or classical republicanism dominates her writing. Gary Kelly, for instance, sees Scott as a thoroughgoing civic humanist by training and by inclination. He points out that she was connected to Conyers Middleton, a "Cambridge scholar and leading voice of classical republicanism" who was Scott's grandmother's second husband and influenced the education of Scott and her siblings. Scott's best-known novel *Millenium Hall,* Kelly observes, can "be read as a feminized and feminist version of the commonwealth and classical republican tradition" seeking to discredit courtly culture and modify gentry capitalism. Harriet Guest, along these lines, argues that Millenium Hall represents an "ideal retreat from commerce." Despite the Millenium Hall women's "commercial view of society," they withdraw to engage in "nostalgic feudalism." Alfred Lutz, too, sees Scott's work through a civic-humanist lens and reads *Sir George*

Ellison "as an unsuccessful attempt to contain commercial capitalism within classical republicanism" through privatization of civic virtue.[2]

By leaning so heavily on civic humanism, such interpretations risk conflating notions of republican virtue and conduct-book domesticity and overemphasizing the separation of spheres; they give too little weight to the social meanings of religion and charity and the pervasive forms of exchange in Scott's work. Scott actually stressed jurisprudential discourse—that of natural law and contractualism—because it offered a more congenial model for women. Because the idea of reciprocity in the contract requires willing agreement, jurisprudential notions make room for the exercise of women's will and assertion of women's rights. Contractualism, for Scott, made possible a sociopolitical place for female subjects. At the same time, however, Scott recognized problematic aspects of contractualism and therefore instilled the language of Christian charity into the language of contractual reciprocity to create a utopian dialect. The contractualist considerations in her novels reveal her antipatriarchal political commitments, but her Christian beliefs aided in reconceiving those contracts. She combined the spiritual and the economic to imagine an ideal contractualism that set in motion an endless sequence of reformative transactions. As a result, her work depicts a self-replicating and ever-expanding utopia.

In her embrace of contractualism Scott departed from Mary Astell, who otherwise so influenced her. Astell disparaged contractual theories. "If *all Men are born Free,*" she asked, "how is it that all Women are born Slaves?" As Ruth Perry has explained, Astell "thought the doctrine of individualism selfish and asocial and was suspicious of the way genetic theories of citizenship beginning with a 'state of nature' erased the social and political meaning of maternity. She also recognized that women lost their political rights when they married—along with their property rights—and she advised women not to marry."[3]

Contemporary feminist theorists have continued to critique contractualism in the same vein. Carole Pateman describes the ways in which the social contract obscures the sexual contract on which it depends. It genders the sexes, establishes hierarchy, overlooks the political nature of marriage and family life, envisions the civil individual as male, and constructs him as one whose identity arises by means of destructive competition rather than community association.[4] Scott was critical of the contract even as she embraced it. Indeed, she detected its antifeminist bias and reconceived it on three related levels: the political, the marital, and the charitable. Those reconceptions allowed her to imagine the utopian transformation of Britain.

Political Contracts

First, Scott adapted the social contract. The initial social contract is the agreement posited by contractarian philosophers as the genesis of the state. People banded together out of the state of nature and granted an authority to rule over them. Despite the differences between Hobbes and Locke, both saw each person as an individual; each subject had a voice, at least initially, in determining the parameters of the collectivity and extent of the sovereign's authority. Although Hobbes and Locke, in theory, did not exclude women, the contract, in effect, was made among men, as Pateman and other feminist critics have pointed out. Liberal theorist Martha Nussbaum, however, has emphasized that it is "custom and political arrangement," not the theory itself, that perpetuates women's oppression, and she argues that the theory therefore can retain radical transformative power. Scott, too, felt that the jurisprudential model offers possibilities for women that the civic-humanist model does not, primarily because there is no reason—apart from custom—why women should not have participated in the original contract.[5]

That left room for Scott to reformulate the social compact, because her utopian community emerged from Hobbesian circumstances. Miss Mancel in *Millenium Hall* asks, "How little society is there to be found in what you call the world? It might more properly be compared to that state of war, which Hobbes supposes the first condition of mankind."[6] Scott depicted horrible families: fathers insist that children marry ogres for money rather than their sweethearts for love; mothers are weak, spoil rather than teach their children, and fail to stand up to the misguided fathers; stepmothers do what stepmothers tend to do in fiction, turning their weak-willed spouses' feelings away from their first wives' children; uncles who become the guardians of young orphan girls raise them only for their own sexual pleasure; sisters play tricks on brothers to thwart their romances while rivaling their own female siblings for the attention of parents and suitors; and brothers who have inherited estates forget the claims of sisters and leave them destitute, usually at the behest of money-hungry wives. The family proves a treacherous organization in Scott's fiction, and readers following the paths of her battered protagonists can only wonder at the ingenious malice that confounds innocents time and again. Her main characters are expelled from unreliable families and seek fellowship among friends and strangers. In the process they reenact the creation of the initial social contract, creating new communities based on emotional, educational, and moral ties rather than legal or biological ones.

Scott's disdain for biological ties had sources in her own experience. She had good reasons to complain of her father, Matthew Robinson, who repeatedly refused to offer her financial support.[7] She also expressed disappointment in her brother, William: "I let him into my way of thinking before he left this place, telling him that if a Brother behaved to me like a Stranger, I shou'd never see him in any other light than that of a Stranger. I have not that regard to blood some good people have, perhaps it may be that I have so drained my Veins that certainly there does not remain in my whole body one drop of what I brought into the World with me, therefore I feel little from Relationship, my affection is proportioned to the merits & behaviour of my kindred."[8]

Blood similarly complicated the life of her partner, Lady Barbara Montagu. Scott lamented that despite high rank and family fortune, Lady Bab's blood let her down: "Had she been heir to the Estates of all family of Montagu's it wou'd not have been an equivalent in the article of happiness for the Gout she has inherited; she pays dear for great blood, & what is hard no one ever look'd on great blood with less inward complacency."[9] Taking undue pride in blood is a matter of contempt in Scott's writing. In *The Test of Filial Duty,* for example, the heroine, Emilia, ridicules the conceited ap Rees family, who display "mildewed armour, rusty swords and spears, and broken guns, all fixed to a wainscot, so rotten from age and want of air, that what once served for the defence of the bodies of the great ap Rees, now threaten destruction to their descendants."[10]

Utopian characters in Scott's novels embrace her derision of blood as they join a community and follow rational standards of behavior instead of trumpeting ancestry and venerating crumbling tokens of lineage. If the world at large operates in the manner of a Hobbesian state of war, the ideal community embraces a social contract that ensures fairness even as it supports distinctions of rank. In George Ellison's opinion, England, "with all its faults is conspicuously generous, frank, and merciful, because it is free; no subordination exists there, but what is for the benefit of the lower as well as the higher ranks; all live in a state of reciprocal services, the great and the poor are linked in compact; each side has its obligations to perform; and if I make use of another man's labour, it is on condition that I shall pay him such a price for it, as will enable him to purchase all the comforts of life; and whenever he finds it eligible to change his master, he is as free as I am."[11]

Given that Scott offers such a ringing assertion of liberty in *Sir George Ellison,* her apparent reluctance to advocate abolition in the novel begs for explanation. Indeed, Scott's treatment of chattel slavery has elicited extensive critical commentary as scholars struggle to define the nature of her opposition to the practice. George Ellison, uneasy at the idea of owning and punishing slaves, insists that they are his "fellow creatures." "I must call them so," he tells his cruel and incredulous wife, "till you can prove to me, that the distinguishing marks of humanity lie in the complexion or turn of features. When you and I are laid in the grave, our lowest black slave will be as great as we are; in the next world perhaps much greater; the present difference is merely adventitious, not natural" (13).

Eve Stoddard sees *Sir George Ellison* as a reformist text that seeks to improve "plantation management with an eye toward the eventual education and manumission of slaves."[12] Betty Rizzo agrees, stressing that Scott "calculated those reforms she could safely advocate (and still hope to be influential) and those she could not."[13] Markman Ellis accepts the novel as innovative and ameliorist but contends that its sentimental logic "seeks to transform the peculiar asymmetries of power endemic to the slavery economies . . . without destroying the ideology or economy of slavery."[14] Scott, Ellis argues, was not as interested in making a coherent political argument as she was in "hitting as many sentimental notes as she can."[15] Felicity Nussbaum also calls the novel "ameliorist" and "committed to gradual social and moral improvement." She focuses not on sentimentality, however, but on how the idea of complexion in the novel brings together discourses of race, gender, and class to expose emerging definitions of Britishness and whiteness.[16] Scott, able to identify with victims, nonetheless sided with dominant ranks and patriotic ambitions. She decried an essentialist stance, furthered Christian notions on the equality of souls, and supported the idea of social ranks, created by God, that imply particular social obligations.

Considered in the context of Scott's entire novel (the Jamaica episode occurs only in the first quarter of *Sir George Ellison*) and, more broadly still, as part of her oeuvre as a whole, Scott's concerns about race and slavery illuminated and buttressed larger arguments about tyranny and gender inequality.[17] Her argument on behalf of slaves was based on what ought to be the reciprocal nature of a relationship—the contractual model grounded in a religious idea of spiritual equality—which sheds light on the parallel she created between chattel slavery and slavery in marriage. Ellison emphasizes the irony of the slave-owner enslaved, which forces readers to confront the issue of marital servitude. His wife exercises "arbitrary power" over him and makes him "that slave which he would suffer no one to be to him" (35, 22).

Scott, like Fielding, took a microscope to domestic power relations and exposed the emotional as well as the political meanings of domestic domination. Ellison can to some extent improve the conditions for his slaves, but he cannot alter his marriage. He must return to England because Jamaica, a place run on coercion and unjustifiable forms of subordination, lacks the ideological ground on which he might build a fair community. In England, his first wife conveniently dead, Ellison can take advantage of a place that is ripe for transformation, a nation with "all its faults," to be sure, but one with a contract system in place. It is a country where a self-replicating utopia can be set in motion.

Ellison's manners are clearly central to this project. Scott employed the image of the Protestant hero who could create a community of peace and harmony by reforming behavior and regulating the ways of society. Interest in such a figure would seem to account for her historical attention to men like Gustavus Ericson and Theodore Agrippa d'Aubigné, whose histories she wrote at about the same time as *Millenium Hall* and *The Test of Filial Duty*. To an extent, their representations partake of the popular mid-eighteenth-century vision of the patriot. Bolingbroke's famous *Idea of a Patriot King* described him as the "most powerful of all reformers: . . . a sort of standing miracle" who transformed his people, causing "admiration and love in every honest breast, confusion and terror to every guilty conscience, but submission and resignation in all. A new people will seem to arise with a new king. Innumerable metamorphoses, like those which poets feign, will happen in the very deed: and, while men are conscious that they are the same individuals, the difference of their sentiments will almost persuade them that they are changed into different beings."[18]

Bolingbroke's vision drew on the civic-humanist tradition, the emphasis of which on virtue and the public good Scott certainly espoused. And as Christine Gerrard has noted, "Charismatic monarchs are as much part of the Whig tradition as they are of the Tory."[19] Scott, however, did not believe in magic but in hard work; Bolingbroke's appealing idea suffered from abstraction. In the case of Gustavus Ericson, for instance, Scott emphasizes specific achievements. "Gustavus, though as great a general and of as intrepid a spirit as any prince of that or the succeeding age, yet was free from the restless disposition of a conqueror. . . . [He] wished to enjoy in peace the kingdom he had conquered by his sword, and was more bent on civilizing than extending it."[20]

Gustavus sets about introducing Lutheranism to Sweden in order to free people from the insidious and costly grip of the Roman clergy. He builds palaces all over the country so the wealth of the nation is not concentrated in a single capital but circulates throughout the kingdom. Decentralization contributes to a greater justice because "no province was subjected to the tyranny of a governor, or the venality of judges; the whole was under his immediate jurisdiction, and he was the supreme judge in every cause." In addition, his presence throughout the country civilizes the people. "By engaging them in milder intercourse and more delicate pleasures" Gustavus teaches "the gentle delights arising from a well regulated and benevolent society" (377–78). He encourages trade, builds hospitals and schools, supports the University of Uppsala, and erects forts on the frontiers of the kingdom to prevent enemy incursions.[21]

Such a charismatic reformer is rare—George Ellison emphasizes that such a man appears only once in a hundred years.[22] Consequently, Scott suggested that people must rely on local leaders and contractual interactions among themselves to ensure virtue and fairness. And authors must invent imitable heroes. Therefore, in *Sir George Ellison,* Scott demonstrated how a character similar to Gustavus Ericson, but "within the reach of imitation" and possessing real limitations, responds to a more familiar environment. Like the women of Astell's monastery who have access to the shining example of Lady Catherine Jones, Scott's readers profit from proximity to Ellison. They are also, as in Fielding, instructed in reading toward imitation. Indeed, Gustavus Ericson refuses to remove from his people; he travels constantly throughout the kingdom, the better to reform manners and dispense justice. This interest in local leadership and example explains Scott's focus on the position of the justice of the peace, "which, if the office were executed with discretion, vigilance, and integrity, would prove one of the most valuable blessings in the British constitution" (70). A justice of the peace, by virtue of connection to the community, understands and has the capacity to influence those within reach. Both George Ellison and Owen ap Griffith, in *The Test of Filial Duty,* attain this political post and use it, Scott maintains, to great advantage for the community. Ellison, who is eventually knighted, is urged to run for Parliament. When he explains to friends that he knows his limitations and would rather remain in a sphere where he can "laudably acquit" himself, they "smiled at his scruples, and told him he was fit for Utopia" (132, 133).

Scott's emphasis on the actions of the justice of the peace demonstrated belief in the centrality of human interrelations to achieve social reform; only through contact will people become educated in the principles necessary to participate in the new social contract. Consequently, education of all kinds was central to Scott's utopian plans. It constructed and bound together communities while forming young people of all classes to perpetuate the utopian groups that protagonists fight so hard to establish. But education's part in Scott's utopianism goes further; it questions the dichotomization of private and public that scholars have identified in the emerging sociopolitical order.[23] By making a family—indeed, a school—of her communities and then having her utopian subjects move out beyond the boundaries into new territories, Scott allowed education to replicate virtue in the economic, social, political, and even literary realms while it justified women's intellectual interests and political engagement.

Scott's understanding of education thus reinforced her political and feminist goals as it encompassed organized schooling and informal learning. When George Ellison returns to visit his friends at Millenium Hall, the women tell him about the school system they are setting up for girls, designed to promote women's independence as well as buttress class and status.[24] "Third-rank" women, going into service or becoming "wives to men in small trades," are to be taught writing and accounts, washing, baking, brewing, milking, and so forth. Their schools will be placed at "the out-skirts of large country towns" so they can become part of the local economy, taking in needlework and clear-starching "at the common prices" so schoolmistresses are "enabled to take the children at a very moderate price." No dancing master should be allowed at these schools, and the girls should not call each other Miss because that "teaches them to confound the distinction that ought to be kept up between them and their superiors" (96–97). Third-rank children ought not to be ignored, then, but their class position must be clearly defined and continually reinforced.

The same goes for second-rank schools for women who have "no prospect of considerable fortunes." Such schools are to offer a curriculum focused on economics and practical subjects such as sewing and cooking. Although drawing "might prove a useful and profitable art" for these girls because they might sell their pictures to the upper classes, music should not be permitted in the curriculum. Unlike drawing, which can be separated from a person and sold, musical performance demands that the person appear in, and therefore inject herself into, the upper ranks. A young middle-class woman trained in music might imagine raising herself by playing for her superiors and perhaps marrying one of them. But all her financial investment—lessons, instruments, and clothes in which to perform—"must ruin her fortune." Moreover, having been taken advantage of by her superiors, who perhaps enjoyed her playing but had no intention of marrying her, the young woman would end up distressed to the point that "neglect or insult [would] become all her portion" (95). Second-rank schools, like those of the third rank, should encourage women to be useful but bolster class distinctions.

By contrast, first-rank schools should offer the gentry and aristocracy ambitious academic curricula. Dance instruction should be farmed out, but the four young teachers of twenty boarding students should excel in music, drawing, writing, arithmetic, and science. They should also give instruction in religion, languages, "good reading," history, geography, and chronology, not to mention "the less abstruse parts of astronomy, natural philosophy, ethics, and the rational parts of metaphysics" (95).

The careful distinctions between social ranks and their appropriate lessons make clear that, to the Millenium Hall women, utopia depended not on the banishment of hierarchy but on the far-reaching educational project itself. When George Ellison says he admires the plans for the women's school but doubts whether people will accept them, Mrs. Morgan responds, "We are grown such Utopians, that what you urge might have appeared very strange to us, if we had not heard the same observations from another friend . . . therefore we are prepared for all the discouragement our schemes can encounter" (98). Yet in the utopian story the scheme actually works, and Ellison promptly sends his neighbor's daughters to the top-rank school. Education ensures that young people, particularly women of the first rank, will become individuals of "good sense," utopian subjects whose knowledge, reason, and devotion to learning work to perpetuate the socially stratified utopian community.

Because serious intellectual work and moral example are reserved for the women of the first rank, it is unsurprising that the Millenium Hall women decide that most parents cannot be trusted to teach their children adequately. The women argue, predictably for people dismissive of blood relationships, that it is right to take children away from the narrow-minded, unthinking mothers and fathers who inhabit the Hobbesian families Scott so abhorred.[25] Better to have exemplary substitute parents as teachers, because time is of the essence. It cannot be wasted, nor can frivolous activities be justified. On the contrary, education to utopia depends on children learning that everything they do has an impact, not only on people immediately around them but also on others far removed:

> Every action of our lives ought to be useful. Upon these common, and frequent acts, depends in great measure the happiness of those connected with us. Great injuries or great benefits are seldom in our power; the opportunities for either are few; but by a number of small vexations, we may render a person more miserable than we could by one great injury. There is an elasticity in our spirits, which enables them to rise again after a great and sudden blow, while a frequent repetition of vexations keeps them down, and deprives them of all power of exertion: but a narrow mind sees not the iniquity of such oppression in a right light, because the evils it inflicts are not expressly included either in the prohibitions in the Decalogue or the laws of the land; blind to the spirit of the law, they attend only to the words. Those, therefore, whose ideas are circumscribed within such narrow bounds, are ill qualified to cultivate the minds of their children. (91)

That statement moves in telling ways to convey Scott's Fieldingesque approach to life in a Hobbesian world, taking account of the psychology of tyranny, the inability of doctrine and law alone to forestall oppression, and the dangerous deficiencies of literal-minded, unskilled readers.

The passage warrants closer attention because it not only echoes Fielding but also touches on views of psychology, epistemology, and history that shed light on Scott's utopianism. As people are affected by the accumulation of small experiences, so, too, Scott felt, is history shaped by the collection of individual actions. The grand gesture or powerful political figure, like the Decalogue and the laws of the land, can indeed have a large impact, but seemingly invisible events can equally or more totally destroy the individual, the community, or the nation. For instance, Scott observed to her sister that people are more likely to be undermined by psychological erosion than by an unexpected shock: "I have always found . . . sudden misfortunes to be best borne as they find the mind in a stronger & more vigorous state; whereas the fear of evils we foresee depress & wear out our spirits & render them less able to support them when they happen."[26] Such invisible erosion can debilitate an entire country. Conflicts and wars, Scott argues in her preface to *Gustavus Ericson,* often find origins in the unseen vice of an insignificant individual:

> Kingdoms are often set at variance by trifles. . . . the covetous encroachments of a man whom the minister either favours or fears [can] embroil two powerful nations; and . . . what is looked upon by the public eye as the effects of national resentment for national injuries, and spreads the most extensive destruction, sometimes originally arises from the private views of the lowest officer in the monarch's service, as the greatest river has its source under ground; in its first appearance little more than a bubbling rivulet, scarcely perceptible, till uniting with every stream it meets in its progress, it swells gradually into a river, whose torrent at length destroys every thing that opposes its course. (v–vi)

The idea of the potential power of what is "scarcely perceptible"—a view articulated by an obscure, impoverished, reform-minded woman writer—grew into a theory of historiography. It shaped one of Scott's arguments for writing biography, a genre, she felt, that brought to light the hidden detail "which more properly developes the human mind."

In *Gustavus Ericson,* Scott weighed the merits of "general" and "biographical history" and argued for a middle way between the two.[27] Biography, focusing perhaps too closely on the individual, needs general history to complete it, whereas general history, that conveyor of public discourse, has some grave disadvantages that biography eliminates. Scott pointed out that general histories offer the big picture but cannot take account of difference and desire; as a consequence, they cannot effectively teach and thereby change readers. Even as they describe larger political events and trends they lack the capacity themselves to incite political change. But biography also falls short and has disadvantages.[28] They include:

> [T]he partial knowledge it gives of history, distinguishing some particular periods with great lights, while intermediate ages are left in obscurity. These detached pieces of history are like redoubts in fortification; each may serve to employ for some time those who design to become masters of them; but if there is no line of communication whereby they are united, they can give no assistance to each other. A reader may by this sort of study become acquainted with the characters and actions of some particular kings of any country, but will remain totally ignorant of the history of the kingdom. (ix)

For Scott, truth could only be arrived at by negotiating between the two, so she decided that she must combine both in her life of Gustavus Ericson and began the biography with a lengthy "Introductory History of Sweden, from the Middle of the Twelfth Century."

Her metaphors of the river and the fortification testify to the utopian quality of her thought in emphasizing the need for "communication" and "assistance." General history can at its peril ignore the hidden sources, the various underground streams and rivulets that join into a river "whose torrent at length destroys every thing that opposes its course" (vi). At the same time, biography at its peril ignores the force of general history, for the individual redoubts in fortification can supply some resistance against "those who design to become masters of them." However, "If there is no line of communication whereby they are united, they can give no assistance to each other" (viii–ix).

While the one suggests that the monolithic—in this case, the general history—needs to recognize the various sources of its strength lest it be washed away by them, the other suggests that an individual source of strength—in this case, biography—can alone provide very little resistance and be overcome. In other words, in both instances a failure to acknowledge connection results in destruction. It might seem odd for Scott to make metaphors of history and a reader's knowledge of history in terms so ominous that destruction looms, always menacingly, in the background. Her persistent conviction that failure to acknowledge interconnectedness ends in ruin, however, corresponds to her idealistic utopian outlook. A person of "good sense," a utopian subject, understands how critical are the often unseen connections between individual people or moments of history, whether unnoted, persistent vexations or hidden, underground streams. These can become sources of destruction. At the same time, hidden links represent sites of potential utopian transformation. Reading between the lines of the Decalogue and the laws of the land, taking into account the ignored interlinear space that holds those together, Scott's broadminded utopian subject recognizes their true spirit, the meaningful utopian place or topos that defies a literal and confining interpretation.

Like Fielding, Scott advocated careful education—in the interpretation of history as well as the present—to create productive utopian subjects who perceive isolated words and events and the connections between them. They read not to decipher letters but to grasp the meaning of the whole and to act on it.[29]

Marriage Contracts

The Hobbesian situations Scott's characters endure most often arise from heterosexual courtship and marriage, so the second level of Scott's analysis confronts the marriage contract by insisting on women's status as self-directing individuals. If women are to possess property in their own persons, then they must be able to enter into contractual arrangements by voluntary choice. Women should be able to marry for "a natural liking" rather than for money, the single life should remain a viable alternative, and women should have the option of living with other women. Scott fully recognized the political nature of the marriage contract. It is true that her focus on love did not prevent her from emphasizing obedience to parents. Her last novel in particular, *The Test of Filial Duty,* stresses the need to follow parental commands.[30] But the admonition rings hollow because Emilia and Charlotte finally marry the men they desire. The implication is that if a couple waits long enough, parents will come around, fate will intervene, and the lovers will enjoy the right match.[31]

Scott promoted marriage for love, not because she wished to reinforce domesticity and separation of the private sphere from the public, but because people should be free to join appealing families in order to participate in even exchanges of emotion as well as resources. Scott consistently returned to the implications for individual liberty of the marriage contract, drawing on ideas of "voluntary choice" to imagine a woman who is simultaneously self-possessing and social. Political theorist Marilyn Friedman has analyzed "voluntary choice," a concept she traces to Enlightenment jurisprudential discourse. For her, it "refers to motivations arising out of one's own needs, desires, interests, values, and attractions, in contrast to motivations arising from what is socially assigned, ascribed, expected, or demanded." Friendships based on voluntary choice are "more likely . . . to be grounded in and sustained by shared interests and values, mutual affection, and possibilities for generating mutual respect and esteem."[32]

Scott attached particular importance to choosing a community because people could then participate in the mental exchange—that intellectual, moral, and emotional fellow-feeling—Scott found critical to self-possession and identity. Furthermore, it would ensure an equitable distribution of resources that would sustain material existence and charitable Christian activity. As Miss Mancel proclaims in *Millenium Hall*, "What I understand by society is a state of mutual confidence, reciprocal services, and correspondent affections; where numbers are thus united, there will be a free communication of sentiments" (111). The effects of equitable exchange thus extend beyond the home and have a political impact, making George Ellison's neighborhood or Millenium Hall simultaneously a family, a school, and a society.

That Scott looked beyond domesticity is confirmed by her attitudes about affection and sexuality. Friedman's analysis of "voluntary choice" focuses on women's friendships and women's communities, associations that represent "creative disorder" and the potential for social change.[33] Women's friendships in Scott have precisely such implications. Although the fellow-feeling in her utopian communities often appears asexual, she depicts moments of obvious eroticism and deep devotion between women. The "romantic friendships" in Millenium Hall, especially that of Miss Mancel and Miss Melvyn, have received the greatest scholarly attention, but there are other noteworthy examples.[34] Leonora and Louisa in *A Journey* run away together and pose as brother and sister before Leonora is to be married off for money to an odious old man, and Cornelia and Julia in *The History of Cornelia* develop a passionate friendship, with Cornelia trying to deter Julia "from fixing your affections too strongly on any man."[35] Julia eventually does marry Mr. De Rhone, but Scott's ideal is revealed earlier in the prenuptial community: "Mr. De Rhone never passed a day without enjoying some of the conversation of the two friends. They lived together almost with the same ease as if one house had contained them. They often read together. At other times, he would assist them in cultivating their garden, and accompany them to the poor, whom they visited, and whose necessities they took a delight in relieving" (175–76). Mr. De Rhone thus takes up what would appear to be Scott's ideal male position, one shared with Mr. d'Avora in *Millenium Hall*. He is a benevolent and trusted man in a society of women who remain free to bestow their affections as they wish. George Haggerty argues that this figure "understands that the relationship between these two women has inherent value outside the usual terms for quantification in this society; and he helps them to achieve their desire of mutual independence."[36]

The expression "mutual independence" may sound oxymoronic, but it explains why the most conspicuous mark of friendship, for Scott, was equal access to money. As Cornelia says to the impecunious Julia, "Shew me that you look on me as another self, and upon every thing I have as yours" (118). In Millenium Hall, Miss Melvyn realizes she was wrong to think Louisa too young to be "capable of . . . so perfect a friendship, as was requisite to constitute [the] unity of property" (93). True friends, married or not, share their resources. In a letter to her sister, Scott wrote approvingly, "One may see that he [Elizabeth's husband, Montagu] looks upon the money he has lately acquired as much at your command when in his purse as if in your own, according to the proper union between Man & Wife."[37] The same was true of Scott's relationship with Lady Bab: "I speak of L[ad]y Babs Pension as if it were my own, & in truth it is as much mine as hers, we having as little distinction of property as any married couple."[38] Partnerships depend on the free circulation of not only feeling but also funds, not only caring but also cash.

Further, Scott represented the single life for women not as spinsterhood but as an opportunity for a purposeful, engaged Christian life. As Charlotte argues in *The Test of Filial Duty,* "Some of the happiest, as well as most useful persons that I know are old maids; and such I much wish to be, if my heart always keeps as indifferent to the other sex as it has yet been. To cast a ridicule on that state has been a great piece of male policy; but I hope I shall never be the dupe of so poor an artifice" (6:20). "Male policy" is a ruse designed to keep women from the chance to choose happy and worthwhile lives.

Male policy also unjustifiably thwarts establishment of productive communities of single women. Scott's utopia, like Mary Astell's monastery, may appear to some as threateningly conventual, but she insisted that its educational mission, its pragmatic, charitable aims, and its replicating, outward-moving capacity distinguished it from a nunnery. Even though Elizabeth Montagu characterized her sister's life at Batheaston as resembling that of a "convent," Scott insisted that a closed nunnery was not her model community because it infringed on women's liberty and lacked contact with the world.[39] As she wrote to her brother in a letter dated May 26, 1762 (the year of *Millenium Hall*'s publication):

> It is strange that Beings whose inclinations are so changeable, & whose minds generally so much want variety shou'd ever with chearfulness enter a Cloister, where they have nothing to behold but the same faces, within the same walls, during their whole life. When a Heathen devoted himself to death the distress was soon over, but to devote oneself to a death-like life which may last three-score Years is a rasher act than ever a Decius or a Curtius performed. Every Man has such nice dependencies on various People & Circumstances, that no one can be very free, but it is strange that any should endeavour to render themselves absolute Slaves, without a possibility of Manumission; & as strange that people shou'd think an useless Life, a Life of religion.[40]

She reiterated hatred of slavery and belief in useful activity and human connectedness even as she disparaged convent life.

The same criticism recurred in her fiction. In the *History of Cornelia* two young women need to be rescued from that "unnatural state" (169–70). Mr. De Rhone, upon helping one of them escape, sounds much like Scott when he says, "I never liked convents, which seemed to me calculated to make numbers really miserable, and only to hide from the world that they were so. I could never suppose, that God had given us talents to exercise many duties necessary to the happiness of the community, and yet had ordained that the surest way for the attainment of salvation should be shutting ourselves up from the world, and neglecting all the duties for which we were qualified" (161).

As it turned out, Scott's unsurprising solution for such young women involved living in the country in one of her ideal communities. For the convent-ridden Lucinda it would be better to "enjoy liberty in obscurity and retirement, than be confined to the rules invented by mad founders, and enforced by peevish abbesses" (139). Hence Scott insisted on a distinction between, on the one hand, the kinds of active and educational communities she proposed that are freely chosen and definitely of this world, and, on the other hand, the Catholic and largely French convents that confined members and did not participate in community life. She took care to set in relief the distinction Astell had emphasized between conventual and nonconventual life in the *Serious Proposal, Part II,* for her aim consistently remained the worldly, the active, and the utilitarian. Scott's utopias therefore not only provided a pragmatic justification for the idea of freely selecting a community as she had done but also furnished a new way of viewing the continuity between partnerships, the family, and the community that makes "voluntary choice" an attractive possibility for others.

Benevolent Exchange

In addition to adapting the political and the marital, Scott also reimagined charitable relations as "benevolent exchange." In her Hobbesian world, the benevolent moment is another moment in the exchange of power, with custom exacting from recipients a price for charity. Indeed, Hobbes had analyzed the situation in *Leviathan,* where he described the plight of the "desperate debtor": "benefits oblige; and obligation is thraldome; and unrequitable obligation, perpetuall thraldome."[41] Scott extended Fielding's analysis of dependence and tyranny to show how generosity and gifts support the patriarchal order.

In so doing, she adumbrated twentieth-century historians and anthropologists. Marcel Mauss, in his 1950 classic *The Gift,* argued that gift-giving is "apparently free and disinterested but nevertheless constrained and self-interested." He defined a gift as "the present generously given even when, in the gesture accompanying the transaction, there is only a polite fiction, formalism, and social deceit, and when really there is obligation and economic self-interest." Gift-giving is a means of negotiating power relations. In her study of the Trobriand islanders, Annette Weiner discovered that Trobriand women "control their own system of wealth, whose importance is publicly acknowledged," and the power they enjoy is established and maintained through gift-giving. Although Mauss and Weiner focused on premodern societies, their fundamental insights have more recently been extended to early modern Europe, as in Natalie Zemon Davis's *The Gift in Sixteenth-Century France.* Scott essentially agreed that when generosity moves in only one direction, the person on whom gifts are lavished is in bondage.[42]

Scott not only recognized the Hobbesian effects of customs of gratitude but also identified their gendered nature. In a letter to her sister, she confided that "it is not agreeable to be in any way in debt."[43] In the novels, Cornelia refuses to accept aid, even from the kind Mr. De Rhone because "her rule was never to receive an obligation, for which the giver could possibly, any moment of his life, wish for a return she could not grant" (46). One young woman in *Sir George Ellison* learns that "a giving hand, and a generous heart, are distinct things" (113). Emilia in *The Test of Filial Duty* responds to the bullying generosity of a suitor: "That gratitude obliges us to a return of love, is male doctrine; and those who maintain it do not consider how dangerous it is, except they are sure none but themselves will ever love us" (6:41). With witty defiance, Emilia thus exposes how such gratitude, bound up with heterosexual courtship, compromises women's selfhood. At the same time, it implies a danger to men—the threat of other suitors who might successfully extort women's love. Customs of gratitude not only create "desperate debtors" but also pit women against men and men against each other.

Scott, however, took the notion of gratitude seriously and continued to support ideas of benevolence and mutuality. Instead of yielding to Hobbesian reality, she imagined a world in which benevolent exchange includes everyone equally. In Scott's utopian communities, gift-giving is simultaneously a way of gaining power and fulfilling Christian duty, because Christ empowers women through others: "Give, and it shall be given unto you. . . . For with the same measure that ye mete withal it shall be measured to you again" (Luke 6:38).

Scott read Luke 6 to support a type of balanced exchange. It was reciprocity based on the contractual model that encouraged true charity and undermined patriarchy. Mrs. Alton, a destitute gentlewoman, describes her motivation for joining the group at Millenium Hall—being taken advantage of by her brother and sister-in-law, who resented supporting her after her parents died. She admits, "A person must be of a sordid temper who can keep an account of debtor and creditor in generosity; but yet I could not refrain from making some little degree of comparison, which shewed me that my services deserved as payment from my brother, what my relationship to him might alone sufficiently entitle me to. I wished to make all the return in my power for what he should be pleased to do for me; but to be made a slave, and yet reproached as a burden, was more than I could well bear" (*Sir George Ellison* 22, 23).

That such cost-benefit analyses were central to Scott's thinking is evident in her letters. To her sister, she wrote, "Where have you acquir'd a new Neighbour? an acquisition that according to Mr Dryden is both loss & gain, but the ballance of the account is on the wrong side, since the time you will lose by it in all human probability is more valuable than the conversation you will gain."[44] Similarly, she considered whether it pays to maintain a friendship with sickly people: "to forego the friendship of very amiable people because we cou'd not hope to enjoy it many years might be bad oeconomy in happiness, as it woud be giving up certain pleasure from a fear of probable grief, but when that grief does come it seems the heavier scale."[45]

Commercial language accompanied the cost-benefit analyses. George Ellison thinks that his first wife has "a just title to his gratitude." To the friends who mock his subordination he says, "'They must not wonder if his long application to merchandize had taught him to see every thing in the light of traffic; and his wife had bought him at so great a price, that he thought she had a right to make the best of the purchase'" (244). What ought to be a relationship based on mutuality is in fact more like the slavery Ellison so abhors. But if economic power of some over others allows them to manipulate and engage in domestic tyranny, the economic language Scott employed suggests not a wish to evade the financial but to ensure fair distribution. She repeatedly "see[s] every thing in the light of traffic," talks of "debtor," "creditor," "services," "payment," and "just title."

Such words would appear to be the idiom of the "public sphere," but Scott applied them to private relationships. She infused intersubjective relations with commercial language as a way of demonstrating the need for fair exchange to be brought to bear on private human relationships. Susan Moller Okin concludes that liberal ideology, having over the years created a separation of the public and domestic spheres, has left women vulnerable to becoming victims of domestic violence. As a consequence, the rights of privacy must be reconsidered so justice for women can be brought into significant segments of the private sphere.[46] In Scott, a similar argument flows from her observation that interpersonal exchanges are not removed but continuous with commerce and must be viewed in that light in order to introduce justice and a fair movement of resources. By appropriating the economic model to create a notion of benevolent exchange, she sought to describe how domestic relationships can result in a utopian balance between obligations and benefits. Mrs. Alton may be reluctant to talk about "debtor and creditor in generosity," but she does so nonetheless. What is wrong with the phrase is not so much its economic reference as the imbalance, the lopsidedness, that "debtor" and "creditor" imply. Ideally—and, in the utopian community, normally—people do favors for others. In so doing, they receive the consideration of gratitude and respect; the objects of the benevolence have their lives improved and, in turn, oblige others in the same way. This utopian extension of the idea of Christian charity recognizes emotional give-and-take, a balance of payments and benefits as it were, thus theorizing the perfect charitable Christian, who, receiving as much as giving, can remain a self.[47]

Scott's deeply rooted notions of benevolence ran counter to interpretations that consigned women to the role of desperate debtor and construed their duty as passively giving of themselves, selves not really even their own because they were already owed to men. In a sense, Scott appropriated the Lockean idea that an individual enjoys a property in her person, not only for reasons based on natural right but also because her Christian duty to be charitable requires it. God "commands us to feed the hungry, to cloath the naked, to relieve the prisoner, and to take care of the sick. Those who have not an inheritance that enables them to do this are commanded to labour, in order to obtain the means to relieve those who are incapable of gaining the necessaries of life" (*Millenium Hall* 244). As she further considered Luke 6 in *A Journey,* Scott encouraged women, in the voice of Carinthia, not to interpret Christian duty as passivity but as activity:

> Patience is a great Virtue, no doubt, but it is a suffering one, and to use it in any but desperate Cases is Pusillanimity; its Office is to teach us to endure only those Evils we cannot prevent. I admire a Woman who chuses to avoid Injuries rather than indolently to grieve under them, and to work for a Support instead of weeping for want of one. A Person long used to act thro' Love, could not easily give up the Reins of Government to Fear; and when People practise that Excess of Christian Meekness, which is now thought only a female Virtue, of turning the other Cheek to him who has smote the one; and to him who has taken Part of her Right and Property, giving the rest also, only from want of Courage to resist, she may be a greater Coward than others, and perhaps a better Wife in the Opinion of some Men, but not a better Christian.[48]

Christian duty "to act thro' Love" requires women to resist the tyranny and abuse of husbands and to earn their own bread, as Scott attempted to do by writing. The political language of this passage—"Reins of Government," "Right and Property"—reinforces the ways the spiritual and material, the emotional and political, are always linked in Scott.

Scott transformed the Christian call for charity into a justification for women's ownership, self-possession, and agency. Even under the most pressing circumstances, that active engagement with the world generally was expressed as benevolent utopia-building. As Cornelia flees an uncle and the pernicious Mr. De Rhee, who both want to rape her, she sets about managing and making prosperous the poor families she encounters. Cornelia begets Leonora in *A Journey*, who earns a living in ways that create peaceful and loving communities, and Mrs. Traverse, who has a child out of wedlock, hides herself in the country, and sets about organizing the village there. These figures multiply into the Millenium Hall women, who inspire the destitute gentlewomen to go on and buy another house for more gentlewomen, and motivate Sir George Ellison, whose neighborhood is then reincarnated among the Welsh ap Griffiths in *The Test of Filial Duty*.

Utopia is not a privileged person's theoretical construct set into practice, but a cascading, reproductive movement forged of individual effort in the face of personal pain and recognition of the pains of others. All of Scott's utopian characters, positioned as women and sometimes granted the fictional freedom of being men, take up Carinthia's call for activity rather than passivity. They make the best of bad situations by applying themselves benevolently in the economic, contractual realm to attain recognition as independent, self-possessing Christians. In a letter to her sister, Scott noted that she took "more pleasure in practical than speculative divinity. However short my faith will sometimes fall of what orthodox writers require, yet all the doctrine I subscribe to, & as I woud wish to live by it, I rather prefer that to speculative matters, as more useful."[49]

Sarah Scott thus embraced liberal ideas of individual rights and property and then imagined the development of utopian communities in which these rights furthered the capacity, most often of women, to carry out Christian responsibilities. Far from depicting an inaccessible arcadia, Scott pragmatically navigated the political, social, and economic realities of her time to propose fairer, more desirable, ways of living for women, the poor, and the sick. Her utopias have been described as "limited."[50] In fact, however, Scott's interest in the imitation of Christ, Astell's model combined with a belief in the efficacy of English contractualism, allowed her to depict ideal societies that through accumulation, education, and imitation would replicate themselves endlessly throughout the kingdom.

5. Mary Hamilton: Plagiarizing Utopia

Sarah Scott reproduced utopias both within her fictions and without as she created ideal societies that increased in extent and membership and then proliferated textually into sequels. Mary Hamilton's works also grew out of one another; my focus, however, will be on the ways she reproduced utopia by plagiarizing. Her tendency to copy fellow authors does not imply a self-serving intention to pass others' work off as her own but reveals what she saw as a public-spirited will to share and democratize. Her liberal utopian idea is set in greater relief than the earlier authors' because it responds to the revolutionary era in which she lived and worked. The Duchess de Crui, at the opening of Hamilton's first novel, published in 1777, urges a correspondent not to "call me a plagiarist, for sometimes having recourse to my common place-book, and for taking the freedom of using such sentiments as will tend to illustrate my ideas; from whatever author I may have borrowed them, I shall give their names, when I recollect them: but to trace the origin of my ideas, would be an endless task."[1]

Hamilton's commonplace book served as a reading journal into which she copied edifying passages from various writers and from which she then copied as she composed her novels. I will discuss the significance of her borrowing from Daniel Defoe's *Political History of the Devil.* This move, viewed from one angle, represents homage to authority. Viewed from another, it paradoxically shows how Hamilton wrote her own story, recontextualizing Defoe's words and, in particular, challenging his notions about gender roles. Her use of Defoe's ideas, surprisingly, uncovered a critical stance toward received language.

Hamilton's plagiarism therefore offers important insights concerning her aims and the feminist utopian project she furthered. First, Hamilton underscored female utopists' uneasy relationship to the discourses within which they operated: Mary Astell revised John Norris, Sarah Fielding took on moral sense philosophy, and Sarah Scott reconceived the contract. In the manner of Michel de Certeau's *bricoleuses* who "make . . . innumerable and infinitesimal transformations of and within the dominant cultural economy in order to adapt it to their own interests and their own rules," these writers made space for utopian imagining.[2] Hamilton simultaneously ventriloquized and opposed Defoe, and in so doing she offered the most extreme example of working within an established dialect. She not only drew on Defoe's ideas but also employed his words. In the process, she underscored the double quality of the reproductive utopian project, a doubleness that distresses some critics of eighteenth-century feminist utopias because it refuses to attack the status quo outright and relies on "scarcely perceptible" resistance, to use the idiom of Sarah Scott. Hamilton reinforced convention as she boldly stole received language in order to revise it and reorient readers' perceptions.

Second, Hamilton, along with her feminist colleagues, sought to reroute discourses of nation-building into utopia-building. Patriotism supplied the spirit to further a cosmopolitan rather than a narrowly national agenda. During the eighteenth century, John Brewer has argued, artistic production expanded so prodigiously that a market for literary compendia developed and the defeat of perpetual copyright legislation encouraged the publication of anthologies and new kinds of allusion and pastiche. "Any success was likely to be copied, parodied, plagiarized, reworked in other media and broken apart, split into fragments and extracts for easy consumption. . . . What modern critics call inter-textuality had arrived with a vengeance."[3] Brewer points to John Gay's *Beggar's Opera,* explaining the ways it drew on and alluded to a plethora of materials and how it, in turn, generated widespread allusions, popular poems, ballads, and satires. The tendency to collect and critique eventually gave rise to a vast critical literature, an attempt "to give a coherent, critical and historical account of literature, music and painting that placed present-day achievements in a larger context."[4] The upshot, Brewer maintains, was the institutionalization of culture and the creation of a national heritage.

Mary Hamilton's work certainly took part in this movement. Although her aims coincided with the process insofar as she intended to improve public taste, her feminism and Christianity inclined her toward inclusion rather than exclusiveness. The increase in taste was always intended to promote the expansion of virtue rather than create an elite clique of connoisseurs. Hamilton wished to found a virtuous national community that culled the positive qualities of other countries and shunned vices, whether characteristic English or foreign ones. As in Astell, Scott, and Fielding, education would achieve the expansion of virtue. Consequently, Hamilton asserted that the creation of community and social harmony depended upon the free circulation of intellectual property. Plagiarism, therefore, does not represent theft or intellectual colonization; instead, it remains the sincerest form of flattery. To Hamilton as to many of her contemporaries, real genius consisted of artful imitation: "the true way to advance another's virtue is to copy it."[5]

Hamilton carried feminist utopian ideas into the last quarter of the eighteenth century; attempted to prolong cosmopolitanism after the Seven Years' War and the outbreak of the American War for Independence; and influenced significant feminists such as Mary Wollstonecraft and Catharine Macaulay, who brought the utopists' notions of the political nature of female education, women's rights, and equality into the period of the French Revolution.

* * *

As Clare Brant has pointed out, "Anyone trying to comprehend the variety of women's writing [in the eighteenth century] has to re-consider anonymity, pseudonymity, and (un)originality. The commonplace book, for instance, used by many readers to make copies of favourite texts or extracts, could involve more than functional transcription."[6] Gender emerges as the central issue in Mary Hamilton's appropriation of language from Daniel Defoe. The plagiarized passage on the left is from Hamilton's *Munster Village* (1778). She took it from Defoe's *Political History of the Devil* (1726), which appears on the right:

It must be confessed there is a strong propensity in man's nature, to assign every thing uncommon to supernatural means. But though I am very apt to believe there is greater credulity in most minds, than will be candidly acknowledged, yet the degree of it must be in proportion to people's ignorance and want of information. Thus the famous doctors of the faculty at Paris, when John Faustus brought the first printed books that had then been seen in the world, or at least seen there, and sold them for manuscripts, were surprised at the performance, and ques-

It must be confess'd there is a strong Propensity in Man's Nature, especially the more ignorant Part of Mankind, to resolve every strange Thing, or whether really strange or no, if it be but strange to us, into Devilism, and to say every Thing is the *Devil,* that they can give no Account of.

Thus the famous Doctors of the Faculty at *Paris,* when *John Faustus* brought the first printed Books that had then been seen in the World, or at least seen there, into the City, and sold them for Manuscripts: They were surpriz'd at the Performance, and

tioned Faustus about it, but he affirming they were manuscripts, and that he kept a great many clerks employed to write them, they were satisfied. Looking further, however, into the work, and observing such an exact uniformity throughout the whole, that if there was a blot in one, it was the same in all, etc. etc. etc. their doubts were revived. The learned divines not being able to comprehend the thing, (and that was always sufficient) concluded it must be the *devil;* that it was done by magic and witchcraft; and that, in short, poor Faustus (who was indeed nothing but a mere printer) dealt with the *devil.*

They accordingly took him up for a *magician* and a *conjurer,* and one that worked by the *Black Art,* that is to say, by the help of the devil—and threatened to hang him; commencing a process against him in their criminal courts; when the fear of the gallows induced Faustus to *discover the secret*—that he had been a compositor to Koster of Harlem, the first inventor of printing.[7]

question'd *Faustus* about it; but he affirming they were Manuscripts, and that he kept a great many Clerks employ'd to write them, they were satisfied for a while.

But looking farther into the Work, they observ'd the exact Agreement of every Book, one with another, that every Line stood in the same Place, every Page a like Number of Lines, every Line a like Number of Words; if a Word was mis-spelt in one, it was mis-spelt also in all, nay, that if there was a Blot in one, it was alike in all; they began again to muse, how should this be? in a Word, the learned Divines not being able to comprehend the Thing (and that was always sufficient) concluded it must be the *Devil,* that it was done by Magic and Witchcraft, and that in short, poor *Faustus,* (who was indeed nothing but a meer Printer) dealt with the *Devil.*

N. B. *John Faustus* was Servant, or Journeyman, or Compositor, or what you please to call it, to *Koster* of *Harlem,* the first inventor of Printing, and having printed the Psalter, sold them at *Paris* as Manuscripts; because as such they yielded a better Price.

But the learned Doctors not being able to understand how the Work was perform'd, concluded as above, it was all *the Devil,* and that the Man was a *Witch;* accordingly they took him up for a *Magician* and a *Conjurer,* and one that work'd by the *Black Art,* that is to say, by the help of the *Devil;* and in a Word, they threaten'd to hang him for a Witch, and in Order to it, commenc'd a Process against him in their criminal Courts, which made such a Noise in the World as rais'd the Fame of poor *John Faustus* to a frightful Height 'till at last he was oblig'd, for fear of the Gallows, to discover the whole Secret to them.

N.B. This is the true original of the famous Dr. *Faustus* or *Foster,* of whom we have believ'd such strange Things, as that it is become a Proverb, *as great as the* Devil *and Dr.* Foster: Whereas poor *Faustus* was no Doctor, and knew no more of the *Devil* than another Body.[8]

Mary Hamilton thus condensed and slightly reordered Defoe's account. She maintained his expressions but avoided notes or asides and edited out details, for example consigning Defoe's lively treatment of the line-for-line, word-for-word correspondences found in Faustus's books to a perfunctory "etc. etc. etc." Perhaps the omission indicates not only impatience on her part but also recognition of the irony implied in duplicating a passage about duplication.

As indicated in the remarks of the Duchess de Crui, Hamilton's method of composition involved reference to a commonplace book into which she would copy passages from her reading that struck her fancy. These passages then supplied apt anecdotes or aphorisms as she pieced together her own text. Indeed, her patchwork writings give the impression that she mined a number of authors, something suggested by the *Feminist Companion to Literature in English,* which points out Hamilton's many learned footnotes, her characters' drawing on commonplace books, and the "unmarked passages" and unattributed borrowings from Hester Chapone.[9] Such references and plagiarisms were frequent in eighteenth-century literary life because the concepts of authorship, literary property, and copyright were only gradually gaining clear legal and social definition.[10] Hamilton appears to have pilfered not from a medieval respect for authority or the need to fill pages hastily in order to publish and feed her hungry children (although she lived under such pressure) but from the desire to enrich the didactic force of her writing.

The form of her novel *Munster Village* suggests that the story exists primarily to provide occasion for moral evaluation and social commentary. The central narrative thread involves the heroine's creation of a utopian artists' colony. Lady Frances puts off marriage in order to maintain control of her inheritance so she can construct Munster Village and raise her nephew and niece. The artists' colony contains a library, a hospital, and places for two hundred men and twenty women. Explaining this enterprise allows Hamilton to comment on the sorry state of libraries in England (*MV* 23); the need for public hospitals (29); and the importance of education for women—in this case, especially those whom Lady Frances thinks "labour under any imperfection of body" and would be enabled to increase "their resources *within themselves,* to compensate for their *outward defects*" (25). Less likely than attractive women to make a satisfactory bargain in the marriage market, these women ought to have a satisfying alternative.

Hamilton also had occasion to muse on the desirability of an aristocracy based on virtue (*MV* 37); debate the interaction of reason and passion in human happiness (13); propose a retirement home for animals (33); defend the theater against detractors (43, 145); discuss inequalities in marriage and reject the idea of divorce but endorse separation in the case of marital discord (50 ff., 150); support charity for worthy persons (70); lament the vulnerability of women's reputations (73–74); ponder the ill-effects of women's attempts to hide their pregnancies (112–13); and (117–22) support the notion of equal worth, hold up a black couple as an example of respectability, and decry the treatment of galley slaves. She demonstrated a liberal pragmatist's view of the attitudes and actions necessary to create a better England.

Her approach to social problems corresponded in important ways with that of Daniel Defoe, who delighted in the vigor of the "Projecting Age" and wrote many proposals for improving English society. His first major publication, *An Essay upon Projects* (1697), was devoted to schemes for improving banking, bettering roads, providing insurance, and establishing academies. Thirty years later he was still issuing proposals for retirement homes, madhouses, and foundling hospitals in *The Protestant Monastery* (1727) and *Augusta Triumphans* (1728), among other works.[11] Hamilton evidently shared Defoe's spirit and, as this instance of plagiarism would suggest, was willing to adopt some of his views—and words—as her own.

Hamilton was not the only debtor in this particular instance of literary borrowing. Defoe, of course, appropriated the Faustus story. By the eighteenth century it had apparently become a legend, one said to have been perpetuated by "John Walchius."[12] A contemporary account appeared in an article by John Bagford in the *Philosophical Transactions* of 1706–7.[13] As in Defoe's version, that article repeated the notion that printing originated in Holland with Coster rather than in Germany with Gutenberg, and it confused the printer Johan Fust with the Renaissance magician Dr. Faustus. The history of printing thus gained the element of sorcery and magic. That element was missing from the source Bagford cited, the work of Gabriel Naudé. In Naudé's earlier version of the Fust story only the economic issue is said to account for Fust's prosecution by Paris authorities; the element of magic does not appear. By selling printed books as manuscripts, Fust was overcharging (i.e., gouging) customers:

> On this point we must first remark that the style in which this Bible was fashioned . . . was very similar to the handwriting one used at that time; that the said Jean Fust had carried a large number to distribute in Paris, the majority of which were also on vellum, and decorated with large letters and gold illuminations, he sold them initially as manuscripts, and charged at least sixty ecus each: but later letting them go for twenty or thirty, and those who had bought the first ones having realized that there was too great a number of them and [that they were] too similar to have been written by hand, they brought an action of overcharging against him, and they pursued him so hotly that he ran away from Paris to Mainz, and not finding himself safe enough there, he went to Strasbourg where he stayed some time, and taught his art to Jean Mentelin, who lived in said city.[14]

Bagford's summary therefore misrepresents the work of Naudé: "Naudeus's Life of Lewis the Eleventh hath an Account of Faust's Printing the Bible in the Latin Tongue, his bringing them to Paris, and vending them there for MSS. his Troubles and Accusations before the Parliament, being tried for a Conjurer, which I conceive gave occasion for that foolish Book, that goes under the Name of Dr. Faustus's Life."[15] What Bagford included as an anecdote about the history of printing, Defoe interpreted as an example of human folly in the face of the unknown. And that quality also attracted Hamilton, who nonetheless repeated it with the paradoxical intent of arguing against some of Defoe's opinions.

How? Although the plagiarism would suggest similar attitudes and concurrence between Hamilton and Defoe on the issue of the supernatural, the context nonetheless reveals a significantly different gender argument. Women had long been associated with the supernatural.[16] In the *Political History of the Devil,* Defoe satirically equated old maids with witches and attractive young women with devils. "It seems the *Devil* has always pick'd out the most ugly and frightful old Women to do his Business" (262), whereas "the fair looking World are generally *Devils,* that is to say, are in his Management" (240); and, "In a word, the walking *Devils* that we have generally among us, are of the female Sex" (313). Defoe went so far as to call men involved in occult activities "Old Women-Men" because their dealings with the devil render them feminine (254). What is more, the devil was said to transform old men into old women when he needed them (263–64).

Defoe's other writings on magic and apparitions reinforced these ideas.[17] In *A System of Magick* he describes antediluvian women as "the Devils of the Age" (13), tells about old women's predilections for "raising the *Devil*" (135), and explains why magic "is generally practis'd by old Women only" (223). It is interesting to explore Defoe's gendering of occult activities. While men turn into Old Women-Men for practicing witchery, female witches can become wizards. Mother Shipton "was not a Witch . . . but a *Warlock* or Wizard" because she performed the masculine function "to reveal and discover Conspiracies, and to govern the greater things of Life; as to blast or succeed the Enterprizes of Princes and People" (224). By contrast with wizards, witches work on a personal scale and, according to Defoe, cause greater evil because they gratify "the vilest Passions of Men," bewitching "Men, Cattle, Places and Things" (223). In the passage under discussion, Faustus is charged with being a "witch." In *An Essay on the History and Reality of Apparitions* Defoe refers to the "idle Heads of the old Women" (280), who, like the old women in the *Journal of the Plague Year*, are preoccupied with signs of the supernatural. Such signs appear consistently in Defoe's novels and pamphlets.

By contrast, Mary Hamilton's point in *Munster Village* was precisely to demonstrate an attractive spinster's initiative, to show that a single woman can actively pursue the arts, education, and social reform in a matter-of-fact way that is far from unnatural and mysterious. She plagiarized Defoe in the context of an argument about Greek superstitions and suggested that Munster Village represents a more enlightened environment. "She was advised to call her elegant village by the name of *Athens;* but this she declined, naming it *Munster Village:* but she justly thought it deserved it; with this difference, that the inhabitants are too well informed to give into such gross superstitions, and so easily suffer themselves to be imposed upon by astrologers, divines, soothsayers, and many other sorts of conjurers, as the Grecians did" (31). Munster Village imitates the Greeks but deviates; *Munster Village* takes from Defoe but with a difference. As she appropriated Defoe's language, Hamilton was simultaneously arguing against his ideas about females as devils. Women should have the chance to act, she suggested, free of the suspicion suffered by a man like John Faustus for doing something as new and extraordinary as Lady Frances does in creating Munster Village, and as Hamilton demonstrated in fashioning a novel that has an enterprising heroine.

Consequently, several inferences can be drawn from Hamilton's use of Defoe. First, her borrowing illustrates the popularity of Defoe's *Political History of the Devil,* of which there were a dozen editions in eighteenth-century England as well as translations into French and German. Reprints continued in the nineteenth century, both in England and America. Second, the borrowing indicates that Defoe's work not only enjoyed public favor as entertainment but also could be taken seriously, if not as a "Political History" of the devil then as a historical satire on human ignorance in various periods. Third, the theft suggests that Defoe's style, his satirical-pragmatic mode, appealed to a woman author advancing female initiative because it provided a lively argument against viewing unusual behavior as irreligious or satanic.

Finally, the disparity in the larger gender arguments of the two texts suggests that we can profit from probing the gender valences of writing in which similar elements or even the same passages appear. Women's and men's literary productions did not belong to separate realms in eighteenth-century England. Male readers assimilated texts by women writers and vice versa; more recent work in literary history shows just how often female as well as male authors borrowed from and influenced each other.[18] Nonetheless, a woman writer may well be arguing against the social position constructed for her in books like the very one from which she steals. Hamilton shared Defoe's projecting spirit and his identification with Faust—a devious artisan taken to task for his projects. At the same time, her recognition of gender inequality led her to recontextualize the stolen anecdote. She may have appropriated Defoe's words, but she rejected the gendering of his voice.

* * *

If Hamilton rejected the voice of Defoe, she spoke the language of her feminist antecedents. Like Sarah Fielding and Sarah Scott, she espoused the reproductive utopian paradigm, finding in it a way to promote a liberal, feminist agenda in a new socioeconomic climate. Consequently, Hamilton recalled the utopists' central concerns. First and foremost, she stressed the issue of education, especially for women, because "education . . . is productive of infinite advantages, extending its influence to society, and may operate upon posterity to the end of the world" (*D* 1:42). Lady Frances admits twenty female scholars in Munster Village. Although they are few in comparison to the two hundred male students, the women enjoy full support for life, and their instruction, as in Scott's *Sir George Ellison*, is tailored to their social status. Hamilton thus did not introduce full equality between the sexes and among classes, although, like Scott and Fielding, she wished to expose the tyranny and injustices of patriarchal absolute rule.[19] Even as she departed from Mary Astell's politics, she echoed her, chiding men for disparaging women; such scoffing men "are of the *mushroom kind*, sprang up out of a dunghill, and never had mother, sister, nor daughter" (*M* 2:162).[20] The tolerant Sir John Bolton points out that "the mind is enlarged or contracted by the exercise of thoughts" and women and subordinates are kept down by being forbidden such exercise. "There is a maxim in France, never to promote officers whose patience hath languished in subaltern offices; they regard them as persons whose understandings are straitened by a narrow sphere of action, and who, accustomed to little things, are become (like women) incapable of greater" (*M* 1:104–5).

As a way of demonstrating women's capacities, Hamilton's heroines display wit and learning, offer lengthy reading lists, and share carefully devised courses of instruction. In *Letters from the Duchess de Crui* we are given the elaborate curriculum of Lady Harriet as well as Lady Filmer's "plan of education" (1:175–94, 5:71), and *Memoirs of the Marchioness de Louvoi* is so full of syllabi and critical commentary that it would appear to be Hamilton's primary purpose that the novel serve as a literary review and send female readers expeditiously to the most profitable texts. Education for women remained the central feminist issue for Hamilton because "had women the same advantages of education as men, there would be no room to doubt but that they would be equal to them" (*D* 1:71).

Hamilton agreed with Fielding and Scott that education must provide gentlewomen and aristocrats the means to earn a living if doing so became necessary. The new economy too often left women vulnerable. When Lord Munster's son and his new wife, Lord and Lady Finlay, are suffering in poverty, she sells two of her own paintings, having "too much good sense to be ashamed of employing those talents, bestowed on her by nature for *so natural a purpose*" as supporting her family. "Good blood," the narrator concludes, "cannot be kept up, without the shambles of the market, so it is no scandal to procure *that* by ingenuity or industry, when the appendages of gentility are so far reduced as not to afford it otherwise" (*MV* 16).

The new economic order had thus profoundly realigned the obligations of and expectations about class and gender. According to Hamilton, the civic-humanist ideal, which located virtue too narrowly in masculine upper ranks, belonged to an outdated system. Because men no longer practiced the classical republican virtues, women could not be expected to adhere to that model either. Almeria Surry points out that women in Roman times chastely ran their households while their brave husbands defended the nation; such a moral order was as equitable as it was desirable. Those days, however, are gone: "Let the *other sex* return to the temperance and frugality, the probity and honour of ancient times, and I would undertake to promise that ours should not only emulate their virtues, but sometimes exceed them" (*M* 2:176). Hamilton both echoed Astell and anticipated Wollstonecraft.

At the same time, Hamilton conveyed the same pragmatic approach to the new economy evinced in Fielding and Scott. She saw need to reconcile wealth and virtue, and therefore emphasized the notion of an aristocracy not of birth but of merit. Virtue does not move vertically, on a hierarchical model, but is promoted horizontally through application in the world and interactions among individuals. Young Lord Munster is told that he will not inherit Lady Frances's fortune and is sent to Holland to learn business. When he questions whether trade is not "destructive of the social virtues," Lady Frances replies that, on the contrary, "it [is] not unusual for men of high birth to enrich their family *by trade*" and that he should endeavor, by his "temper, application, and personal accomplishments," to gain "advancement and honor" (*MV* 38–39).

People of high rank, in fact, are under greater pressure than others to act irreproachably. Hamilton repeats that they otherwise not only shame themselves but also sully the reputations of their illustrious progenitors (*M* 1:83, 3:94). Sir John Filmer tries to temper his wife's partiality for people of rank: "we cannot all be *great,* but every body may be *good.* I respect the circumstance of birth, only as it is an additional motive to virtue" (*D* 1:22). Again, it is education that will promote rectitude; Sir John opens a school for "twenty of each sex" that will give "a double benefit to the *public,* as it adds to the number of the *hopeful* what it takes from that of the *profligate*" (1:27). *Letters from the Duchess, Memoirs of the Marchioness,* and *Munster Village* all emphasize the ways education expands virtue and increases the number of utopian subjects.

The middle-class virtues of hard work and pragmatism thus outweigh the prerogatives of class. Utopia is decidedly not an aristocratic life of leisure and plenty: "The care, attention, and labour incumbent on men for their support, invigorate both the soul and the body, and they are the natural causes of health and sagacity. Virtue itself would be indolent if she had no passions to conquer and regulate. It is every way our advantage that we have no such slothful paradise as the poets feigned in the golden age" (*MV* 38). Wollstonecraft emphasized the same point: "Hereditary property sophisticates the mind, and the unfortunate victims to it . . . swathed from their birth, seldom exert the locomotive faculty . . . [and] are unable to discern in what true merit and happiness consist."[21]

In that view, women, because of their dependence and lack of exertion, are like idle aristocrats. Hamilton accordingly insisted that women realize there is no guarantee that they will, through marriage, forever be supported, just as aristocrats cannot assume they will always command wealth. Women must protect themselves by creating a supportive community. The Finlays' enlightened daughter Lady Eliza determines not to suffer the same fate as her mother. Marriage will not force her to leave the society of her friends because it is from that community that she will draw strength if her marriage falters. Eliza tells her suitor, "From all her observations in life, no love ever lasted long enough to make it worth while to sacrifice every thing else to it; the *Paradi-*

siac vision of eternal constancy having long vanished from these sublunary regions:—and that unless he would reside in England—she never would be his!" (*MV* 124). Lady Frances, Eliza's substitute mother and the living exemplar of maternal virtues in the text, shares Eliza's savvy about the unacceptable sacrifices of marriage and breaks off her engagement to Lord Darnley while she sets up Munster Village; he waits patiently for sixteen years to obtain her hand.[22] Hamilton's surviving heroines, as practical as the women of Millenium Hall, will not allow the myth of paradisal matrimony to tear them from their support network or thwart plans to apply themselves, improve their circumstances, and attempt to create a rational utopia. Unafraid of work, smart, level-headed, and confident, they take a practical approach to life decisions, with the implication that the middle-class ethos stands to benefit women, single or married, of all ranks.

Further, like Scott's visions, Hamilton's are grounded in the notion of benevolent exchange, or mutual assistance, and that idea, as in Scott, is taken beyond the mutual dependence of people to express the more intangible interconnection of things. Lady Frances holds that "society is manifestly maintained by a circulation of kindness: we are all of us, in some way or other, wanting assistance, and in like manner qualified to give it. . . . All men are by nature equal: their common passions and affections, their common infirmities, their common wants, give such constant remembrances of this equality, even to those who are most disposed to forget it, that they cannot, with all their endeavours, render themselves unmindful of it" (*MV* 20–21).

Hamilton thus sought to convince the powerful of their vulnerability and that, although they would rather not acknowledge it, they are actually dependent on underlings. That is true of marriage, which makes partners "dependent on each other" (*D* 3:171); of social life ("The great depend on the little, the little on the great" [*M* 3:54–55]); and of politics ("The epithet of *great,* so liberally bestowed on princes, would, in most cases, if narrowly scanned, belong rather to their ministers" [*MV* 57]). Like Scott, Hamilton focused on the potential transformative effects of the underling. Where Scott referred to the "lowest officer in the monarch's service" who can bring about a revolution and employed the metaphor of underground streams creating a torrent to express how something invisible can have momentous results, Hamilton contended that "it is not always great and adequate causes that produce strange and surprising events; on the contrary, they often are the result of things seemingly small" (*MV* 20). That fact, according to Hamilton, needed to be registered in methods of historiography, which, as in Scott, are too apt to overlook what is devalued, private, and feminized. "Love and gallantry have frequently thrown whole countries into flames, and proved the real causes of the war, very different from those assigned in manifestoes, instructions, and instruments, preserved in the archives of princes" (*M* 1:70).[23] Hamilton therefore furthered appreciation of biography, in the vein of Scott and Johnson, "as containing facts, which, attended to, and properly digested, may serve to direct us in the conduct of our lives" (*D* 1:156). She also opened space for women's agency and influence. "Ladies are the principal movers of great events" (*D* 1:151), she maintained, and "women are one of the secret springs which regulate the universe" (*M* 2:153).

Hamilton's arguments reinforced the feminist utopist emphasis on equality in the state of nature, echoed ideas of Shaftesburian system, and were grounded in Christian notions about the utility and significance of all individuals. "In the general scale of beings, the lowest is as useful, and as much a link of the great chain, as the highest," says Sir John (*D* 1:22), echoing I Corinthians 12:14, 21–22: "For the body is not one member, but many . . . the eye cannot say unto the hand, I have no need of thee: nor again the head to the feet, I have no need of you. Nay, much more those members of the body, which seem to be more feeble, are necessary." Because women, the poor, and the sick matter as much as anyone else, benevolence is essential (not merely ornamental, as Adam Smith argued) and must be reciprocal. Hamilton, like Scott, wished to counter what she perceived as the Hobbesian realities of her world, where generosity did not express benevolent reciprocity but rather unrequitable obligation. Seeing altruism from the perspective of the recipient, Annette le Reillet, like Fielding's and Scott's toadeaters, tells how a benefactress continually makes her feel obliged, and, she concludes, such interested giving "leaves a sting behind, a pain in the mind, perhaps little inferior to that [it] has removed" (*M* 1:187).

So closely does Hamilton follow Fielding's analysis that she even plagiarized the passage on "double slavery" from *David Simple:* "But in my opinion, those persons who give up their time, and sacrifice all their inclinations to the humours of others, cannot be over-paid by any thing we can do for them. Men never think a slave obliged to them, for giving him bread when he has performed his task. And certainly it is a double slavery to be made servile under the mask of friendship" (4:88–89).[24] The only suggestive alteration was Hamilton's use of the word *mask* where Fielding had written "to be made *servile* under the pretence of *Friendship.*" Fielding's interest was in teaching readers to distinguish real friends from false ones, whereas Hamilton's metaphor implied a reader who already knows what friendship really means. Following a Fieldingesque pattern, Annette le Reillet becomes a "humble companion" to the Countess de Ris and laments, "Disinterestedness and generosity are things which nobody now understands" (*M* 2:16,

2:30). Instead, she claims, "traffick" infects charity: "He who serves his friend cancels the obligation by putting him in mind of it; if he expects a return, he is kind to himself and not his friend, and then it is traffick and not beneficence" (3:59). Hamilton, like Fielding and Scott, marked the changing nature of charity in the period and wished to reinstill in readers the idea of its centrality to the nation: "Charity is a duty, the fulfilling of which is absolutely necessary to the being and support of society" (*M* 3:71).

Creating charitable souls requires emotional education. The arts furnish Lady Frances with a method to effect such a transformation in Munster Village, and she expands the interpersonal approach depicted in the ideal tutors of Scott and Fielding. Scott had suggested that the emotional identification characters experience as they read, role-play, and unwittingly participate in games facilitates their transformation into people of "good sense."[25] Scott's protagonists, as teachers, are always on the spot to make the most of those potentially epiphanic moments when characters' personalities are open and ready to be changed. In the "History of Leonora and Louisa" in *A Journey through Every Stage of Life,* Leonora counsels a young couple having marital problems. The husband is jealous, the wife coquettish and vain. Leonora tells them to go into the country. There, the wife should read romances, which will take her out of herself, stimulating desires she will then redirect toward her husband and curtailing her egotistic wishes to be desired by other men. "They agreed Romances might be of Use, when the Endeavour was to make Affection over-balance Vanity, which had hitherto rendered her Heart almost insensible to tender Impressions; and where she would see nothing besides her Husband, except the Beasts of the Field and the Fowls of the Air, he might depend on being the Hero of her Romance; for which his excessive Fondness very well qualified him, altho' her Husband."[26] After romances, "more rational Studies were to succeed; that after being taught how to love, she might learn what was lovely, the better to place her Affections, and to deserve those of others."[27] Emotional education forms a significant part of education in general, and books like romances have value in that they can open individuals to new sensations and create an appetite for other transforming literature. If Charlotte Lennox used the effects of romance to heighten comedy in *The Female Quixote,* Scott, Fielding, and Hamilton employed reading and the arts to didactic ends.

Where Scott had worked on an interpersonal and local scale, however, Hamilton ambitiously analyzed the problem of arts education on a national level. The Royal Society unjustifiably ignored the arts, she maintained. The young Lord Munster, traveling abroad, finds that other nations consider "the English cheap. I can account for this in no other way, than that they form their judgment of us only by the *philosophical transactions*," that is, the publication of the Royal Society (*MV* 83). As a result, Lady Frances's creation of Munster Village makes up for an English deficiency: "It was left to her ladyship to revive the agreeable arts, for which her name must be handed down to posterity with honor" (133).

Lady Frances argues for democratization of artistic production and consumption, which, she contends, will have morally beneficial effects. Paintings and other representations must be available to students, Lady Frances argues in a Shaftesburian vein, if they are to improve as artists and develop spiritually, because viewing great art helps direct people's passions toward moral ends. In religious worship, for example, "externals" such as rituals and representations are necessary to elicit proper devotion. They "become real assistances; because the connection between the body and soul, between the senses and the imagination, between the passions and the reason of mankind, is so strong and mutual, that they uniformly act and re-act upon one another, and mutually raise the soul to new and higher degrees of fervor" (*MV* 30–31). Accordingly, Lady Frances places "fine pieces of painting in her chapel, which is also a very fine new building" (31). Viewing art "give[s] a turn to the mind advantageous to society . . . awakens a congenial sensation, and quickens us to . . . acts of humanity and benevolence" (*M*2:68–69). Through the uplifting connections between mind and body inspired by viewing good art in a beautiful setting, the inner person is improved, charity encouraged, and social harmony increased.

Arts education will also enhance the "national taste in *painting*." Hamilton's narrator in *Munster Village* comments on the dearth of indigenous artists and the mismanagement of the art market. In Lady Frances's utopian community, the arts foster development of the individual as well as transformation of the nation, so Britain can finally "rival the Italian, the Flemish, or even the French school" (30). Lady Frances refers to the British Society for the Encouragement of Arts, Manufacturers, and Commerce and insists that this organization "is well calculated to diffuse a spirit of taste" in England. Moreover, "had such a society been instituted fifty years ago, London, perhaps by this time, would have been the grand seat of the arts, as it is the envied seat of freedom" (132). She thus seconds Joshua Reynolds's arguments in favor of establishing a Royal Academy.[28]

She also expresses frustration at "the bad consequences of the duty laid on pictures imported into great Britain" (*MV* 30). In the late seventeenth century it was illegal to import paintings; regulations were intended to protect the livelihoods of indigenous artisans and craftsmen. Unevenly enforced, the laws were revised by the early eighteenth century to allow importation but to impose duties that were, first, based on the quality of the painting and then, when that was recognized to be arbitrary, on the basis of the work's size. Records of imports are extant for the mid-eighteenth century. In the period following the Seven Years' War and before the appearance of *Munster Village,* the average number of pictures brought into England per year was about one thousand.[29]

Hamilton rejected the mercantilist approach and advocated a free art market because increased circulation of, and access to, great art inspires greatness of soul, which, in turn, incites production of distinguished art that promotes viewers' inner improvement. Exceptional artistic models must be in circulation and made available to the public. In *Memoirs of the Marchioness* that conviction accounts for a long passage of praise for the art of engraving, by which means "all the celebrated performances and inventions of the most celebrated masters are exceedingly well imitated" and can be disseminated "to the whole world" (2:72–73).

In the final masque of *Munster Village,* a figure of Michelangelo commends Lady Frances for displaying copies of Raphael's Stanze paintings from the Vatican. Raphael himself interjects, suggesting that "*the cartoons* were the best of his performances."[30] These, instead of the Stanze work, ought to ornament Munster Village. The king, however, possesses the cartoons and is unjustly "lock[ing] them up from public observations" (132–33). William III had made the cartoons accessible to the public at Hampton Court, but George III removed them to Buckingham House. In 1777, the year before *Munster Village* appeared, the controversial populist John Wilkes addressed the House of Commons to protest the removal of Raphael's monumental drawings:

> At present [the cartoons] are perishing in a late baronet's smoky house at the end of a great smoky town. They are entirely secreted from the public eye; yet, Sir, they were purchased with public money, before the accession of the Brunswick linc, not brought from Herrenhausen. Can there be, Sir, a greater mortification to any English gentleman of taste, than to be thus deprived of feasting his delighted view with what he most desired, and had always considered as the pride of our island, as an invaluable national treasure, as a common blessing, not as private property?[31]

Hamilton endorsed the call to give the public access to Raphael's masterpieces. Lady Frances, "unwilling either to refuse her sovereign *taste* or *philanthropy!*" (*MV* 133) implies that he lacks precisely those qualities by refusing to display the cartoons. Hamilton's discussions of art thus revealed her democratizing tendencies, and the statements on tariffs and duties underscored her liberal economic views. The improvement and force of the nation depended upon liberty and free circulation of, as well as unrestricted access to, images and ideas.

While patriotism drove her liberal outlook, Hamilton displayed striking cosmopolitanism. True, she repeatedly supported British potential and distinction. "Heaven has placed us in a most advantageous situation," she observed, "unless we are divided at home, attacks from abroad may molest but cannot ruin us" (*MV* 41). Young Lord Munster's travels to other countries, like those of so many graduates of the Grand Tour, make him more, not less, patriotic (41–42). Yet the Grand Tour ought to teach appreciation for virtue and distaste for vice, wherever these are found. Mr. Denham is lauded for differing from "modern travellers, who weed foreign countries, importing German drunkenness, Spanish pride, French levity, and Italian deceit, while they leave behind, German industry, Spanish loyalty, and Italian frugality: thus they suffer interiorly from their travels, what they gain exteriorly" (*M* 1:181). By contrast, he is "a citizen of the world, and totally unfettered by the little mean distinctions of climate, or of country, which diminish the benevolence of the heart, and set bounds to philanthropy" (1:175).

Hamilton endorsed a cosmopolitan outlook on the grounds that a wider perspective offers more possibilities for detecting models of virtue and more opportunities for exercising benevolence. Travel fosters tolerance: "It is extremely useful to go abroad sometimes to wear off prejudices" (*D* 1:221). Hamilton's novels are set all over Europe and bear references to the entire globe. She everywhere found excellence in other cultures. "Petersburgh, Rome, and Sweden" receive praise in *Memoirs of the Marchioness* because doctors there are, reasonably, required to sign prescriptions for medicines (1:30–31), and in *Munster Village* the English are encouraged to "rival" the Italians and the Flemish but not overtake or subdue them.

Hamilton's plan for an ideal community may have been based on ancient models, but when it was built and she was urged to name it Athens she decided instead to call it Munster Village. The point was not to trump and prevail, but, as in Astell and Scott, to seek imitable models and create something new and useful.[32] Again, the underlying idea was progress through mutual assistance; a scholar or artist gains from the work of predecessors and then, in turn, contributes to the ongoing process of increasing knowledge and expanding virtue. It means simultaneously recognizing dependence on earlier thinkers and artists while making an original contribution:

> Be his abilities ever so great, he will need the assistance of others, and ought to be very thankful for it. We must indeed make use of our own reason, but we ought also to take in all the helps and advantages we can get; and he that is careful to improve those helps which are afforded him, and who, without submitting

> implicitly to the judgment and opinion of others, endeavours to make the best use he can of their labours and studies, as well as of his own thoughts, is in a far more likely way of improving his knowledge, than he, who, from a vain confidence in his own judgment, despises and rejects those helps. (*M* 1:99–100)

Hamilton agreed with Scott that failure to acknowledge the need for models and thereby recognize ties and dependencies results in ruin. The notion was so firmly held that it colored the authors' discussions of nation-building and colonial enterprises. *Munster Village* and *Sir George Ellison*, patriotic and utopian texts that have a confident embrace of England's constitution, trade, and economy, may well have contributed to eighteenth-century justifications of British imperialism. As Hamilton noted, "We have a natural force to *defend* and *maintain* the empire of the seas." Yet she qualified that sentiment by insisting, "We enjoy wealth and possessions in both the Indies, if we do not lose them by our own misconduct" (*MV* 41).

That call to virtue referred also to America and the recent Declaration of Independence and underscored the ways in which Hamilton viewed things from below, from the perspective of the female, the subaltern, and the disadvantaged. Hamilton called for religious tolerance because people should "consider themselves to be creatures of one God" (*D* 1:220) as well as on the dubious grounds that religious minorities promote virtue because they must work harder to achieve recognition and acceptance (*M* 1:74–75). Her Scottish background also sensitized her to the issue of dialect prejudice, as when Lady Filmer checks her tendency to condemn others' accents: "She recollected the use of language is only to convey our ideas to one another: and as every country has its own peculiar dialect, to speak the purest is only a kind of local merit" (*D* 1:29). Feminist utopists failed to abolish slavery or curtail the exploitation of foreign lands, but they nonetheless consistently demanded sensitivity to, and mitigation of, the suffering of non-British people. It is wrong "to confine the instance of humanity within the narrow circle of a few European nations," Hamilton insisted (*MV* 121). As usual, the links among people were emphasized rather than the distances separating them.

Characters who fail to recognize interdependence, mutuality, and the need for reciprocity are made to pay. The first Lord Munster, for example, is as tyrannical as the figures in Scott's Hobbesian families. A widower and an arbitrary ruler driven by unbridled passion, he commands that he be given the hand of Miss Burt, the young daughter of his son's tutor. Tragedy ensues as he disinherits the son, Lord Finlay, when he finds out that Finlay has secretly courted Miss Burt, who eventually paints and sells *Arcadia* to support her family. The young couple dies in poverty—"for want of proper assistance" (*MV* 17)—and Lord Munster commits suicide.

Underscoring this grim conclusion, Hamilton obsessively revisited the argument against tyranny by telling dispiriting biographies. Adelaude suffers from a despotic guardian, who, like Lord Munster, refuses to let his son marry her and desires her for himself. Mrs. Lee's husband proves so self-centered, "spending his whole time between women, racing, and gaming" (*MV* 46), that she is compelled to separate. The Duke de Salis abandons and then publicly degrades and abuses his innocent duchess. On the final page of the novel, Mrs. Lee caps off the theme of woman's "loss of liberty" in marriage, decries her subjection to "an arbitrary lord" (150), and laments the lack of mutuality in the marriage tie. As a way of offering alternatives, Hamilton portrayed virtuous behavior in men such as Lord Darnley, Mr. Villars, young Lord Munster, and the Marquis de Villeroy. They are men of feeling who respect women, allow them to express themselves and assert their wills, and suffer for their sakes.

If masculine absolute rule proves tyrannous, Hamilton warned, so, too, does a lack of authority lead to disaster. Christine Rees has pointed out that Hamilton had "problems in integrating her more progressive utopian views with her conservative morality."[33] Perhaps the conflict between a belief in equality and liberty, on the one hand, and in submission to principle, on the other, best illustrates that tension. Although full integration is not achieved in Hamilton, she sought above all to further mutuality and reinforce human links. For example, Miss Harris's father, unlike the other despotic brutes, is not a philistine, but passion has nonetheless gotten the better of him. An enthusiast, he will stop at nothing to gain coveted ancient objects, and it is chance only that prevents him from selling his daughter to obtain manuscripts. His desire to own the items is a sign of mania; he has come to ignore the real value of antique things. Young Lord Munster, trained to business in Amsterdam, emphasizes the need for moderation and concludes that Dutch virtues turn into vices when people "exert them to excess"; "their industry becomes rapine, their vigilance fraud, their wariness cunning" (*MV* 67–68).

Unlike Lady Frances, who turns her interest in the ancients not to excess but to the advantage of those about her, Mr. Harris's covetousness only lets him see the value of a thing, the thrill of possession rather than the enlightening beauty or wisdom the object conveys. Mr. Burt, too, offers a counterexample. Like Scott's admired mentor figures, d'Avora and De Rhone, he freely dispenses knowledge and good will instead of hoarding them, and his shared erudition makes him trustworthy and sympathetic. The story of Mr. Harris thus warns that interest can turn into obsession and desire into mania if not balanced by an ethic of mutuality. Hamilton, like Scott, emphasized such an ethic to counter individual selfishness, and she focused on the arts as a means of reining in self-centered passions and directing them into beneficial reciprocal avenues. In this way Hobbesian social relationships could be transformed into utopian ones. As in Scott, the benevolent management of a pragmatic heroine who promotes the arts and organizes community life will civilize the manners of the people.

Hamilton's views on the arts and economics, grounded in notions of reciprocity and exchange, furthered liberal and democratic aims. Like the other female utopists, she saw the reconciliation of wealth and virtue by means of Christian benevolent reciprocity. Despite Hamilton's patriotism and apparently conventional ideas about gender roles and propriety, she was anchored by potentially radical Christian beliefs that—like Mary Astell's magnetism—favored redistributing power and resources even beyond Britain. As in Astell, imitation was morally charged and indicated self-betterment and spiritual improvement. Young artists are to view and imitate great art so that they, in turn, can paint in ways that will direct people's passions to meaningful spiritual ends.

Ruth Perry has argued that "the library is a perfect emblem of . . . *Munster Village,* whose dominating impulse is collecting, creating a repository of knowledge, gathering up the treasures of art and science in one place."[34] John Brewer has further suggested that the tendency toward "borrowing, copying, and collecting" serves to create a national heritage.[35] Collecting and displaying, in Hamilton, are intended as spurs to excellence. Following Scottish ideas of political economy, Hamilton saw the value of literature deriving from its circulation and exchange, with competition encouraging improvement. "Rivalling" the artistic production of other nations was better for everyone and, guided by the ethic of mutuality, did not represent a drive to conquer and subordinate.

It is in this light that we can best view Hamilton's plagiarism. On one level, her theft represents democratic access; her use of Defoe, Fielding, and others was part and parcel of her utopian vision. When, in the masque that concludes *Munster Village,* the figure of Michelangelo admires the way that she has displayed copies of Raphael, Lady Frances modestly insists that her work is "proof how much we fall short, how faintly we copy originals!" (132). Lorenzo de Medici also compliments her achievements, and she humbly repeats that she only seeks to follow his example: "the imitation [is] *a faint one*" (132). Yet the humility does not entirely ring true. She endorses imitation of earlier models in the Augustan manner—"To copy Nature is to copy them."[36] And she simultaneously agrees with Edward Young that such transcription involves a transmutation.[37] She proudly created a context and added her stamp to carefully selected material. In Lady Frances's hands, imitation of earlier models yields something notable but different. She creates Munster Village rather than a new Athens.

The efficacy of Lady Frances's imitation is echoed in Hamilton's plagiarism of Defoe. As Lady Frances draws on past examples, so, too, Hamilton incorporated Defoe's arguments. Both admire the productions of their predecessors, yet they recontextualize the material and make it their own, presenting it in a new guise and under a different name. Defoe's text spoke to and through Hamilton, even as she reworked it; the intertextuality of her novels reinforced a conviction that books, like human beings, become more profitable as they become more intricately linked. Texts, like people, depend upon each other, and in their friendly rivaling achieve an interconnection—via the efforts of a shaping author like Hamilton—that fosters mutual assistance in improvement. Literature and the arts speak to people and are "real assistances" in enhancing connections within and among human beings; they also offer "proper assistance" to those in need and displace forces of tyranny.

As in the masque celebrating Lady Frances at the end of the story, as in the commonplace book on which Hamilton drew, and as in her novels themselves, notable figures come together and encourage laudable efforts at individual and social rejuvenation. The commonplace book thus represents a utopian space where authority and ideas mingle, to be rereleased into the world by Hamilton in a new way before being read and carried on in the mind and manners of the reader. The pattern of reauthorization never stops, and the education can "operate upon posterity to the end of the world" (*D* 1:42). Later women writers took Hamilton's message to heart as they helped themselves to her work. Ann Radcliffe drew on *Munster Village* in *The Mysteries of Udolpho,* and Jane Austen reintroduced Eliza, the Bennets and the Bingleys in *Pride and Prejudice.*[38] Mary Hamilton's plagiarism was coextensive with her impulse to create community. It expressed belief in the free circulation of artistic and intellectual property as a way of reproducing utopia.

6. Reproducing Utopia beyond Britain: Jeanne Marie Leprince de Beaumont's *The New Clarissa* and Sophie von La Roche's *Events at Lake Oneida*

The significance of eighteenth-century British feminist utopists becomes evident in the ways French author Jeanne Marie Leprince de Beaumont and German writer Sophie von La Roche imitated the English model and thus reinscribed reproductive utopianism. Such a comparison is further called for because literary influences in this period were never confined geographically or linguistically. Sarah Scott's *History of Cornelia* appeared in German in 1762, *Millenium Hall* in 1768, and *Sir George Ellison* in 1774. Sarah Fielding's *Familiar Letters* were translated into German in 1759, and her *David Simple* and *Ophelia* appeared in French in 1782 and 1797. Leprince de Beaumont's writings appeared nearly simultaneously in French and in English, they were virtually all translated into German, and a compilation—her *Vermischte Werke* in two volumes—was published in Leipzig in 1779. La Roche's works were also widely available; *Die Geschichte des Fräuleins von Sternheim* was quickly translated into English, French, Dutch, Russian, Swedish, and Danish.[1] Mary Hamilton's *Munster Village* appeared in French in 1782.

All of the English women whom I have discussed could understand French—Scott published a translation of Pierre de la Place's *La laideur aimable*—and therefore need not have relied on translations at all.[2] Sophie von La Roche was fluent in both French and English. French was the language of the court, and La Roche wrote French with greater ease than German, the orthography of which she learned only later in life. Leprince de Beaumont, who lived many years in England, must have been able to read and converse in the language. Hamilton, who lived the last period of her life in Amiens and whose daughters married Frenchmen, peppered her writing with untranslated passages from the French. Despite political and military conflicts between countries, the literary market of the time was pan-European. Although national literatures were beginning to be institutionalized and promoted in the late eighteenth and nineteenth centuries, literary influences across the Channel during the Enlightenment were substantial and are too often ignored. The work of Jeanne Marie Leprince de Beaumont and Sophie von La Roche demonstrates how cosmopolitanism lent impetus to female authors' feminist and moral project and how women's utopianism in the eighteenth century was a western European phenomenon.

Further, a study of their novels suggests how European women formed a community of female authorship; they met, they corresponded, and they read each other's writing. Leprince de Beaumont worked as a governess in the British royal household just at the time Scott's husband was employed as a tutor. Because the women moved in the same circles, it is likely they would at least have crossed paths. A decade later Scott wrote to her sister, "I have received Madame Beaumont's history, & thank You, I was in hopes more of her Magazin des Enfans had been published. I have had but 4 Numbers."[3] Sophie von La Roche, in her periodical *Pomona für Teutschlands Töchter*, discussed British authors at length—"Madame Rowe," "Milady Worthley Montague," "Madame Macauly," "Mis[s] Hahna Moore," "Mis[s] Carter," "Madame Chaponne," "Madame Barbault," "Madame [Elizabeth] Montague," "Madame Scott," "Mademoiselle Dopson," "Madame Brookes," and "Mis[s] Talbot." She had special regard for "einer jungen liebenswürdigen Engelländerin Burney" and translated Cornelia Knight's Roman poem, "In the Room of the Emperors at the Capitole."[4] Her Anglophilia is well known.[5] On travels to England, La Roche sought out literary circles and was especially delighted to meet Frances Burney.[6]

The connections among German, British, and French authors suggest that the most productive approach to their utopian writings is a comparative one. Analysis of Leprince de Beaumont and La Roche not only demonstrates the influence of British utopists on Continental writers and expands the sisterhood of Enlightenment authorship but also emphasizes the need to look past nineteenth-century nationalist paradigms and see the international awareness inherent even in patriotic eighteenth-century texts.

Jeanne Marie Leprince de Beaumont

In Leprince de Beaumont's *The New Clarissa* (1767), the reproduction of utopia comprises both the sexual and the textual. Her revision of Samuel Richardson's *Clarissa* and Jean-Jacques Rousseau's *The New Heloise* represents a woman's intervention in French debates about depopulation, which intensified following the devastation of the Seven Years' War (1756–63). Her novel point of view went beyond the theories about moral decay or the pernicious effects of social institutions proffered by Montesquieu, Rousseau, and their followers. With her images of a utopian French countryside contrived by the indefatigable Baroness d'Astie, Leprince de Beaumont amended women's maternal role in increasing France's population; she also stressed the instrumentality of women in discourses of national reform and international exchange, creating room for them as reformers, polemicists, and heroes.

In responding to Richardson's acclaimed *Clarissa,* which had first appeared in London in 1747–48, Leprince de Beaumont designed a female-centered utopia that leaves its heroine alive within a burgeoning family, very much in control of her fate and community. She countered Richardson's protagonist, who, unable to attach herself to any community or enlist the aid of relatives or female friends, is raped and dies alone. In this way *The New Clarissa* simultaneously rewrote Jean-Jacques Rousseau's *The New Heloise* (1761), which also created a popular model of female subjectivity in its intelligent and amorous yet tormented and—ultimately—dead heroine.

Leprince de Beaumont offered a partial vision of the sort described by Angelika Bammer, even as she insisted on its universality; she took advantage of woman's indeterminate political position to articulate local reforms with global repercussions.[7] Patriotically seeking to solve France's postwar depopulation problem, Leprince de Beaumont envisaged sociopolitical changes that would increase fertility and strengthen France's economic and military might. Yet these national improvements would at the same time create a place for women as international reformers. One of her central female characters justifies her political goals by claiming that she is "a citizen of the universe." Through a reproductive utopian process Leprince de Beaumont's community materially modeled a utopian solution whose ripples were to alter global conditions. She offered her imagined cure for concrete local and distant international injustices, economic imbalances, and political ills. An early feminist text although not a radical one, *The New Clarissa* paradoxically privileges women's nationlessness as it justifies their instrumentality as citizens, creating for them a political domicile in whatever nation they see fit to ensconce themselves.

Details about Leprince de Beaumont's life are scarce. She was born in Rouen in 1711 and died in Annecy in 1780. A marriage to an irresponsible and inconstant husband was annulled in 1745, and she was forced to earn her own support. From 1748 to 1762 she lived in England, working as governess to several aristocratic families as well as in the household of the Prince of Wales.

She must have been well respected and well liked because a number of girls she instructed, among them Sophie Carteret, later made her a surprise visit in France for her sixtieth birthday.[8] Leprince de Beaumont enjoyed moving in elite circles among the Oglethorpes, Lady Pomfret, Lady Egremont, and Lady North; she met Horace Walpole; and Madame du Boccage, who visited London, commented on Leprince's opportunity to discuss metaphysical subjects with Lord Chesterfield.[9]

It is during her English sojourn that she seriously began to write. Her best-known publication, a periodical, *Le Magasin des Enfans* (1758), first appeared in English as the *Young Misses' Magazine* (1757) and was written with an English audience in mind. "Beauty and the Beast" is the most famous story from the *Magasin des Enfans;* it is not the first extant version of the tale, but it is the form in which it became popular and was most often reprinted.[10] *Le Magasin des Enfans* was succeeded by *Le Magasin des Adolescents* (1760), *Instructions pour les Jeunes Dames* (1764), and *Les Américaines* (1770). In addition, Leprince de Beaumont wrote educational works for boys as well as for artisans, country people, and the poor: *Le Mentor Moderne* (1772) and *Le Magasin des Pauvres, des Artisans, des Domestiques et des Gens de Campagne* (1768). Her novels were also popular: *Lettres de Madame du Montier* (1756), *Mémoires de Madame la Baronne de Batteville* (1756), *Civan, roi de Bungo, histoire Japonoise; ou, Tableau de l'education d'un prince* (1758), and *Lettres d'Emerance à Lucie* (1774).[11]

The New Clarissa may follow Richardson and Rousseau in using the epistolary form to depict the fate of a moral heroine who seeks to escape an undesirable arranged marriage, but it nevertheless offers a plot in which the English heroine need not die passively and unprotected. Instead, Clarissa comes to enjoy the sanctuary of a virtuous mother-in-law who enlists Clarissa's energies in creating a utopian community. Leprince de Beaumont's Clarissa, unlike Richardson's heroine, takes stock of her unlucky situation, chooses her own husband—a disguised French baron—and settles in the Bordeaux region with her mother-in-law, the Baroness d'Astie. Clarissa, thrilled by the baroness's improvements to the countryside, describes the reforms in letters to her mother and to a lively friend, Harriet.[12]

Because Clarissa has been taken in as a daughter by her mother-in-law, and because Clarissa's mother, Mrs. Darby, comes to Paris and for vague reasons adopts Harriet, the women create a supportive familial community characterized by the epistolary exchange of moral and utopian ideas. It is a situation meant to oppose the quandary of Richardson's lonely protagonist, vainly seeking shelter and protection and forever unable to act on her own behalf, let alone on behalf of others. In their letters, the women applaud the baroness's innovations; she has studied agricultural methods, livestock diseases, and remedies and has increased the area's productivity by introducing new ways of fertilizing, composting, and irrigating. Every poor family is given a cow, and the baroness ensures that babies can be fed the milk—so mothers are "freed" for agricultural labor—by fashioning ceramic nipples to attach to bottles, which older nurses can then use for feeding the infants. The tireless Baroness d'Astie even develops incubators for chickens and organizes dairy and cattle cooperatives to secure farmers' livelihoods. The innovations enhance productivity, lessen poverty, improve nutrition, and thus increase the population. The enthusiastic farmers praise and bless their benefactress (2:14).

Leprince de Beaumont makes clear the impact that the baroness's example should have on readers, one in keeping with the imitation of Christ and the reproductive utopian project outlined in earlier chapters. Harriet and Mrs. Darby model this response as they study the baroness's projects and attempt to initiate their own reforms. "You have reconciled me to the right path," writes Harriet, who takes up spinning in her house, "and, if God has not found me worthy to become legislator of a whole village, I am, at least, determined to play this part in my family; and on my estate when my affairs are finished [in Paris]" (2:64). Mrs. Darby, for her part, visits the general hospital in the city and offers ideas about caring for orphans, educating girls, getting people to work, and rehabilitating fallen women (2:160).

If Harriet's and Mrs. Darby's proposals appear conservative and modest, Clarissa counters with a radical plan. She hopes to found a Christian Union "where these words [*meum et tuum*] should never enter, and of whose happy inhabitants, it might be said as of primitive christians, their goods were in common, they had but one mind, one heart" (2:76–77). Like Astell, Fielding, and Scott, Leprince de Beaumont's Clarissa looks to the early church for a model. She imagines herself and her husband at the head of this community, which will include sixty families, where meals—mostly vegetarian—are to be taken in common, clothing is to be uniform, the sick will be cared for in a sanatorium, and aged women will play fully active roles.

The plan for a Christian Union furthered the novel's central aim—to outline conditions that augment the country's population. This demographic theme placed Leprince de Beaumont's novel in the middle of eighteenth-century debates over France's perceived demographic decline. Her project participated in the "useful and public discourses" Foucault has described in the *History of Sexuality* and that in the eighteenth century worked to manage sex in the interests of the state.[13]

Although her arguments seconded many of those proffered by the philosophes, they focused on women's political instrumentality and required women to become citizen-reformers. To that end, Mrs. Darby points out that Clarissa's Christian Unions would be preferable to unproductive monasteries: "I should like every village to have an hamlet of christian union, where those who were desirous of practising the gospel literally, might retire: these would be true monasteries useful to the state. These people would furnish an healthy numerous race, for fruitfulness and health are the consequence of labor and a sober way of life. Their children, by entering into society, would bring there virtues which would change the face of the earth; our country places would become an heaven" (2:93). Christian Unions would produce ideal citizens whose migration to other regions ensured the expansion of utopia. The process perfectly mimicked the visions of Fielding and Scott.

Leprince de Beaumont, however, must make concessions to accommodate Clarissa's social position. Because the scant nutrition and excessive labor of peasant life would endanger Clarissa's fertility, Mrs. Darby and the baroness insist that she retain the amenities of the rank to which she was born and had become accustomed. "God has made different conditions in life, and wills that each should live according to his station" (2:94). Moreover, "It would be contrary to the order of Providence to live as peasants do" (2:129–30). Consequently, Clarissa must be satisfied with a reduction to three-course meals (two courses of meat, one vegetable); plain clothing; decent, not spartan, lodging; eight hours of sleep a night; and only a few servants. Leprince de Beaumont flirted with radical ideas but finally buttressed the class system and glorified bourgeois virtues. Indeed, when Clarissa is about to marry the penniless Baron d'Astie, who is posing as a wigmaker's assistant, she decides, "We shall live in the mediocrity which nourishes virtue, preserves it, and produces happiness," for in the middle class "one generally finds people of better morals, than among those in more exalted stations" (1:192, 1:176).

The comments anticipate those of Mary Hamilton because they suggest that all should work, contributing according to their capacities; that farmers should engage in vigorous manual labor; and the wealthy and the high-ranking, with supposedly superior educations, ought to organize the lives of workers and set an example. The Baroness d'Astie provides one successful model, having organized her village in the most efficient and cost-effective way. The Christian Unions—even as they incorporate established class and rank hierarchies—will help "furnish an healthy numerous race" (2:93). Unproductive social elements must be moved into productive work. Monasteries in France devolved and disintegrated, Mrs. Darby argues, partly because the monks gave up manual labor; they no longer fulfilled "the duties . . . owed society" (2:92, 2:90). No social place existed for such people in Leprince de

Beaumont's vision, and no room was provided for those who sought to live meditatively or economically apart from the rest of society. Leprince de Beaumont's active interest in contemporary debates is evident in her anti-monasticism and her emphasis on trade, but these issues, including her conservative views about class, all furthered her arguments about population.

Leprince de Beaumont's intervention in contemporary debates about depopulation included a patriotic call for empowering France after its defeat in the Seven Years' War. In that conflict, Britain, Prussia, and Hanover stripped France of the most substantial of its overseas colonies, which led to French demands for national reform. Proposals for improvements addressed fundamental change in laws, taxation, trade, tariffs, and financial institutions. Although concerns over depopulation had been raised years earlier, the post-war situation brought those fears to a new level. Previously framed as a global problem, it now came to be seen, as Leprince de Beaumont's text demonstrates, as a national imperative.[14] Indeed, for some time depopulation had been ascribed to moral decay, and she tackled the problem accordingly. She agreed with Montesquieu's *Lettres persanes* (1721), which argued the need to remedy France's depopulation through social and political reforms. These reforms included abolishing primogeniture, promoting commerce, limiting permanent immigration to foreign colonies, and doing away with monasteries and priestly celibacy. Because Leprince de Beaumont raised the depopulation issue and placed some of her solutions in precisely the same framework, she could well have been responding to Montesquieu's arguments.[15]

Although Leprince de Beaumont took part in the Enlightenment debate about depopulation, she modified its terms. In *The New Clarissa*, her concerns about French vigor are bound up with questions of woman's social weakness and the dearth of Christian values. Her contribution to depopulationist discourse was complicated by her gender identification and religious idealism, both of which moved her beyond Montesquieu and concern for national boundaries. Thus the text exhibits an unusual blend of specificity and generality, of ideas for practical local reform with an eye to universal change. That she spent the period of the Seven Years' War in England may explain why *The New Clarissa* combines respect for British ways and desperate faith in France's potential ascendancy. The utopia acquired British characteristics even though her goal was to refashion France into the "first nation in the universe":

> Cities would be desolated to the advantage of the provinces; the rich and the nobility would drive from their antechambers three parts of the idle fellows whom they detain from labour: France would become the treasury, the magazine, the granary of Europe; not an inch of ground would be left uncultivated.

> Population would be doubled with labour, and produce for the king a numerous people, hardened by labour, fit for the fatigues of war. Plenty would take the place of poverty, always dreadful when it is the consequence of sloth: in a word, we should become the first nation in the universe, without exciting the envy of our neighbours. (2:152–53)

Given her residence in England, Leprince de Beaumont must have witnessed the early effects of Britain's industrial revolution and the impact of new agricultural techniques, which involved reorganizing the land and improving methods of cultivation to enhance productivity. The plan she outlined indicates as well that she sought to initiate similar reforms without causing the displacement enclosures forced on English peasants. A passage from the preface to the French edition of the *Magasin des Enfans,* which did not appear in the earlier English version, confirms her view of English economic development and its moral effects:

> To what should we attribute the progress of commerce in England? To the destruction of that prejudice which makes one regard commerce as a profession unworthy of the nobility. An honest and productive merchant can aspire to any honor. Dukes and counts are not embarrassed to associate with him, to treat him with distinction, to show him respect. The most powerful influences upon the human mind, interest and self-love, thus combine to make commerce flourish. Commerce leads to wealth and esteem. But the English go further: agriculture too is a path to distinction for anyone who excels in making it flourish. A farmer able to enrich himself through his industry takes his place among the gentlemen; the lord admits him to his table, to his friendship, to his amusements. If I were the distributor of signs of honor, I would not hesitate to erect a statue to the first person who had the courage to rise above the ridiculous prejudice which makes one disdain commerce and agriculture. This person did more for his country than he would have done by winning ten battles: he unblocked the fertile springs of true wealth.[16]

Impatient with the aristocracy yet bound to the notion of social hierarchy, Leprince de Beaumont postulated a gentrification of French farmers and industrialists as well as aristocrats. England might have been leading the way, but France need not remain behind.

Leprince de Beaumont hoped to see France overtake her rival and become dominant while at the same time avoiding Britain's envy. Her nationalism proved paradoxically internationalist. France's strength depended not on expanding beyond its borders to colonize other regions but on retaining and multiplying its population. Rather than viewing the acquisition of foreign territories as increasing the scope of the nation and the number of its subjects, Leprince de Beaumont—like Montesquieu—judged such developments a burden. "We are eager to find islands in the new world at a great expence," Clarissa declares. "France is depopulated to people these climes; and we have, in the very centre of the kingdom, desert places which might be rendered fertile" (2:218). Agricultural and procreative fecundity were thus inextricably linked while centrifugal colonial movement dispersed national resources. A strong France could only emerge if its inhabitants mustered their rural productive and reproductive forces, and set aside colonial rivalries with Britain.

The New Clarissa addressed issues of international politics even as it concentrated on national strength; it not only looked to contemporary issues but also critiqued past positions. In particular, it points to the damaging consequences of the revocation of the Edict of Nantes in 1685, when more than four hundred thousand Huguenots emigrated to Britain, Prussia, Holland, Switzerland, and America. A strong advocate of religious tolerance, Leprince de Beaumont called for toleration of Protestants within France and asked English readers to grant the same for Catholics across the Channel. Yet tolerance remained secondary to demographic concerns. Although emigrating Huguenots represented fewer than 2 percent of France's population in the late seventeenth century, the revocation nonetheless worked against population growth. Characteristically, Leprince de Beaumont offered a solution: Children of beggars and orphans should not be neglected or sent off to monasteries. Instead, they should be nurtured by French society, educated, and encouraged to marry and have children. She even projected the positive results of such a policy. It would produce 128,000 families. Then, if each family averaged four children, France would have 512,000 additional inhabitants in twenty years (2:176). In one generation the revocation's harm could be undone.

Impelled by these hopeful numbers, Clarissa details what type of education might bring about desired change. "Colleges of husbandmen" should be established where orphans could live in common and thereby save expenses. The increase in trained agricultural workers would raise productivity, lower prices, and free others to engage in manufacturing. As a result, France would produce all its own necessities, which would increase exports, decrease imports, and ensure that "the French would become the purveyors of all Europe" (2:178–79). That largely agricultural image of France included industrial activity at the novel's end, confirming that the economic comparison with Britain remained constantly in the author's mind.

Women's special reproductive, maternal role in increasing France's population thus moved on in *The New Clarissa* to concern about the instrumentality of women in discourses of national reform and international exchange. Leprince de Beaumont's position as advocate resembled that of her contemporary, Madame du Coudray, the "king's midwife" who was appointed to lecture on obstetrics in the countryside in order to increase rural birthrates.[17] The activities of these women, rural, hidden, and barely mentioned in contemporary sources, are the kinds of "scarcely perceptible," "seemingly small" events that Sarah Scott and Mary Hamilton argued were insufficiently noted in the official historical record and at the same time represented potential sources of social transformation.

Leprince de Beaumont's text is thus a "partial vision" in Angelika Bammer's sense. It reveals the extent to which customs and social institutions limited women's horizons and consequently the records of their lives, forcing their texts to be "partial"—fragmentary or incomplete. At the same time, it was "partial" in its interested aims, seeking changes in the customs and institutions that caused the limitations. Leprince de Beaumont thematized that sentiment, and her novel becomes a reflection on reformist goals as Mrs. Darby considers the status of a woman's views on social change. The mother cheers on Clarissa's plans for increasing population and hopes that those in power will recognize their value and implement them. "But, as this is not to be expected," she advises, "do yourself in miniature, what you could wish was done in great; perhaps, your good example will excite some rich persons to second you" (2:192). She, too, will aid in this process: "If you cannot engage others to execute in great your good projects, we will endeavour to offer models of them in miniature" (2:159). Leprince de Beaumont, like Bammer, thus described hopeful gradualism rather than revolutionary substitution, where a local model, capable of universal application, would point the way to national and international reform.[18]

To this extent, then, Leprince de Beaumont gave in to the necessity of a woman's "partiality," her need to attempt social change "in miniature." Although small, these attempts are complete; her innovations may begin in the provinces, but they have the potential, she insisted, to transform the nation and even have international impact. In this respect her utopian project was not "partial," a plan that demonstrated its "feminine" quality by refusing universalizing or totalizing strategies. Quite the contrary, although she avoided a totalizing approach or method, she still imagined an ambitious community offering a model that would cure social injustices, economic imbalances, and political ills. Reflecting on how some might think it silly for uninfluential women to "set themselves up for reformers," especially women who are not natives (they are English, not French), Mrs. Darby concludes, "Ah! I feel, from the emotions of my heart, that I am a citizen of the universe; and all mankind, whatever they are, are my brethren" (2:165–66). Leprince de Beaumont recognized women's predicament. Whether English or French, they were not citizens, and, like the poor, might well have felt no connection to their countries (2:172). They possessed little power or capacity for effecting substantial change. Yet lack of citizenship in a particular nation meant that women could claim greater loyalty to humankind in general.[19]

The condition of nationlessness thus paradoxically offered a place from which to articulate ideas for national reform. Concrete ideas for social change, in turn, demonstrated why women should be taken seriously by those in power and be viewed as active subjects. Further, Leprince de Beaumont suggested, women's ideas for reform offered a model of conditions under which women would want to become citizens in the first place. Rampant colonial ambitions, an idle aristocracy, and unproductive cities exploiting underpaid and overworked country laborers all worked, according to Leprince de Beaumont, to weaken France's demographic, economic, military, and moral force. Citizenship could only be meaningful if these wrongs were righted, and undoing them would reconcile other women to the nation so that they, too, would energetically participate in its growth and improvement.

The New Clarissa, therefore, simultaneously argues that the cosmic outlook of women—whether French or English—can fashion a nation that will set an example to be copied by all others, and that France in particular can become the "first nation in the universe," a singular model country in which all people will desire to participate, even Englishwomen such as Clarissa, Mrs. Darby, and Harriet. Leprince de Beaumont expressed a feminist utopianism—one drawing on British forebears and foreshadowing the "partial visions" of twentieth-century feminist utopian authors—that would counter France's unique setbacks after the Seven Years' War and create a space for women as citizen-reformers of whatever country they inhabited.

Sophie von La Roche

Movement beyond national boundaries is even more evident in the work of Sophie von La Roche. On travels through America in 1831, Alexis de Tocqueville insisted on taking a detour to Lake Oneida in upstate New York, a place, he wrote, that "my imagination had transformed into a new Eden." What prompted a vision so powerful? As a child, Tocqueville had read an abridged French version of Sophie von La Roche's novel *Events at Lake Oneida* (1798).[20] His pilgrimage provides a striking occasion for interpreting the novel as La Roche's successful reproduction of a sympathetic empirical reader and as an answer to Fielding's call that readers be instructed in order to become utopian subjects. Motivated by the book, Tocqueville acted on utopian longings, as La Roche had done when she learned from her traveling son's letters of a

Frenchman who had settled the island in Lake Oneida and later when she decided to write about him. Her novel is at once a robinsonade, a tale of survival on a lone island, and a story about the principles needed for building a peaceful, international community after the disappointments that followed the French Revolution.

Sophie von La Roche was easily Germany's most famous eighteenth-century woman writer. After an engagement with her cousin Christoph Martin Wieland was broken, she married into court life, a theme that became the subject of her first and best-known novel, *Die Geschichte des Fräuleins von Sternheim* (1771). That book was an instant sensation, and she was applauded by Herder, Goethe, and Lenz. Yet her acclaim did not last because she rejected the overwhelmingly individualist preoccupations of the Sturm und Drang movement and instead tackled practical social subjects such as education, morality, and social virtues. She promoted other women writers, wrote travel literature as well as journalism, and finally composed her memoirs. Her writings were intended to be didactic, a factor that contributed to the neglect she suffered from critics until late in the twentieth century.[21]

Fräulein von Sternheim is the story of the education of a young woman, Sophie, in the ways of the world, including the benevolent improvement of a country village, a project with strong resemblances to those in Sarah Scott's novels. The parents of the heroine ensure that "justice and beneficence [are] practiced in equal measure within the boundaries of their small domain."[22] They conduct agricultural experiments and establish a poorhouse and an orphanage (67–68). Sophie later imitates her parents in drawing up a plan for a girls' school that should offer instruction in domestic service, "where poor girls could be trained to become good and skilled servants" (179); after she marries, her English husband wants to "build a school and a hospital modeled on those at Sternheim" (242).[23] As Barbara Becker-Cantarino suggests, *Sternheim* concludes "with a feminine utopia" that replaces the "masculine" court and its corrupt ways.[24] Although La Roche, like Scott, suggested that a good example begets further utopian experiments, these formed only a small part of her novel. Indeed, *Sternheim* has been called a *"Freundschaftsutopie,"* a utopia of intimacy rather than a full invented society.

A more extended and broader political example of La Roche's utopianism appears in *Erscheinungen am See Oneida* (1798). The focus of *Erscheinungen* is not only the education of a character, the narrator, but also of the reader. La Roche, like Sarah Fielding, looked to teaching methods of interpretation as the key element in creating utopian subjects. The narrator, the implied reader, models a method of sympathetic empiricism. He travels to America "to witness the beginning and progress of the cultivation of reason and the soil" and "to compare nature and art at their borders."[25] Europeans who are placed in a natural wilderness, he imagines, will return to a state of nature, a simpler and more virtuous way of life, and will reject the luxury and idleness of cities. He therefore leaves the overcultivated city of Philadelphia to view the poor log cabins at Lake Oneida in upstate New York. There he finds what he is looking for in the conduct of the Wattineses, a French aristocratic couple from Flanders who have been displaced by the French Revolution. Before the arrival of other Europeans, they lived alone on an island in Lake Oneida for four years. Their tale of survival, characterized by hard work, self-discipline, and long-suffering patience, is told from several perspectives and forms the largest part of the narrative.

That this utopian story differs dramatically from La Roche's earlier novel *Sternheim* has much to do with the manner in which La Roche received the tale and, like Mary Hamilton, reworked the material at hand. It is not a story based on her experience but on reports from others, accounts she, like her narrator, heard about, investigated, and interpreted. The Wattines family—in the reports called Vatine, Desvatines, or Des Wattines—inhabited an island ("Frenchman's Island") in Lake Oneida and were occasionally visited by travelers during the 1790s. La Roche never traveled to New York, but she eagerly sought reports from her son, Fritz, and daughter-in-law, Elsina, who spent about five years in America, trying to improve their fortune. They journeyed to upstate New York and met with a friend and adviser, an enterprising Dutchman by the name of Van der Kemp (the model for a character named Vandek in the novel), who must have told them about the Des Wattines. Van der Kemp had found the family inhabiting the island as he surveyed the land with an eye to purchase. In 1794 Fritz and Elsina finally visited the Des Wattineses, who had bought a hundred acres on the northern shore of the lake (the present Constantia). Although we no longer have Fritz and Elsina's record, that of Van der Kemp remains.

Francis Adrian Van der Kemp's account of his 1792 "Journey to Lake Ontario" is highly romanticized. He depicts the island in Lake Oneida as "the happy seat of a Goddess . . . of a Magician—or, a Fairy's residence in the times of chivalry. . . . All what the Poets did sing of the gardens of Alcinous—all the scenery of those of Armida, so highly decorated by Virgil and Ariosto, could scarce have made upon me, who was captivated unawares and bewildered, a more deep impression than this spectacle of nature. . . . It seemed a Paradise."[26]

The mythic and fabular quality of Van der Kemp's description must have enticed La Roche, as did the scene of domesticity— extensively echoed in her novel—that introduces the Des Wattines family. His manners are "those of a Gentleman" despite his ragged appearance, and Madame des Wattines is portrayed with "chessnut brown hair, flung back in ringlets over her shoulders, her eyes fixed on her darling Camille—a native of this Isle—at her breast; while two children, standing at each side of her, play'd in her lap." Van der Kemp's moralizing tendency and profound reverence for this man also dominated the tone of La Roche's novel: "Esteem for the man filled our bosom, and when you considered, how indefatigably he must have exerted himself! what sacrifices he must have made! what hardships endured, to render her situation comfortable, and rear roses for her on this Island—so deep in the western wilderness—then, notwithstanding all the foibles, which a fastidious cool observer might discover at his fireside, in a character and conduct as that of Des Wattines, he becomes an object of admiration: I at least gazed at him in wonder" (81). Unwilling to focus on Des Wattines' "foibles," Van der Kemp chose to emphasize the neatness of his house and garden. Although "it was all in miniature," what was noteworthy was the "indefatigable industry" necessary "to accomplish all this to such a degree of perfection" (83). Like Leprince de Beaumont, Van der Kemp described a small example that could enthrall a witness and expand the meaning of the particular. The myths and fables that draw in the viewer give way to a story of the hard work and application required to achieve perfection.

A more "fastidious, cool observer" than Van der Kemp did indeed visit the Des Wattines, one who read the circumstance not through romance but through comedy. La Rochefoucauld portrayed Des Wattines as a spendthrift who, having wasted a fortune of 24,000 livres on "expensive follies and inconsiderate enterprises," was forced into the wilderness to recoup. "He had first sold his jewels, then his garments, then his linen, and finally was obliged to part with his library" to none other than Van der Kemp, according to La Rochefoucauld. Des Wattines was less tender to his wife than she to him, sold the products of his little garden "as dear as possible," disliked Americans, and was overwhelmed by nostalgia for his native land: "He dreams of nothing but France. . . . He would rather live miserably there, than to dwell in any other country. . . . This feeling is common with all Frenchmen."[27] For La Rochefoucauld, national identification and character finally proved of greater interest than even the comic traits of a scoundrel.

Yet another account comes from Frenchmen Simon Desjardins, Pierre Pharoux, and Geoffrey Desjardins, officials of the "New York Company," who kept a journal of their travels from 1793 to 1797 as they surveyed land along the Black River. Their reading of Des Wattines was in keeping with their business interests and financial concerns. To them, he was a "French Robinson Crusoe" who "presents another example of the class of Frenchmen who are not enough guarded against ill fortune in this country." In their account, Des Wattines was not wasteful but had been cheated of his fortune by people who overcharged him for land, and he was finally robbed of his last resources by a duplicitous business partner. Although Des Wattines had been forced to sell his furniture, the travelers insisted, he kept his library. In keeping with the other accounts, however, he spent his first year with the Indians. When the travelers witnessed how Des Wattines was teased by other inhabitants at Lake Oneida, they observed that he did not "fail to throw back as much," and they sought "to conciliate affairs" as much as they could.[28] Like the other writers, the visitors viewed the scene through a literary lens colored by their interests and enumerated how a "French Robinson Crusoe" was coping with material and social deprivation.

La Roche most closely followed Van der Kemp's romanticized version, but at the same time she dwelt on the story's inherent thematic conflicts. First, La Roche, like the travelers, moved between images of primitive simplicity and refined civilization and used the opportunity for moral commentary on the virtues of industry. On the one hand, she applauds the honesty and straightforwardness of the Wattines' island existence, of a precapitalist economy where value derives self-evidently from usefulness or moral worth. The Wattineses suffer no confusion about what is needed, what is helpful, what is beautiful, and what is good. On the other hand, they could never have endured without the products of European civilization. They depend on tools and implements purchased in Philadelphia before their trip to Oneida, and on long winter nights they read rapaciously from the three hundred volumes they hauled along. The *Encyclopédie* proves as essential as their hoe and rake.

The narrator complains about the hasty development that has taken place since the arrival of more families in Oneida and fears that it will soon display the excesses of Philadelphia. But Vandek, recently arrived from Holland, counters, "We begin with hard work, knowing that we are doing it for ourselves, and we toil all the more assiduously, always keeping future pleasures before our eyes, as we have seen others savor the success of their labors; for such ideas and feelings are never lost. And why should we forever only replay the roles of the first scenes of culture to satisfy some philosophical notion?"[29] The narrator replies that he meant only to retard encroachment of the destructive passions that always dash happiness. Vandek responds that such a sentiment resembles the absurd hope that a seafarer will encounter no winds. Is it not more reasonable, he suggests, to provide oneself with a good navigator? "We will do this by educating our children, helping as much as possible to strengthen their reason so that ship and sail will reach the intended harbor in wind or in calm."[30]

This belief in the power of education, so central to all feminist utopists, reveals a second conflict, because, as Emilie Wattines demonstrates, education cannot guarantee moral behavior. In broaching this topic, La Roche echoes Fielding's reservations about the likelihood of successfully teaching people hardened by the world. She also questions La Rochefoucauld's conclusions that the Des Wattineses disliked American ways and longed for the companionship of Frenchmen: "This kind of disgust for Americans, is a very common trait with the French, whom we meet in this part of the world. Agreeable forms, polite expression, sweetness, gayety and openness of manners, are always necessary to please them, however they may have been assailed by fortune."[31] La Roche, by contrast, allows Emilie Wattines to lament that the French, despite their high level of cultivation, nonetheless beheaded a monarch and murdered her husband's family. The Oneida, in comparison, are uncivilized, yet they aided her with the births of her two children. "Weren't the Oneidas, with whom I had found protection and help, angels compared to thc Parisians?" Yet Emilie would never forego cultivation and learning in order to take up the ways of the Indians: "But to renounce learning and improved manners and to return to the lowest level of reason,—oh no, no, better to die than to lose hardwon knowledge."[32]

La Roche neither romanticized nor dismissed the Indians and their ways, although she always retained a European outlook and European allegiances. Her representation of the "contact zone," where Europeans and Indians meet, corresponds with Mary Louise Pratt's rendering of actual women explorers who "emplot quests for self-realization and fantasies of social harmony" instead of inscribing visions of dominance and conversion.[33] She mused that perhaps eventually Indians would come to know the delights of learning; perhaps it would only be a matter of time until they produced a thinker of the stature of Newton. Just as the Wattineses were driven from their homeland, so the Indians were gradually being driven from theirs. Yet their contact may, "if they are not exterminated by the Europeans," mean influences that will help the Indians increase their own types of knowledge.[34]

La Roche therefore retained hope that education and cultivation, in general, would lead to improvement and moral behavior, even though the bloodshed of the French Revolution and the tendency of history to repeat itself called such a wish into question.[35] Vandek, who supported the revolution, feels that political changes have brought no progress. "Where there are people, there is imperfection," he says, and warns the narrator against holding on to ideals because "real life suffers from it; we become unjust and harsh towards our neighbor and our fate, and what is worse, one seldom does good."[36]

La Roche thus simultaneously approached and avoided ideals, which are critical as motivators but can lead to despair. She departed from Hamilton's optimistic view "that whoever does not attempt perfection, will sink far below mediocrity."[37] Instead, in the wake of the French Revolution, she invoked the dangers of such thinking. Vandek would limit the number of people who might be entrusted with these notions: "I have wished for years that only poets and artists might know the dangerous enticement of a capacity for representing ideals, because they thereby establish their own happiness and, in creating beautiful images, they promote the pleasure of others."[38] Clinging to ideals can only disappoint, making people ineffectual or even intolerant toward others. At the same time, Vandek suggests, ideals are essential because they make life beautiful and worthwhile. As a result, he decides, ideals will be the safest if restricted to the hands of a few sensitive poets, who will presumably not misuse them and instigate bloodshed and revolution but ornament life instead. In *On the Aesthetic Education of the Human Race* (1794), Friedrich Schiller observed that upheavals such as the French Revolution could be avoided through aesthetic education, which would teach liberty. La Roche echoed that idea in Vandek's argument but avoided retreating into a purely aesthetic realm.[39]

With Vandek's thesis La Roche justified publication of *Events at Lake Oneida*. As an author representing ideals, she offered beautiful images for readers to contemplate. Disappointments, especially over the French Revolution, were transformed into an aesthetic impulse. But La Roche had more than aesthetic enjoyment in mind, and her attempt to convert a strong didactic message into delightful sensations reveals a central ambivalence—an unresolved weighing of sentiment and reason, philosophical and pragmatic aims—that results in tensions and conflicts within the text. Where earlier feminist utopian authors more confidently undertook to balance wealth and virtue, sensibility and rationality, La Roche was unsettled.

Her ambivalence is the more apparent if one compares La Roche's novel to the fiction that most inspired it. The characters in *Erscheinungen* wax enthusiastic over the works of Jacques-Henri Bernardin de Saint-Pierre, but La Roche constructed a plot that had significant departures from his robinsonade *Paul et Virginie* (1788). This best-selling tale popularized the philosophy of Bernardin's friend Rousseau. It depicts the natural upbringing of Paul and Virginie on the island of Mauritius (called Ile-de-France at the time), involving activities similar to those in Rousseau's *Emile*. Both children do not learn to read or write until they are teenagers; instead, they master practical skills by planting a garden and tending to domestic chores. Free of the corrupting influences of civilization, they can allow their innate virtues to flourish, and they become generous, naive, and sentimental adolescents. Without fathers—

Paul's having abandoned his pregnant mother and Virginie's having died before her birth—Paul and Virginie grow up with two mothers and are fed from the breasts of both. Paternal influence comes from the narrator, a neighboring hermit who has rejected European civilization and recommends solitude even as he enjoys the company of Paul's unusual family. Each mother owns a slave to do heavy labor.

Paul and Virginie grow from being brother and sister into fiancés, but their "natural" way of life and the contentment they and the others feel come to an end when Virginie is forced by the governor and the priest, representatives of the corrupt state and church, to travel to France and live with a great aunt from whom she is to inherit a fortune. Virginie, thoroughly unhappy and ill at ease in Europe, is finally disinherited by the aunt and seeks to return home. Tragically, just before the ship reaches the harbor of Mauritius, a violent storm arises. Virginie drowns because she will not allow a strong sailor to undress her in order to save her (European ways apparently influenced her after all). All of her family, including the slaves Domingo and Marie and the dog Fidèle, dies of grief within a few months of her death. Only the hermit remains to tell a solitary traveler the sad story behind the two abandoned huts on the island hillside.

The contrasts between Sophie von La Roche's *Erscheinungen am See Oneida* and Bernardin's *Paul et Virginie* help demonstrate how, despite her strong sentimentalism, domesticity, and enthusiasm for nature, La Roche nonetheless echoed the pragmatism and self-sufficiency of earlier female utopists. Although Bernardin's protagonists, growing children of nature, are characterized by sensibility and an innate feeling for virtue, La Roche's are a young married couple who use reason to survive. Nature in *Paul et Virginie* invokes images of pastoral arcadia; it is bounteous and beneficent. In La Roche, nature may be beautiful, but it will only yield rewards if the Wattineses work hard and demonstrate self-discipline and patience. Further, reason and education prove critical to their survival. They endure long and painful winter nights by reading the *Encyclopédie* and honing their Latin skills, while summer months offer Emilie the chance to learn to swim. Not only does she not drown, as does the innocent and ignorant Virginie, but she can also give birth safely to her two children by swimming to the Indian settlement and getting help there.[40]

La Roche's characters show respect for other people, even if her applause is sometimes reserved for Europeanized behavior. Emilie praises Mexican conduct books and explains how well-behaved she found the girls at the Negro School in Philadelphia; she admires the Indians even though she says she could never live in their manner. By contrast, Bernardin, although lamenting the ill-treatment of slaves, takes slavery for granted and implies that

Africans are destined for it. His sentimental book, intended to bring on tears and anger at the generalized corrupt forces of civilization, power, and money that render good people impotent, is told by a narrator who has rejected Europe. La Roche's novel is a moral story intended to inspire tolerance and virtuous actions. Its narrator is a sentimental investigator who empathetically seeks the truth through eyewitnesses and empirical evidence. He has not rejected Europe but returns to it in the end. Having benefited from a moral and sentimental example, he can go on to improve instead of dismiss the ways of his homeland.

As befits an author writing in the early years of Romanticism, La Roche displayed comparative pragmatism and activist impulses at the same time she inscribed a tale of heightened sensation and pious feeling. Yet she demonstrated her predominant Enlightenment allegiances in discussions of individual merit and empirical method, themes foregrounded in Mary Hamilton. As Emilie Wattines describes giving birth to her son among the Indians, she reflects that people are equal in natural feelings and needs alone. Only in these traits does one witness "the sole true equality that France's new philosophers would like to see in all of life and in all relationships between people."[41] Later it is pointed out that although circumstances position all the colonists equally, their ways of living and their virtues introduce difference among them (2:178). Scriba, a German merchant who initially bought the land on which the new settlement is developing, worries that Wattines' aristocratic background might upset the community by introducing inequalities "where the name of colonist would give everyone the same rights and obligations." The narrator, however, offers an answer to the problem. A solution would lie, he says, "in adopting and holding firmly to the basic laws of England . . . [that allow] the freedom to do as one wishes with oneself and one's property, providing it does not harm the common good or others. This would make all and every one happy."[42] La Roche's character is named "Wattines" rather than the more common "Des Wattines" of the travel accounts, and "Van der Kemp" becomes "Vandek." It is a way of downplaying the issue of blood and title.

La Roche's letters show that she systematically studied Swiss, French, and English laws and concluded that the English constitution offered the greatest potential for the greatest good. In 1793 she wrote to a correspondent that England offered the only hope for society and that as a consequence she was reading only English books at the time.[43] People should be equal in theory, she maintained, just as, in the state of nature, they are in circumstances, and they ought to possess the same rights. They will not, however, prove equals from within. Some are more virtuous, more talented, more intelligent, or more hardworking than others, as is Carl Wattines, who insists that his son, Carmil, should never mention his noble rank but should "demonstrate the moral nobility of his soul in knowledge and manly virtue."[44]

La Roche outlined a meritocratic theory of equality that accounts for difference, and in this she strongly echoed Mary Hamilton. If she ignored gender difference to convey tacit compliance with bourgeois women's increasingly subordinate and privatized role, she nonetheless underscored the convictions of Scott and Leprince de Beaumont as well as Hamilton in embracing natural law and a view of individual merit.[45] At times she even exceeded their perspective in questioning hierarchies of social rank despite her opposition to the leveling effects of revolution. The novel thus confirms La Roche's Anglophilia. She had a strong and lasting tendency to look across the English Channel rather than to France for models of manners and mores.

In addition to the question of equality, La Roche was firm in her belief in empiricism and individual capacity through effort and reason to find out what is true and good. If formal education and cultivation can sometimes lead to artificiality and excess, an individual's sincere search for truth can only lead to understanding and tolerance. La Roche's affirmation of Enlightenment conventions was colored by her Pietistic background. Her narrator must conduct thorough empirical research and hear the Wattineses' story from several perspectives before he can record it as history. He is ardent in his efforts to learn what happened with the family on the island. First, he goes with the Dutchman Vandek to the island to be shown where Vandek discovered the Wattineses and how he persuaded them to help found an onshore community (1:60). The narrator then studies the notes that Mrs. Vandek has jotted down after conversations with Emilie Wattines (1:95, 1:111), and he reads an essay that Carl Wattines has written especially for him about the family's four years of isolation (1:112). In addition to the written account, he receives his live narration (1:205) and travels with Wattines twice to the island for on-site tours (2:63, 3:81). The narrator questions Emilie on her version of their first year, interested especially in her perspective on the visit to the Indians to give birth to Carmil (2:140 ff.).

All along, the narrator has been writing down his findings in the form of a letter to his German cousin, and Carl Wattines asks to read the report (3:29). The written version offers Wattines a broader, more interesting account even than his own experience, and it will allow him a fuller memory—not merely a partial one—of what happened on the island. Historiography, La Roche implies, involves careful research, many perspectives, and a sympathetic interpreter. She asks why only "business people, conquerors, physicists and painters" should travel, interpret, and represent far-flung parts of the world. "Why not a sentimental traveler, like Laurence Sterne's?" (1:2).

The many views from which the story is told have been seen as a technical and structural weakness of La Roche's novel, but that criticism ignores the extent to which this "formal" trait carries ideological content.[46] La Roche advocated an epistemology that carries a tension—of sympathy and empiricism, subjectivity and objectivity—that will involve the heart and the intellect of the reader in order to lead simultaneously to historical understanding and moral enlightenment. I am, therefore, tempted to render the title, *Erscheinungen am See Oneida,* more freely as *Revelations at Lake Oneida,* because La Roche conveys a sense of epiphany (à la James Joyce's *Dubliners*), of intellectual and spiritual illumination, that a telling of the events is to impart.

The narrator's careful investigation parallels La Roche's method of constructing her novel as she drank in her son and daughter-in-law's reports from New York and supplemented their record by reading books on America.[47] The narrator ferrets out every detail of the story and all the while allows his heart to be moved by the virtue and dignity of characters under the strains of pioneer life. Alexis de Tocqueville merged with the implied reader figured by the narrator when he sought out the island in Lake Oneida on his travels through America: "It was with hearts full of emotion, racked by fear and hope, and inspired by some sort of a religious feeling, that we began our meticulous searches and followed up the traces of those two beings whose name and family and part of whose story was unknown to us."[48]

But Tocqueville's "Journey to Lake Oneida," his written account of the trip, suggests that the lesson he gleaned was not the universal one La Roche sought to impart about the active virtues that buttress civilization, even though Tocqueville's political views corresponded significantly with La Roche's. What he took away instead was a romantic vision of Wattines as a supremely happy, self-sufficient being enjoying with his wife their "new Eden," and then, after the wife dies, an isolated and torn individual:

> Is there wretchedness greater than that of this man!
> Here is an unfortunate whom human society has shunned: his fellows have rejected him, banished him, and forced him to renounce their intercourse and flee into the wilds. Only one being has remained attached to him, followed him into solitude, and come to dress the wounds of his soul and to give him, in exchange for the joys of the world, the more pervading emotions of the heart. There he is reconciled to his fate. He has forgotten revolutions, parties, cities, his family, his rank and his fortune; he breathes again. His wife dies. Death comes to strike her and spares him. Poor wretch! What can become of him? Will he stay alone in the wilds, or will he go back to society where he has long been forgotten? He is no longer adapted either for solitude or for the world; he does not know how to live either with men or without them; he is neither a savage nor a civilised man: he is nothing but a piece of debris, like those trees in the

American forests which the wind has had the power to uproot, but not to blow down. He stands erect, but he lives no more.[49]

Tocqueville and his fellow traveler Beaumont read themselves into the isolated figure of Wattines and were terrified of the tragic possibility of becoming exiled themselves. As Beaumont wrote to his sister, "We were curious to see the solitary retreat of our compatriot. Who knows if some day we shall not be glad to find asylum there."[50] Indeed, La Roche's story might first have captured Tocqueville's attention because of the fate of the protagonists. Like the Wattineses of the tale, Tocqueville was an aristocrat whose family members had been driven into exile, harassed, and guillotined during the revolution. More recently, the July Revolution of 1830 had brought to power a regime from which his family, longtime administrators under the Bourbons, chose to distance themselves. Although Tocqueville signed an oath of loyalty, he was "at war with [himself]" over doing so, and his unease with the new regime spurred his decision (and that of Beaumont) to undertake the journey to America at just this juncture. They were commissioned to study American prisons to find models for reforming the French penal system, and they gathered the materials for later writings, notably Tocqueville's celebrated *Democracy in America.* Spurred by the memory of the book that had "left a deep and lasting impression on my mind" when he was a child, Tocqueville and Beaumont made a sizable detour to seek out "our two French people, if they were still alive, or at least visit their home."[51] After the canoe trip to the island, Tocqueville jotted in his pocket notebook: "This expedition is what has most vividly interested and moved me, not only since I have been in America, but since I have been travelling."[52]

Unlike their official visits to evaluate prisons and other American institutions, the trip to Lake Oneida appealed to Tocqueville and Beaumont on levels personal, social, and political all at once, arguing the individual emotional foundations of social and political alliances and the fundamental vulnerability of human associations.[53] Having left France on account of another revolution and because of discomfort with the new regime, they confronted at Oneida the possibility of exile and the potential failure of their arduous trip—their fact-finding mission with the aim of establishing institutions that would perpetuate the liberal principles they both held dear.

Tocqueville returned home from America, wrote out the story of his "Journey to Lake Oneida," the most memorable and poignant event in his travels, and then tucked it away in a drawer. It only appeared in the complete works in 1861, edited by Beaumont, two years after Tocqueville had died. Tocqueville must have felt it was a personal and emotional tale unassimilable to the sociopolitical and institutional analyses of *Democracy in America.*

Yet even though he did not tell the whole story in that book, the Oneida experience appears briefly in a chapter on how the geography of the United States supports democracy, allowing citizens to move west in order to improve their lots. The island represented an abandoned Old World left to ruin by impetuous settlers seeking their fortunes. It expressed the power of nature to overwhelm human civilization:

> I was far from supposing that this spot had ever been inhabited, so completely did Nature seem to be left to herself; but when I reached the center of the isle, I thought that I discovered some traces of man. I then proceeded to examine the surrounding objects with care, and I soon perceived that a European had undoubtedly been led to seek a refuge in this place. Yet what changes had taken place in the scene of his labors! The logs which he had hastily hewn to build himself a shed had sprouted afresh; the very props were intertwined with living verdure, and his cabin was transformed into a bower. In the midst of these shrubs a few stones were to be seen, blackened with fire and sprinkled with thin ashes; here the hearth had no doubt been, and the chimney in falling had covered it with rubbish. I stood for some time in silent admiration of the resources of Nature and the littleness of man; and when I was obliged to leave that enchanting solitude, I exclaimed with sadness: "Are ruins, then, already here?"[54]

Where the "Journey to Lake Oneida" expressed the "littleness" of Tocqueville and Beaumont in the wake of the July Revolution, this version of the trip to the island became generalized to a tale of human frailty in the face of a wild, uncontrollable nature. In this transformation, Tocqueville's passage in *Democracy in America,* unlike that in "Journey," reinforced La Roche's moral about the tenacity and integrity needed to establish human community and sustain civilization. To that extent, the all-but-forgotten work of a little-known German woman writer, inspired by British models, quietly entered a celebrated French tome.

At the same time, the utopian longing invested in Tocqueville's "Journey to Lake Oneida" was altered in *Democracy in America,* where he analyzed the problems of labor, pain, and punishment in the social world. La Roche's novel, by contrast, integrates both emphases; utopian dreaming is not divorced from practical community-building. Eden is a place requiring hard work, and it is gradually populated. Monika Nenon thus concludes that La Roche offers a "bourgeois utopia" and argues that the novel, far from being conservative, rejects "the older aristocratic order founded on the privileges of birth and inherited rank" and champions a progressive point of view that "will eventually culminate in the idea of a republic."[55]

Forty years later, La Roche had successfully educated her reader, Tocqueville. Moved to extraordinary action by the power of her story, he not only followed the research of the narrator but also shared and cherished the sentiments La Roche's narrator so often articulated in describing the Wattineses. He reproduced the empirical impulse, the liberal sentiments, the recognition of conflict and paradox, and the uncertainties about history that La Roche wove into her 1798 fiction.

The shared interest of La Roche and Tocqueville in how imagination and theory affect life, how sentiment influences action, suggests that both authors would have been pleased to learn that one of the most successful of American utopian experiments, the Oneida Community, was founded a few years later at Oneida itself. The relationship between fiction and reality thus blurred in the creation, reception, and afterlife of La Roche's novel. The Oneida Community, based on Owenite and Fourierist principles, developed successful industries—especially in producing silverware and steel traps—and lasted far longer than most, from 1848 to 1881, when it was reorganized as a joint stock company. It is still known for tableware manufacture.[56]

In *Revelations at Lake Oneida,* La Roche expressed a strong ethical and liberal political perspective while managing to convey uneasiness and insecurity engendered during the post-Revolutionary period. Many of her themes reveal conflict and indecision, which distinguishes the book from her earlier, sure-footed *Geschichte des Fräuleins von Sternheim,* where right and wrong are confidently delineated. In *Erscheinungen,* one perspective is never enough. Feeling is the most trustworthy guide, but words, which can go wrong, must be relied on. The characters are all admirable, but the image of the murderous Parisians remains; they are invoked again and again. Ideals and their delightful representations prove as necessary as breath and light (1:77), and yet they are painful and can lead to harm. History can repeat itself in all its horror (1:104), but perhaps it will not. La Roche was tempted to escape to the aesthetic realm, where all such tensions can be resolved, but she stopped short of abandoning real-world concerns for a transcendent realm of perfection. Like the female utopists before her, she promoted the practical application of one's talents to effect social improvements, even if she felt less certain than her literary forebears about the ideology in which those reforms would be grounded. La Roche's sympathetic empiricism expressed a liberal approach to living and acting in a fluctuating space on the border between Enlightenment and Romantic worlds.

* * *

Both Sophie von La Roche and Jeanne Marie Leprince de Beaumont responded to texts written by men of another nation: Bernardin de Saint-Pierre's *Paul et Virginie,* Richardson's *Clarissa,* and Rousseau's *New Heloise.* They sought to rewrite the position of women by offering heroines who do not suffer and die in order to fulfill a fantasy of virgin innocence and saintliness, but who meet substantial challenges and enjoy productive lives as citizens, wives, and mothers. Both writers offered perspectives on England. In Leprince de Beaumont it was a land in which deception flourishes for good and for ill: Clarissa is nearly tricked into a sham marriage there, yet she escapes by means of a French baron disguised as a wigmaker's apprentice in order to save his life. Britain was also a place where strong middle ranks mediated the distance between the leisured and the working classes, a desirable state of affairs, according to Leprince de Beaumont. La Roche agreed that the English bourgeois model was to be imitated at all levels, including customs, values, and laws. Both the French and the German author wrote pragmatic utopias that recalled the visions of Fielding and Scott and Hamilton, yet at the same time both moved away from a primarily feminist statement to advocate a general morality instead.

Afterword: A Middle Way

Eighteenth-century feminist authors devised innovative utopias that took account of the rapidly changing socioeconomic and political environment and departed from the traditional utopian pattern. Even as they wrote in a liberal idiom, however, they critiqued it; they possessed the intellect, creativity, and literary dexterity necessary to revise received discourses in order to resituate women. They were shown the way by Mary Astell, who moved beyond the theology of John Norris. Sarah Fielding contended with moral sense philosophers, Sarah Scott reconceived the contract, Mary Hamilton plagiarized and recontextualized Defoe, Jeanne Marie Leprince de Beaumont rerouted debates on depopulation in the process of rethinking Richardson's *Clarissa* and Rousseau's *The New Heloise,* and Sophie von La Roche challenged post-Revolution rhetoric by rewriting Bernardin de St. Pierre's *Paul et Virginie.* Drawing on Christian ideas of charity and the imitation of Christ, female utopists became *bricoleuses* like those described by Michel de Certeau and subtly altered cultural discourses to the advantage of women.[1]

Anticipating goals of some twentieth- and twenty-first century feminists, they demanded the consistent application of liberal principles. Seyla Benhabib has argued persuasively that scholars need to devote increased attention to such Enlightenment ideals:

> Revealing the gender subtext of the ideals of reason and the Enlightenment compromises the assumed universality of these ideals. Nonetheless, they should not be thrown aside altogether. Instead we can ask what these categories have meant for the actual lives of women in certain historical periods, and how, if women are to be thought of as subjects and not just as fulfillers of certain functions, the semantic horizon of these categories is transformed. Once we ap-

> proach the tradition to recover from it women's subjectivity and their lives and activities, we hear contradictory voices, competing claims, and see that so-called "descriptive" discourses about the sexes are but "legitimizations" of male power. The traditional view of gender differences is the discourse of those who have won out and who have codified history as we know it. But what would the history of ideas look like from the standpoint of the victims? What ideals, aspirations and utopias of the past ran into a dead-end? Can we recapture their memory from the battleground of history?[2]

It has been the aim of this study to recapture the memory of eighteenth-century women's utopian thought in order to alter our understanding of "the semantic horizon" of ideals in the Enlightenment. Sarah Scott had already called for recognition of "scarcely perceptible" determinants of history in order to demonstrate the ways women and other subalterns were left out of mainstream historiography. If wars and national disasters could be instigated by "seemingly small" catalysts, to use Mary Hamilton's locution, then these invisible influences could also make a positive difference. Women could change households, communities, the nation, and the world through persistent, incremental moves and subversions.

To that end, and to an extent not adequately acknowledged, the "ideals of reason and the Enlightenment" substantially motivated female utopian authors. They believed passionately that education offered the most effective means of social transformation. Their works emphasize instruction in methods of reading and interpretation, spiritual improvement, emotional growth, and intellectual discernment. The success of such a project depended on the Lockean conception of an impressionable individual bent on self-improvement and profitable activity. Female authors drew on ideas of equality, which they attempted to represent in balanced, nonexploitative human relationships across social ranks, between the sexes, and, to a limited extent, between races. They developed increasingly progressive notions about the polis, advocating the redistribution of resources, imagining extensive subsidized education, and seeking increased access to intellectual property and pleasurable as well as didactic forms of art. Their utopian nation would grow strong and expand its influence, not for the purpose of oppressing peoples across the globe but in order to become a more potent model for the world.

To modify the predominantly liberal conception, these women writers occasionally employed classical images of the charismatic hero and the patriot. More often, they embraced the vision of the early church to imagine how communities might be organized and reproduced. Their ambitious, altruistic global order would be achieved through incremental local activity, which would be proliferated through moral, biological, pedagogical, and textual reproduction inspired by the imitation of Christ. The women's motto could well be expressed by today's bumper sticker slogan "think globally, act locally." I agree with Gary Kelly's view that the eighteenth-century focus on the local does not suggest unambitious political goals. "This sphere might seem limited," he writes, "but . . . in a state lacking major national institutions of public welfare, social surveillance, and policing, the local sphere was a—perhaps *the*—major arena of social action."[3] Women's focus on the rural household and village signified the most likely locus for benevolent exchange, education, and the replication of utopian subjects.

Feminist utopianism in the eighteenth century thus sought a middle way that adapted the predominating discourses rather than fully rejecting them. It emphasized the shifting nature of public and private realms despite economic, political, and social tendencies toward rending apart and gendering them. It reinterpreted the family through alternative visions of marriage, domesticity, and community. In so doing it challenged existing sexual arrangements and called into question some aspects of the emerging sociopolitical order. This study has, therefore, sought to recover a forgotten segment of women's history and reveal the cogent measures proposed for regrounding women's political identity, setting in place what the writers felt would constitute a liberating epistemology. Envisioning utopia made it possible for feminist utopists to assume responsibility for their circumstances. Utopia was a place of imaginative anticipation, to draw on Ernst Bloch's characterization, a daydream they felt pointed the way to change.

At the same time, the women also sought to turn their poorly defined political status to profit. Leprince de Beaumont claimed the power of women's nationlessness: Women as "citizen[s] of the universe" could be a part of all nations, could speak out for reform on behalf of people globally.[4] Astell had expressed a related sentiment about single women: "The whole World is a single Lady's Family, her opportunities of doing good are not lessen'd but encreased by her being unconfin'd." These women adumbrate Virginia Woolf, who asserted in the voice of a female outsider: "As a woman, I have no country. As a woman I want no country. As a woman my country is the whole world."[5]

Nationless outsiderdom has been a feminist credo since at least the late seventeenth century. More recently, Rosi Braidotti has called for women to be "nomadic subjects" as an expression of "nonconfidence in the capacity of the 'polis' to undo the power foundations on which it rests." Nomadic subjects, she argues, shun passports and belong to no nation in particular.[6] Benhabib, however, has pointed out how politically enfeebling such a move is, given that people without passports lack any claim to a political voice and, historically, have suffered at the hands of all manner of collective groups. She maintains that the world now offers a "new constellation" that demands people develop a way of maintaining nation, community, and self in productive tension.[7] What is needed is a constant and fluid movement between local, national, and global identifications. It is a capacity that in nascent form appears in the writing of eighteenth-century women.

Such feats of imagination gave women a flexible idea of relations between the private and the public and enabled the formation of what Nancy Fraser, in her correction of Habermas's notion of the public sphere, has called "subaltern counterpublics": "in stratified societies, subaltern counterpublics have a dual character. On the one hand, they function as spaces of withdrawal and regroupment; on the other hand, they also function as bases and training grounds for agitational activities directed toward wider publics. It is precisely in the dialectic between these two functions that their emancipatory potential resides."[8] In spite of their separatist moments, feminist utopias were not limited or blocked off, as some commentators have suggested.[9] Instead, women authors, drawing on a supportive group of fellow writers and readers, aimed "to disseminate [their] discourse into ever-widening arenas."[10] They would thereby garner the recognition and resources necessary to further their plans, extend virtue, and achieve political identity.

It is in large measure the perspective of outsider that allowed eighteenth-century feminists to forge new types of expression that followed a middle way, foreshadowing postmodern critiques even as they were driven by Enlightenment ideas. Considering the postmodern malaise, or what Fraser calls the "postsocialist condition," David Harvey has called for active engagement in ethical and creative imagining. The rejection of utopianism as authoritarian and totalitarian has had "the unfortunate effect of curbing the free play of the imagination in the search for alternatives." We need "to act as conscious architects of our fates rather than as 'helpless puppets' of the institutional and imaginative worlds we inhabit."[11] Women's partial visions, which turned subaltern status to advantage, offer an example of how feminists and others might approach the "vision problem" today.

To be sure, feminist utopian writers did not effect change on a large scale, yet they did influence individuals and literary life against considerable odds. Astell's impact was profound and reverberated throughout the eighteenth century, as I have argued in chapter 1 and as Ruth Perry and Patricia Springborg have discussed in different contexts.[12] The Bath Community, described by Betty Rizzo, undertook substantial charitable work.[13] Sarah Scott not only set up the Hitcham Community but also likely inspired Nathaniel and Anne Cholmley to build a village for their old or married servants and supervise a school for the children.[14]

To a limited extent, the reproduction modeled in women's utopian texts did in fact come to pass. Further, the type of unexpected literary influence La Roche exerted on Tocqueville can be traced from Scott as well. Her characterization of Gustavus Ericson appealed to James Burgh, author of the utopian *Account of the First Settlement, Laws, Form of Government, and Police, of the Cessares* (1764), who cited Scott and echoed her language as he contrasted the reign of Ericson with the tyranny of Louis XIV:

> How different from Lewis the XIV, is the excellent character of Gustavus Ericson, a king of Sweden; who never attempted to extend his successful arms beyond the deliverance of his own country: who carefully studied how to make his power beneficial to his people, compassionating their necessities, redressing their grievances, rectifying their dispositions, and correcting their vices, with the indulgent hand of a tender parent! And though he softened their rough tempers into humanity, by the innocent pleasures of life; he took care that they should not corrupt their manners, constantly restraining them from every abuse and excess, by the example of an irreproachable virtue in his own conduct.[15]

Burgh was a well-known Dissenting reformer and educator, a close associate of Richard Price and the circle around the publisher Joseph Johnson. Mary Wollstonecraft belonged to this group and was influenced by Burgh's work; the depth and extent of her own influence is, of course, well known.[16]

Barbara Taylor, studying early-nineteenth-century Owenism, has contrasted the attention to women in that socialist movement with their neglect in later Marxism, and she has traced this to the feminist influences on Robert Owen through Mary Wollstonecraft and William Godwin. Taylor's work shows how productive it can be to look at pre-Marxian paths for feminist history. Significant feminist discourses existed before the 1780s, and one of these, feminist utopianism, carried within itself a program for its own perpetuation in the next generation.[17]

At century's end the French Revolution appears to have curtailed women's use of utopian narrative as a form of feminist expression. Feminism came to be advanced most powerfully in the polemics and tracts of Mary Hays, Mary Ann Radcliffe, William Thompson, Anna Wheeler, and others.[18] Although feminist utopian impulses continued to be expressed in the spirited enterprises of Fanny Wright and Flora Tristan, women's utopian narratives did not again emerge as frequent, effective, popular expressions of feminist ideas until the end of the nineteenth century.[19]

Angelika Bammer's notion of the "partial vision" explains how women writers of the 1970s adapted utopia in a postmodern context. Although the "partiality" of eighteenth-century utopianism, its incremental, reproductive quality, allies it with what is now perceived as postmodern, antitotalizing, and feminist, it nonetheless reinscribes Enlightenment concepts as well. In so doing it provides an example of an attempt to alter "the semantic horizon," as Benhabib terms it, of the Enlightenment narrative even as that narrative was being written. Feminist utopists of the eighteenth century recognized their partiality and at the same time offered plans that, leaning on Enlightenment ideals, sought to improve the lives of subalterns and create the possibility for women to become active reformers and political subjects. In the process, they revealed the larger challenge that utopian hope could pose in a postmodern age.

Notes

Introduction

1. Jürgen Habermas, *The Structural Transformation of the Public Sphere: An Inquiry into a Category of Bourgeois Society,* trans. Thomas Burger with the assistance of Frederick Lawrence (Cambridge: MIT Press, 1991). For an overview of thinkers who have rung utopia's death knell, see Russell Jacoby, *The End of Utopia: Politics and Culture in an Age of Apathy* (New York: Basic Books, 1999). Among the influential mid-twentieth-century thinkers he singles out are Judith N. Shklar, *After Utopia: The Decline of Political Faith* (Princeton: Princeton University Press, 1957), and Daniel Bell, *End of Ideology: On the Exhaustion of Political Ideas in the Fifties* (Glencoe: Free Press, 1960); these have been echoed in recent years most controversially by Francis Fukuyama, *The End of History and the Last Man* (New York: Free Press, 1992). Supporting utopian thought along with Jürgen Habermas at mid-century were Ernst Bloch, *Das Prinzip Hoffnung,* 3 vols. (Frankfurt: Suhrkamp, 1959) (trans. by Neville Plaice, Stephen Plaice, and Paul Knight as *The Principle of Hope* [Cambridge: MIT Press, 1995]), and Herbert Marcuse, *One-Dimensional Man: Studies in the Ideology of Advanced Industrial Society* (Boston: Beacon Press, 1964). Influential thinkers who have more recently addressed the question of utopia in a postmodern age include Fredric Jameson, *Postmodernism; or, The Cultural Logic of Late Capitalism* (Durham: Duke University Press, 1991); Louis Marin, *Utopics: Spatial Play* trans. Robert A. Vollrath (Atlantic Highlands: Humanities Press, 1984); and Richard Rorty, *Philosophy and Social Hope* (London: Penguin, 1999). Other commentators and perspectives are listed in note 16 of this chapter.

2. Seyla Benhabib, *Situating the Self: Gender, Community, and Postmodernism in Contemporary Ethics* (Cambridge: Polity Press, 1992), 230.

3. Angelika Bammer, *Partial Visions: Feminism and Utopianism in the 1970s* (New York: Routledge, 1991).

4. Michel de Certeau, *The Practice of Everyday Life,* trans. Steven F. Rendall (Berkeley: University of California Press, 1984), xiii–xv. I have employed the feminine form whereas de Certeau uses the masculine, "*bricoleur.*" The term, in the social science context, first

gained familiarity through Claude Lévi-Strauss, *The Savage Mind* (Chicago: University of Chicago Press, 1966), 16–17. On discipline, see Michel Foucault, *Discipline and Punish: The Birth of the Prison,* trans. Alan Sheridan (New York: Vintage, 1977), and Michel Foucault, *The History of Sexuality,* vol. 1: *An Introduction,* trans. Robert Hurley (1978, repr. New York: Vintage, 1990).

5. Bammer, *Partial Visions,* 2.

6. Bloch, *Das Prinzip Hoffnung,* 165. Bammer uses Bloch's concept of concrete utopia but decouples it from its Marxian moorings in order to deploy it for feminist ends. According to Bloch, "The point of contact between dreams and life, without which dreams only yield abstract utopia, life only triviality, is given in the utopian capacity which is set on its feet and connected to the Real-Possible. And which in fact tendentially transcends what exists in each respective case, not only in our nature, but in that of the entire external world of process. Thus the only seemingly paradoxical concept of a concrete utopia would be appropriate here, that is, of an anticipatory kind which by no means coincides with abstract utopian dreaminess" (*Principle of Hope* 1:145–46). Ruth Levitas, *The Concept of Utopia* (Syracuse: Syracuse University Press, 1990), 83–105, esp. 88–90; Jack Zipes, "Introduction," in Ernst Bloch, *The Utopian Function of Art and Literature: Selected Essays,* trans. Jack Zipes and Frank Mecklenburg (Cambridge: MIT Press, 1988), xi–xliii; Vincent Geoghegan, *Ernst Bloch* (New York: Routledge, 1996).

7. Wendy Brown, "The Impossibility of Women's Studies," *Differences: A Journal of Feminist Cultural Studies* 9, no. 3 (1997): 79–101; Rosalind Coward, "Do We Need a New Feminism?" *Women: A Cultural Review* 10, no. 2 (1999): 192–205. These articles appeared in special issues with articles dedicated to the topic of feminism today and the status of academic women's studies programs. See also *Signs: Journal of Women in Culture and Society* 24, no. 2 (1999); *Journal of Women's History* 11, nos. 1–2 (1999); and Olive Banks, "Some Reflections on Gender, Sociology and Women's History," *Women's History Review* 8, no. 3 (1999): 401–10. Coward's article summarizes arguments from her book, *Sacred Cows: Is Feminism Relevant to the New Millennium?* (London: HarperCollins, 1999). Other books evaluating the state of women's studies include Bonnie G. Smith, *The Gender of History: Men, Women, and Historical Practice* (Cambridge: Harvard University Press, 1998); Judith P. Zinsser, *History and Feminism: A Glass Half Full* (New York: Twayne, 1993); and Karen Offen, Ruth Roach Pierson, and Jane Rendall, eds., *Writing Women's History: International Perspectives* (Bloomington: Indiana University Press, 1991). See also Susan Gubar, *Critical Condition: Feminism at the Turn of the Century* (New York: Columbia University Press, 2000).

8. Elizabeth Faue, "Women's History in the New Millennium: A Conversation across Three 'Generations': Part 2," *Journal of Women's History* 11, no. 2 (1999): 211 (including Anne Firor Scott, Sara M. Evans, Susan K. Cahn, and Elizabeth Faue).

9. Jane Spencer, *The Rise of the Woman Novelist: From Aphra Behn to Jane Austen* (Oxford: Basil Blackwell, 1986), xi.

10. Nancy Armstrong, *Desire and Domestic Fiction: A Political History of the Novel* (New York: Oxford University Press, 1987), 3. Leila Silvana May has criticized Armstrong's influential book in "The Strong-Arming of Desire: A Reconsideration of Nancy Armstrong's *Desire and Domestic Fiction,*" *ELH* 68, no. 1 (2001): 267–85, and suggests that Armstrong's arguments are undermined by contradictions and logical lapses.

11. The question of public versus private spheres is addressed in a volume edited by Elizabeth Eger et al., *Women, Writing and the Public Sphere, 1700–1830* (New York: Cambridge University Press, 2001). The Introduction points out that in this period, which "embod[ied] a transitional ideology . . . the idea of the public was inevitably contradictory and ambiguous" (5). Harriet Guest sees the need for critics to retain the private/public distinction, but she argues in favor of greater attention to non-novelistic genres and challenges the idea that "middle-class women were in the second half of the eighteenth century increasingly confined to domesticity by the demands of propriety." Guest, *Small Change: Women, Learning, Patriotism 1750–1810* (Chicago: University of Chicago Press, 2000), 1–18, quotation, 15, see also 85. Among other contributions to expanding the women's canon is Gary Kelly, gen. ed., *Bluestocking Feminism: Writings of the Bluestocking Circle, 1738–1785*, 6 vols. (London: Pickering and Chatto, 1999), which makes available hitherto obscure but critical feminist texts. Devoney Looser's *British Women Writers and the Writing of History, 1670–1820* (Baltimore: Johns Hopkins University Press, 2000) draws attention to the largely neglected area of women's historiographical interventions. A significant collection of essays on women's writing across genres is edited by Vivien Jones, *Women and Literature in Britain, 1700–1800* (New York: Cambridge University Press, 2000). Individual studies that consider how eighteenth-century women's novels interrogated women's sociopolitical positions are listed in note 12.

12. Betty A. Schellenberg makes a similar argument about the aesthetic evaluation of conversational novels, works that "have long been dismissed by critics as aesthetic failures because they do not fit the criteria of plot and character generalized as characteristic of the 'classical' novel," and she concludes that "the resulting history of the early novel increasingly appears restricted and unrepresentative." Betty A. Schellenberg, *The Conversational Circle: Rereading the English Novel, 1740–1775* (Lexington: University Press of Kentucky, 1996), 2–3. She does, however, cite the work of John Bender, *Imagining the Penitentiary: Fiction and the Architecture of Mind in Eighteenth-Century England* (Chicago: University of Chicago Press, 1987), and Michael McKeon, *The Origins of the English Novel, 1600–1740* (Baltimore: Johns Hopkins University Press, 1987) as beginning "to fill the gaps of this partial picture" (3).

Early in the twentieth century, before Ian Watt's *The Rise of the Novel: Studies in Defoe, Richardson, and Fielding* (Berkeley: University of California Press, 1957) set aside women authors, a number of historians of the novel were prepared to recognize women's contribution. These critics sometimes drew on traditional characterizations and evaluations of the genre, but they nonetheless promoted a wider perspective on the early novel. See Joyce M. Horner, *The English Women Novelists and Their Connection with the Feminist Movement, 1699–1797*, Smith College Studies in Modern Languages (Northampton: Collegiate Press, 1929–30); J. M. S. Tompkins, *The Popular Novel in England, 1770–1800* (1932, repr. Lincoln: University of Nebraska Press, 1961); and B. G. MacCarthy, *The Female Pen: Women Writers and Novelists, 1621–1818* (1946–47, repr. New York: New York University Press, 1994).

After Watt's study appeared, critics tended to fashion interpretations in response to his thesis and focus on the canonized "fathers of the novel," but attempts to modify Watt have been copious since the 1980s. See, for example, Armstrong, *Desire and Domestic Fiction;* Lennard J. Davis, *Factual Fictions: The Origins of the English Novel* (New York: Columbia

University Press, 1983); Lennard J. Davis, *Resisting Novels: Ideology and Fiction* (New York: Methuen, 1987); J. Paul Hunter, *Before Novels: The Cultural Contexts of Eighteenth-Century English Fiction* (New York: W. W. Norton, 1990); John Richetti, *Popular Fiction before Richardson: Narrative Patterns, 1700–1739* (1969, repr. New York: Oxford University Press, 1992); John Richetti, *The English Novel in History, 1700–1780* (New York: Routledge, 1999); and William B. Warner, *Licensing Entertainment: The Elevation of Novel Reading in Britain, 1684–1750* (Berkeley: University of California Press, 1998).

Studies emphasizing women's contributions and/or issues of gender difference include Ros Ballaster, *Seductive Forms: Women's Amatory Fiction from 1684 to 1740* (New York: Oxford University Press, 1992); Robert Adams Day, *Told in Letters: Epistolary Fiction before Richardson* (Ann Arbor: University of Michigan Press, 1966); Joan DeJean, *Tender Geographies: Women and the Origins of the Novel in France* (New York: Columbia University Press, 1991); Catherine Gallagher, *Nobody's Story: The Vanishing Acts of Women Writers in the Marketplace, 1670–1820* (Berkeley: University of California Press, 1994); April London, *Women and Property in the Eighteenth-Century English Novel* (New York: Cambridge University Press, 1999); Ruth Perry, *Women, Letters, and the Novel* (New York: AMS Press, 1980); Deborah Ross, *The Excellence of Falsehood: Romance, Realism, and Women's Contribution to the Novel* (Lexington: University Press of Kentucky, 1991); Janet Todd, *The Sign of Angellica: Women, Writing, and Fiction, 1660–1800* (London: Virago Press, 1989); and Spencer, *The Rise of the Woman Novelist.*

For a more recent evaluation of Ian Watt's impact, see "Reconsidering the Rise of the Novel," a special issue of *Eighteenth-Century Fiction* 12, nos. 2–3 (Jan.–April 2000). If women's writing has only since the 1980s received something approaching proportional representation in the criticism, then it is unsurprising that women's utopianism has hardly been broached (for studies on women and utopia, see note 19). In my effort here to convince readers of the cultural significance of eighteenth-century feminist utopian texts, I will pay less attention to women's contributions to the form and structure of the evolving novel than to the ways they use narratives to query philosophical, social, and political discourses and to inscribe a social model with an eye to reform.

13. Sylvia Harcstark Myers, *The Bluestocking Circle: Women, Friendship, and the Life of the Mind in Eighteenth-Century England* (New York: Oxford University Press, 1990); Betty Rizzo, *Companions without Vows: Relationships among Eighteenth-Century British Women* (Athens: University of Georgia Press, 1994); Schellenberg, *Conversational Circle;* Kelly, gen. ed., *Bluestocking Feminism.*

14. Keith Michael Baker and Peter Hanns Reill, "Introduction," in their edited volume, *What's Left of Enlightenment? A Postmodern Question* (Stanford: Stanford University Press, 2001), 1–4, quotation, 1. This volume contains the essays by Dena Goodman ("Difference: An Enlightenment Concept," 129–47, quotation, 146) and Lawrence Klein ("Enlightenment as Conversation," 148–66, quotation, 163). See also Daniel Gordon, "Introduction" and "On the Supposed Obsolescence of the French Enlightenment," both in *Postmodernism and the Enlightenment: New Perspectives in Eighteenth-Century French Intellectual History* (New York: Routledge, 2001), 1–6, quotation, 1, and 201–21, quotation, 204 (published earlier in *Historical Reflections / Réflexions Historiques* 25, no. 2 [1999]); and James Schmidt, ed., *What Is Enlightenment? Eighteenth-Century Answers and Twentieth-Century Questions* (Berkeley: University of California Press, 1996).

15. Frank E. Manuel and Fritzie P. Manuel, *Utopian Thought in the Western World* (Cambridge: Harvard University Press, 1979), 5.

16. Such frameworks represent widely varying intellectual, disciplinary, and political angles, although they share a desire to explicate the motivations for and potential consequences of utopian thinking. Darko Suvin, for example, defines utopia as "the verbal construction of a particular quasi-human community where sociopolitical institutions, norms, and individual relationships are organized according to a more perfect principle than in the author's community, this construction being based on estrangement arising out of an alternative historical hypothesis" (*Metamorphoses of Science Fiction: On the Poetics and History of a Literary Genre* [New Haven: Yale University Press, 1979], 37–62, quotation, 49).

In Louis Marin's Marxist definition, "Utopia is an ideological critique of ideology . . . to the degree to which it reconstructs present or contemporary society by displacing and projecting the latter's structures into a fictive discourse." Because utopian discourse is unscientific in the Marxist sense, however, it can provide no map to show how to alter the material conditions of the society which produces it ("Theses on Ideology and Utopia," trans. Fredric Jameson, *Minnesota Review* 6 [Spring 1976]: 71–75, quotations, 71). Similarly Marxist is the view of A. L. Morton, who defines "Utopia as an imaginary country described in a work of fiction with the object of criticising existing society." Unlike Marin, he sees more of a real-world role for the tradition: "Today the long and honoured stream of utopian writers has entered and made a noble contribution to the great river of the movement for socialism" (*The English Utopia* [London: Lawrence and Wishart, 1969], 12, 275).

Frank Manuel's definition is "latitudinarian and ecumenical." Although "the utopia should perhaps be distinguished from the religious millennium," he sees the tradition as including a wide range of narrative, not all of it necessarily fictional. "The boundaries need not be demarcated with nice precision. It is moreover not the literary form that establishes the universe of discourse . . . but the intent to evoke a vision of the life of man in an earthly paradise that would be radically different from the existing order and would presume to render its inhabitants happier in some significant sense of that ambiguous yet unavoidable word" ("Toward a Psychological History of Utopias," in *Utopias and Utopian Thought: A Timely Appraisal*, ed. Frank E. Manuel [Boston: Beacon Press, 1967], 69–98, quotations, 69, 70).

Miriam Eliav-Feldon similarly "excludes any vision of an ideal existence that is otherworldly, unattainable, or dependent either on wonders of nature or on divine intervention." For her, a utopia is "*a literary work describing an ideal society created by conscious human effort on this earth.*" As a group, utopias are "important as sources of information about the opinions and feelings of contemporaries concerning . . . the problems of their age" (*Realistic Utopias: The Ideal Imaginary Societies of the Renaissance, 1516–1630* [New York: Oxford University Press, 1982], 2, emphasis in original).

For Krishan Kumar, "A strict definition of utopia would serve no useful purpose." Still, "The modern utopia—the modern western utopia invented in the Europe of the Renaissance—is the only utopia. It inherits classical and Christian forms and themes, but it transforms them into a distinctive novelty, a distinctive literary genre carrying a distinctive social philosophy." This modern utopia is distinguished by being "egalitarian, affluent and dynamic" (*Utopia and Anti-Utopia in Modern Times* [Oxford: Basil Blackwell, 1987], 3, 32).

Writing of the Enlightenment, Franco Venturi identifies a specifically communistic strain that "is really one of the most irreversible, unchanging and lasting results the eighteenth century transmitted to the nineteenth" and which he defines as specifically utopian. "In every group of *philosophes,* there was at least one who had a secret sympathy for a world in which the fatal distinction between mine and thine either never existed or had been abolished. . . . The traditional utopia expanded and altered under the stimulus of this typical Enlightenment determination to create paradise on this earth, to create a completely human society which was egalitarian and free" (*Utopia and Reform in the Enlightenment* [New York: Cambridge University Press, 1971], 96–97).

In his reader-oriented study of the tradition, Peter Ruppert follows what he sees as a recent trend in scholarship, which suggests "that, rather than one-dimensional blueprints for social reform or consoling visions of identity, utopias are better understood as open-ended interrogations of social reality that are themselves contradictory and inconsistent." Further, "utopias should be grasped as works of the imagination, as symbolic constructs, which function not to represent islands of social perfection but to serve as thought-provoking catalysts whose value is in their shock effect on readers" (*Reader in a Strange Land: The Activity of Reading Literary Utopias* [Athens: University of Georgia Press, 1986], xii–xiii).

For Northrop Frye, the literary "utopia, in its typical form, contrasts, implicitly or explicitly, the writer's own society with the more desirable one he describes. The desirable society, or the utopia proper, is essentially the writer's own society with its unconscious ritual habits transposed into their conscious equivalents." Hence, the shortcomings of More's England are described at the beginning of *Utopia,* with the rest of the book serving as a rational counterpoint. "The contrast in value between the two societies implies a satire on the writer's own society, and the basis for the satire is the unconsciousness or inconsistency in the social behavior he observes around him" ("Varieties of Literary Utopias," in *Utopias and Utopian Thought: A Timely Appraisal,* ed. Manuel, 25–49, quotation, 27).

The definition developed by Christine Rees applies specifically to the eighteenth century; she seeks to avoid restrictive "demarcation disputes." The "utopia may be ideal, satiric, or ambiguous. It may have traces of pastoral idyll, millennial faith, or Rabelaisian indulgence. Whatever else it reflects, it acts as a mirror tilted by the author to catch new angles on familiar aspects of his or her society. It sets out to induce culture shock, and often succeeds." She settles on a broad definition for the utopias she examines. They "involve the imagining of fictional alternatives—whether entire social structures, or different modes of living—which are deliberately designed to contrast with, and comment on, dominant cultural forms" (*Utopian Imagination and Eighteenth-Century Fiction* [New York: Longman, 1996], 2–3). Such varied definitions make classification difficult, and thus a broad view like Rees's makes much sense; nonetheless, I will venture categories for women's utopian writings.

17. J. C. Davis, *Utopia and the Ideal Society: A Study of English Utopian Writing, 1516–1700* (New York: Cambridge University Press, 1981), ch. 1, 11–40.

18. Davis, *Utopia and the Ideal Society,* 36–38.

19. Morton, *The English Utopia,* 143. Manuel and Manuel's *Utopian Thought in the*

Western World also largely bypassed the eighteenth century. Remedying that lack is Gregory Claeys, ed. and intro., *Modern British Utopias, 1700–1850,* 8 vols. (London: Pickering and Chatto, 1997), quotation, xvi. See also Gregory Claeys, ed., *Utopias of the British Enlightenment* (New York: Cambridge University Press, 1994).

Contributing also to a reevaluation of Enlightenment utopianism in 1991 was Jean-Michel Racault, who published his impressive *L'Utopie narrative en France et en Angleterre, 1675–1761* (Oxford: Voltaire Foundation, 1991). Götz Müller produced *Gegenwelten: Die Utopie in der Deutschen Literatur* (Stuttgart: Metzler, 1989), which included consideration of the eighteenth century. Yet none of these volumes includes women to a significant degree. Of thirty-eight texts in Claeys's large anthology, two are by women, and although Racault analyzes novels by Sarah Scott and Mary Hamilton at the end of his book he dodges the question of gender difference. Müller discusses no women at all.

Of the scholars who do consider women's utopian texts, they tend to ignore the eighteenth century. Nan Bowman Albinski, *Women's Utopias in British and American Fiction* (London: Routledge, 1988), and Darby Lewes, *Dream Revisionaries: Gender and Genre in Women's Utopian Fiction, 1870–1920* (Tuscaloosa: University of Alabama Press, 1995) emphasize the nineteenth century. For twentieth-century texts, see Bammer, *Partial Visions,* Frances Bartkowski, *Feminist Utopias* (Lincoln: University of Nebraska Press, 1989), Mario Klarer, *Frau und Utopie: Feministische Literaturtheorie und Utopischer Diskurs im Anglo-Amerikanischen Roman* (Darmstadt: Wissenschaftliche Buchgesellschaft, 1993), and Monika Schafi, *Utopische Entwürfe in der Literatur von Frauen* (Bern: Lang, 1989). Richard Saage (*Utopieforschung: Eine Bilanz* [Darmstadt: Primus, 1997]), and Lucy Sargisson, (*Contemporary Feminist Utopianism* [New York: Routledge, 1996]) pay most attention to contemporary criticism and theory. As a result, articles on individual texts of the eighteenth century (which I will cite throughout) have been infrequent, and only a few have attempted a limited overview of women's utopias, generally treating only two or three texts. See Barbara Brandon Schnorrenberg, "A Paradise Like Eve's: Three Eighteenth-Century English Female Utopias," *Women's Studies* 9 (1982): 263–73; Ruth Perry, "Bluestockings in Utopia," in *History, Gender and Eighteenth-Century Literature,* ed. Beth Fowkes Tobin (Athens: University of Georgia Press, 1994); Hilary Brown, "Sarah Scott, Sophie von La Roche, and the Female Utopian Tradition," *Journal of English and Germanic Philology* 100 (Oct. 2001): 469–81; and Ute Brandes, "Escape to America: Social Reality and Utopian Schemes in German Women's Novels Around 1800," in *In the Shadow of Olympus: German Women Writers around 1800,* ed. and intro. by Katherine R. Goodman and Edith Waldstein (Albany: State University of New York Press, 1992), 157–71.

20. Rees, *Utopian Imagination and Eighteenth-Century Fiction,* 5.

21. Amy Boesky, *Founding Fictions: Utopias in Early Modern England* (Athens: University of Georgia Press, 1996); Lucy Sargisson, "Contemporary Feminist Utopianism: Practising Utopia on Utopia," in *Literature and the Political Imagination,* ed. John Horton and Andrea T. Baumeister (New York: Routledge, 1996), 238–55, quotation, 245.

22. Benedict Anderson has coined the term *imagined communities,* see *Imagined Communities: Reflections on the Origin and Spread of Nationalism,* rev. ed. (New York: Verso Press, 1991). I am inspired by this locution, but I am not emphasizing nationalism and its development; indeed, I will argue that despite the pronounced patriotism of feminist utopian authors they tend to promote cosmopolitanism in their works. I choose the term

invented because, deriving as it does from the Latin "to come upon," it offers a simultaneous sense of discovery as well as vision and thereby implies an activity as inclined to cross borders as to erect them, concerned to emphasize inclusion over exclusion, to foster process and growth as opposed to stasis.

23. Daniel Defoe, *An Essay upon Projects* (Menston: Scolar Press, 1969). This helps to explain the periodization of my study. Although there are certainly feminist utopian writings that precede the "Projecting Age"—the entrepreneurial era following the Glorious Revolution in England, which Jean-Michel Racault has linked with utopianism (*L'Utopie narrative,* 147)—the character (as well as the content) of the visions changed significantly in response to the new social, economic, and political climate at the end of the seventeenth century. Consequently, I do not offer a full history of feminist utopianism in the West, a task beyond the scope of a single study in any case. Nor do I include late medieval or early modern women by going back to Christine de Pizan's *The Book of the City of Ladies* (1404) or even Margaret Cavendish's *Blazing World* (1666), which, although they may share certain feminist traits with Enlightenment works, do not possess the same pragmatism and possibility of real-world application as do eighteenth-century writings. Kate Lilley, "Blazing Worlds: Seventeenth-Century Women's Utopian Writing," in *Women, Texts, and Histories, 1575–1760,* ed. Clare Brant and Diane Purkiss (New York: Routledge, 1992), 102–33; Elaine Hobby, *Virtue of Necessity: English Women's Writing, 1649–88* (London: Virago Press, 1988); Boesky, *Founding Fictions.*

24. Claeys, ed., *Utopias of the British Enlightenment,* x.

25. Mary Louise Pratt, *Imperial Eyes: Travel Writing and Transculturation* (London: Routledge, 1992), 166–67, 168.

26. Felicity A. Nussbaum, *Torrid Zones: Maternity, Sexuality, and Empire in Eighteenth-Century English Narratives* (Baltimore: Johns Hopkins University Press, 1995), 137, 151, 153.

27. Moira Ferguson, "Introduction," in *First Feminists: British Women Writers, 1578–1799* (Bloomington: Indiana University Press, 1985), 31.

28. Eliza Haywood, *The British Recluse: or, the Secret History of Cleomira, Suppos'd Dead* (1722), in *Popular Fiction by Women, 1660–1730: An Anthology,* ed. Paula R. Backscheider and John J. Richetti (New York: Oxford University Press, 1996), 153–224, quotation, 224.

29. Ferguson, *First Feminists,* 31 and passim. Earlier examples that Ferguson would include in this category are Katherine Philips's friendship poetry, circulated among her "Society of Friendship" (1650s) and Margaret Cavendish, *The Convent of Pleasure,* published in *Plays, Never before Printed* (1668).

30. Mary Astell's *Serious Proposal* is of course no narrative utopia. I discuss it, however, because of its strong influence on later writers, an influence that corresponds not only to the form of utopia imagined but also to the way in which it is theorized. Jean-Michel Racault has analyzed the relationship of projects and utopias; see his discussion of what he calls "utopies-programmes" and "utopies-narratives" and "des glissements possibles d'un type à un autre" (*L'Utopie narrative,* 3–31, quotation, 15).

31. Hilda L. Smith, *Reason's Disciples: Seventeenth-Century English Feminists* (Urbana: University of Illinois Press, 1982); Smith's discussion of Astell can be found on 115–39. See also Margaret J. M. Ezell, *The Patriarch's Wife: Literary Evidence and the History of the Family* (Chapel Hill: University of North Carolina Press, 1987). For an extensive overview of literature on women's education and utopian visions, see Ina Schabert, "Der gesell-

schaftliche Ort weiblicher Gelehrsamkeit: Akademieprojekte, utopische Visionen und praktizierte Formen gelehrter Frauengemeinschaft in England 1660–1800," in *Europäische Sozietätsbewegung und demokratische Tradition: Die europäischen Akademien der Frühen Neuzeit zwischen Frührenaissance und Spätaufklärung,* ed. Klaus Garber and Heinz Wismann (Tübingen: Max Niemeyer Verlag, 1996), 755–89.

32. Clara Reeve, *Plans of Education; with Remarks on the Systems of Other Writers* (London: T. Hookham and J. Carpenter, 1792), 71. Further citations are noted by page number in the text.

33. See also Catharine Macaulay's *Letters on Education* (1790, repr. London: Pickering and Chatto, 1996).

34. Claeys, ed., *Utopias of the British Enlightenment,* xii.

35. But see Boesky, *Founding Fictions,* on Margaret Cavendish, 203n15.

36. Ibid., 86–87. Boesky, studying early modern English utopias, suggests that this departure concerning utopian geography becomes a sign of pragmatic reformism as early as the 1650s.

37. Sarah Fielding, *The Adventures of David Simple* and *Volume the Last,* ed. and intro. by Peter Sabor (1744, 1752, repr. Lexington: University Press of Kentucky, 1998); Sarah Fielding, *The Governess; or, Little Female Academy* (1749, repr. London: Pandora, 1987); Mary Hamilton, *Munster Village* (1778, repr. London: Pandora, 1987). Further citations are noted by page number in the text.

38. Henry Neville, *The Isle of Pines* (London, 1668), 6. This earlier example participates in many of the patterns characteristic of later utopias and has been proposed as a model. Johann Gottfried Schnabel mentions it—along with Robinson Crusoe and Philipp Quarll —in the Preface to *Die Insel Felsenburg* (1731, repr. Frankfurt: Insel Verlag, 1988), 12. Schnabel's text, originally entitled *Wunderliche Fata einiger See-Fahrer,* also involves the ritual telling of the island utopia's history.

39. Robert Paltock, *The Life and Adventures of Peter Wilkins,* ed. Christopher Bentley, intro. James Grantham Turner (1750, repr. New York: Oxford University Press, 1990), 244. Further citations are noted by page number in the text.

40. Claeys notes these "illiberal elements" and agrees that they represent "an ideology of order . . . and of paternal protection": "This patriarchalism divulges once again the price paid in democratic coin for measures designed to enhance social harmony" ("Introduction," in *Utopias of the British Enlightenment,* xvi–xvii).

41. Simon Berington, *The Memoirs of Signior Gaudentio di Lucca* (1737, repr. New York: Garland, 1973), 159. Further citations are noted by page number in the text.

42. Francis Gentleman, *A Trip to the Moon* (York: A. Ward, 1764–65), 1:196–97, 1:127–28. Further citations are noted by page number in the text.

43. For discussion of Bentham and Ledoux, see Bender, *Imagining the Penitentiary,* esp. 201–29. Francis Gentleman is best known for his *Dramatic Censor; or, Critical Companion,* 2 vols. (1770, facs. Westmead, Hants.: Gregg International Publishers, 1969).

44. John Locke, *An Essay Concerning Human Understanding,* ed. Peter H. Nidditch (New York: Oxford University Press, 1975); John Locke, *Some Thoughts Concerning Education,* ed. John W. Yolton and Jean S. Yolton (New York: Oxford University Press, 1989).

45. Sarah Fielding, *The History of the Countess of Dellwyn,* 2 vols. (London: A. Millar, 1759).

46. Sarah Scott, *A Description of Millenium Hall,* ed. Gary Kelly (1762, repr. Peterborough: Broadview, 1995), 114–21.

47. In this respect women's utopias incorporate a feature of the robinsonade, which is characterized by practical responses to contingencies, such as Robinson Crusoe's various building and cooking projects. Tellingly, when Defoe moves into the utopian mode as Crusoe's island is populated in his sequel, *Farther Adventures of Robinson Crusoe,* the characteristics of traditional utopias, with their emphasis on central authority vested in a patriarch, appear. Crusoe finally explains the demise of his island community by virtue of his failure to play the patriarch well enough. For a discussion of this moment, see chapter 2 of my dissertation: Alessa Johns, "Gender and Utopia in Eighteenth-Century England," University of California, Berkeley, 1994. Women's use of robinsonade features links them to notions of the "new economic man."

48. Catherine Gallagher, *Nobody's Story: The Vanishing Acts of Women Writers in the Marketplace, 1670–1820* (Berkeley: University of California Press, 1994), xvi–xvii; Ian Watt, *The Rise of the Novel: Studies in Defoe, Richardson, and Fielding* (Berkeley: University of California Press, 1957).

49. Bridget Hill, ed., *Eighteenth-Century Women: An Anthology* (London: Allen and Unwin, 1984), 12.

50. Kate Lilley has argued that this tendency begins to appear in seventeenth-century female utopian authors: "Men's utopias have focused on political systems and laws; utopian writing by women has tended to focus strategically on the possibilities and problems of gendered social life and the weight of custom—micropolitical questions of sexuality, maternity, education, domesticity and self-government—while declining the burden of representing a fully articulated model of a new political order" ("Blazing Worlds," 102–33, quotation, 118).

51. Max Horkheimer and Theodor W. Adorno, *Dialectic of Enlightenment* (New York: Herder and Herder, 1972).

52. For commentary see Craig Calhoun, ed. and intro., *Habermas and the Public Sphere* (Cambridge: MIT Press, 1992); Johanna Meehan, ed., *Feminists Read Habermas: Gendering the Subject of Discourse* (New York: Routledge, 1995); Stephen K. White, *The Cambridge Companion to Habermas* (New York: Cambridge University Press, 1995). Focusing on the eighteenth century are essays from "The Public and the Nation," a forum in *Eighteenth-Century Studies* 29, no. 1 (Fall 1995); the essays in *Women, Writing and the Public Sphere, 1700–1830,* ed. Eger et al.; Dena Goodman, *The Republic of Letters: A Cultural History of the French Enlightenment* (Ithaca: Cornell University Press, 1994); Guest, *Small Change,* 5–14; and Joan B. Landes, *Women and the Public Sphere in the Age of the French Revolution* (Ithaca: Cornell University Press, 1988). Markman Ellis ("Coffee-women, *The Spectator* and the Public Sphere in the Early Eighteenth Century," in *Women, Writing and the Public Sphere, 1700–1830,* ed. Elizabeth Eger et al., 27–52) argues that Habermas's estimation of the coffee house is conditioned by nostalgic Victorian historians who avoided considering its unruly aspects and instead followed only the images of sociability promoted in *The Spectator.*

53. Lucinda Cole has summarized the postmodern critique of Habermas in "'The Contradictions of Community': Elegy or Manifesto?" *The Eighteenth Century: Theory and Interpretation* 36 (1995): 195–202, esp. 195–97. Habermas's response to postmodern theo-

rists can be found in his *The Philosophical Discourse of Modernity: Twelve Lectures,* trans. Frederick Lawrence (Cambridge: MIT Press, 1987). The defense of philosophy as a discipline appears in "Philosophy as Stand-in and Interpreter," in *After Philosophy: End or Transformation?* ed. Kenneth Baynes, James Bohman, and Thomas McCarthy (Cambridge: MIT Press, 1987), 296–314.

54. Benhabib, *Situating the Self,* 2. Lucinda Cole sees Benhabib as a political theorist who manages "to avoid the Scylla and Charybdis of modernist political naivete and postmodernist political despair" ("'The Contradictions of Community,'" 197).

55. Jessica Benjamin, *Like Subjects, Love Objects: Essays on Recognition and Sexual Difference* (New Haven: Yale University Press, 1995). These essays further discussions she began in her earlier book, *The Bonds of Love: Psychoanalysis, Feminism, and the Problem of Domination* (London: Virago Press, 1990).

56. Benhabib, *Situating the Self,* esp. 203–41.

57. For commentary (and also arguments regarding Anna Wheeler's contribution to Thompson), see Barbara Taylor, *Eve and the New Jerusalem: Socialism and Feminism in the Nineteenth Century* (London: Virago Press, 1983), esp. chs. 1–3. Women's utopian narratives do not again emerge as copious, effective, popular expressions of feminist ideas until the end of the nineteenth century. Darby Lewes, *Dream Revisionaries: Gender and Genre in Women's Utopian Fiction 1870–1920* (Tuscaloosa: University of Alabama Press, 1995).

58. Benhabib, *Situating the Self,* 243.

Chapter 1: Mary Astell's "Excited Needles"

1. See, for example, Astell's *An Impartial Enquiry into the Causes of Rebellion and Civil War in This Kingdom . . . and Vindication of the Royal Martyr* (1704); *A Fair Way with the Dissenters and Their Patrons* (1704); and *Moderation Truly Stated* (1704).

2. Ruth Perry, *The Celebrated Mary Astell: An Early English Feminist* (Chicago: University of Chicago Press, 1986), 269, see also 330–32.

3. Mary Astell, *A Serious Proposal to the Ladies: Parts I and II,* ed. and intro. by Patricia Springborg (London: Pickering and Chatto, 1997), 18, 19.

4. Bishop Burnet's approval in print appears hypocritical in light of his alleged efforts to derail the implementation of Astell's proposal. Bishop Gilbert Burnet, *History of His Own Time,* 6 vols. (Oxford: Oxford University Press, 1823), 6:204; see also Perry, *The Celebrated Mary Astell,* 134, esp. note 35.

5. Daniel Defoe, *An Essay upon Projects* (1697, repr. Menston: Scolar Press, 1969), 282; Mary Wortley Montagu, *Complete Letters,* ed. Robert Halsband, 3 vols. (New York: Oxford University Press, 1965–67), 3:97; Samuel Richardson, *The History of Sir Charles Grandison,* 3 vols. (1753–54, repr. New York: Oxford University Press, 1972), 2:355; Samuel Johnson, *Rasselas, Poems, and Selected Prose,* ed. and intro. by Bertrand Bronson (New York: Holt, Rinehard and Winston, 1958), 611; Sarah Scott, *Millenium Hall,* ed. Gary Kelly (1762, repr. Peterborough, Ontario: Broadview Press, 1995); Sarah Scott, *The History of Sir George Ellison,* ed. Betty Rizzo (Lexington: University Press of Kentucky, 1996).

6. Perry, *The Celebrated Mary Astell,* 106–12, quotation, 112; Moira Ferguson, ed., *First Feminists: British Women Writers, 1578–1799* (Bloomington: Indiana University Press, 1985),

22; Betty Rizzo, *Companions without Vows: Relationships among Eighteenth-Century British Women* (Athens: University of Georgia Press, 1994), 317–19.

7. "A New Plan for an Unexceptionable, Female Coterie. Written by a Lady," *Public Ledger* no. 3282 (July 5, 1770), reprinted in *The Repository or Treasury of Politics and Literature for MDCCLXX. Being a Complete Collection of the Best Letters (Including those of JUNIUS) and Essays from the Daily Papers, so Arranged as to Elucidate Each Other, and Illustrated with Occasional Notes and References,* 2 vols. (London: J. Murray, 1771), 2:191–93. My thanks to April London for bringing this article to my attention. Perry (*The Celebrated Mary Astell,* 329) traces Astell's influence also into the nineteenth and twentieth centuries in Jane Austen, Charlotte Brontë, Virginia Woolf, and George Gissing.

8. A review of this literature would go far beyond the scope of this study. For an overview, see Harold Ogden White, *Plagiarism and Imitation during the English Renaissance: A Study in Critical Distinctions* (New York: Octagon Books, 1965), which surveys classical theorists (3–19). Those commentators are excerpted in Allan H. Gilbert, *Literary Criticism: Plato to Dryden* (Detroit: Wayne State University Press, 1967). For a focus on eighteenth-century British implementation of these ideas, see Joel Weinsheimer, *Imitation* (London: Routledge and Kegan Paul, 1984).

9. Christine de Pizan, *The Book of the City of Ladies,* trans. Earl Jeffrey Richards (New York: Persea Books, 1982), quotations, 38 (I.14.4), 111 (II.7.1), and 257 (III.19.6). Christine participated in the genre of the legendary, following Boccaccio's *Concerning Famous Women* and made a critical contribution to the period's *querelle des femmes.*

10. Thomas Heywood, *The Generall History of Women, Containing the Lives of the Most Holy and Prophane, the Most Famous and Infamous in All Ages, Exactly Described Not Only from Poeticall Fictions, but from the Most Ancient, Modern, and Admired Historians to Our Times* (London: W. Hunt, 1657), A3–4.

11. Plato's objections to admitting representations in the Republic are well known (*Republic* IV). Aristotle also comments on the quality of imitation determining the educative efficacy of artistic productions (*Rhetoric* I.xi.23), and he uses such distinctions to discuss generic issues in literary representation. "Tragedy differs from comedy" in that "the latter sets out to represent people as worse than they are to-day, the former as better" (*Poetics* II.2, trans. W. Hamilton Fyfe [London: William Heinemann, and Cambridge: Harvard University Press, 1960], 11). In the late eighteenth century the schoolmaster Vicesimus Knox, in an essay entitled "Of the Danger of Being Led by Imitation without Principles of Religion," warned against "the INFLUENCE OF GRANDEUR AND WORLDLY POWER, OPERATING ON THE THOUGHTLESS BY A BAD EXAMPLE," even though he felt that good models were indispensable (note 13). Knox, *Winter Evenings; or, Lucubrations on Life and Letters,* 3d ed., 3 vols. (New York: Garland, 1972), 3:69.

12. J. C. Davis, "Utopia and the New World, 1500–1700," in *Utopia: The Search for the Ideal Society in the Western World,* ed. Roland Schaer, Gregory Claeys, and Lyman Tower Sargent (New York: The New York Public Library and Oxford University Press, 2000), 95–118, quotation, 107.

13. Longinus, *On the Sublime,* 2:13, quoted in Gilbert, *Literary Criticism: Plato to Dryden,* 163–64. Astell taught herself by precisely these means. She undertook "imitations" of Abraham Cowley (Perry, *The Celebrated Mary Astell,* 48–49). Vicesimus Knox seconds the notion in "On Imitating a Model for the Conduct of Life": "Let him who wishes to

live well, like him who wishes to write well, *chuse a model,*" adding a sentiment more common to the late eighteenth century: "A caution is necessary, lest the imitation recommended should become an odious species of affected resemblance, lest it should be so close as to destroy all originality, and lest it should degenerate to an apish mimicry" (*Winter Evenings,* 1:117).

14. Samuel Johnson, *The Rambler,* no. 143 (July 30, 1751), in *The Yale Edition of the Works of Samuel Johnson,* ed. W. J. Bate and Albrecht B. Strauss (New Haven: Yale University Press, 1969), 4:399.

15. I discuss these issues in relation to Mary Hamilton's work in chapter 5.

16. Mary Astell, *Some Reflections upon Marriage* (London: John Nutt, 1700), 4th ed. reprinted (New York: Source Book Press, 1970), 38–39. "And since the *French Tongue* is understood by most Ladies, methinks they may much better improve it by the study of Philosophy . . . than by reading idle *Novels* and *Romances.* 'Tis strange we shou'd be so forward to imitate their Fashions and Fopperies, and have no regard to what is really imitable in them!" (Astell, *A Serious Proposal,* 24).

17. For Perry's extended discussion of Astell's love of women, which has influenced my interpretation, see *The Celebrated Mary Astell,* 136–48, quotation, 138.

18. Hilda L. Smith, *Reason's Disciples: Seventeenth-Century English Feminists* (Urbana: University of Illinois Press, 1982), 124.

19. Mary Astell and John Norris, *Letters Concerning the Love of God* (London: Samuel Manship and Richard Wilkin, 1695), b6v. Further citations are noted by page number in the text.

20. Smith, *Reason's Disciples,* 124.

21. Other commentary on Astell's emotional engagement includes Mary Astell, *The First English Feminist: Reflections upon Marriage and Other Writings,* ed. Bridget Hill (London: Gower/Maurice Temple Smith, 1986), 8.

22. See Perry, *The Celebrated Mary Astell,* 173–80, for a discussion of Astell's Jacobite sympathies.

23. Catherine Gallagher, "Embracing the Absolute: The Politics of the Female Subject in Seventeenth-Century England," *Genders* 1 (Spring 1988): 24–39, quotation, 34.

24. Patricia Springborg, "Introduction," in Mary Astell, *A Serious Proposal to the Ladies, Parts I and II* (London: Pickering and Chatto, 1997), ix–xli; see also "Introduction," in Mary Astell, *Political Writings,* ed. Patricia Springborg (New York: Cambridge University Press, 1996).

25. Ruth Perry, "Mary Astell's Response to the Enlightenment," in *Women and the Enlightenment,* ed. Margaret Hunt et al. (New York: Haworth Press, 1984), 13–40, quotation, 22 (also published as *Women and History* 9 [Spring 1984]).

26. Hill, "Introduction," in Astell, *The First English Feminist: Reflections upon Marriage and Other Writings.* For Perry's discussion of Astell's love of women, see *The Celebrated Mary Astell,* 136–48.

27. Norris explained "Seraphic Love" in a letter to a friend and emphasized the way that this love, although passionate, transcends the body. John Norris, "On the Passionate Love of God," in *A Collection of Miscellanies: Consisting of Poems, Essays, Discourses and Letters, Occasionally Written,* 3d ed. (London: S. Manship, 1699), 339–43; John Norris, *Christian Blessedness: or, Discourses upon the Beatitudes of Our Lord and Saviour Jesus*

Christ, 2d ed. (London: S. Manship, 1692), 231–32. Norris insisted in one breath that the love of God "may be not only Passionate, but even *Wonderfully* so, and *exceeding the Love of Women*" and then in the next breath backtracked: "That although the Beauty or Amiableness of God, be not the same with that which we see in Corporeal Beings, and consequently, cannot directly fall within the Sphere of the Imagination, yet it is something Analogous to it; and that very Analogy is enough to excite a Passion" (*A Collection of Miscellanies*, 338–39). For Astell, the distinction between passion for Jones and passion for Christ in Jones defied mere analogy.

28. Perry, *The Celebrated Mary Astell*, 78–79; E. Derek Taylor, "Mary Astell's Ironic Assault on John Locke's Theory of Thinking Matter," *Journal of the History of Ideas* 62 (July 2001): 505–22, quotations, 507, 522.

29. Perry, *The Celebrated Mary Astell*, 138. Perry discusses the *Serious Proposal* as "a vision of community fueled by sublimated desire" (113). My argument suggests that rather than sublimating (or replacing the object onto which she focuses her energy), Astell was consciously formulating a religious plan that would on a spiritual and emotional—as opposed to a physical—level satisfy a desire that she recognized and was ready to acknowledge.

30. Norris, *Christian Blessedness*, 174–75.

31. "If any man will come after me, let him deny himself, and take up his cross daily, and follow me" (Luke 9:23); "Abide in me, and I in you. As the branch cannot bear fruit of itself, except it abide in the vine; no more can ye, except ye abide in me" (John 15:4); "If ye love me, keep my commandments" (John 14:15).

32. C. H. Lawrence, *Medieval Monasticism: Forms of Religious Life in Western Europe in the Middle Ages*, 2d ed. (New York: Longman, 1989), 287.

33. Albert Hyma, *The Brethren of the Common Life* (Grand Rapids: Eerdmans, 1950), 10.

34. Lawrence, *Medieval Monasticism*, 283–84.

35. For a discussion about the conflict over Thomas's authorship, see Giles Constable, "The Ideal of the Imitation of Christ," in *Three Studies in Medieval Religious and Social Thought* (New York: Cambridge University Press, 1995), 143–248, esp. 239–40.

36. Constable, *Three Studies*, 238–43, quotation, 239.

37. C. J. Stranks, *Anglican Devotion: Studies in the Spiritual Life of the Church of England between the Reformation and the Oxford Movement* (London: SCM Press, 1961), 270. See Perry for an account of Astell's wide reading. Even if Astell had somehow escaped direct contact with the *Imitation of Christ* itself, she certainly would have recognized the devotional practice associated with it from sermons, lessons with her uncle, reading in derivative texts, and discussions with friends and clergy. On the remarkable extent of the *Imitation*'s influence, see Hyma, *The Brethren of the Common Life*, 10, also 145.

38. Constable, *Three Studies*, 241.

39. Such ideas about custom are echoed in the *Serious Proposal* (e.g., "'Tis Custom therefore, that Tyrant Custom, which is the grand motive to all those irrational choices which we daily see made in the World" [31]).

40. For Astell's reasons why marriage is unlikely to satisfy women, see her *Some Reflections upon Marriage*. The plan also allowed Astell to get beyond the other pain she experienced, the rejection she received at the hands of her beloved: "None ever loved more

generously than I have done, yet perhaps never any met with more ungrateful Returns" (Astell and Norris, *Letters Concerning the Love of God,* 49).

41. Norris, *Discourses,* 231–32.

42. Perry, *The Celebrated Mary Astell,* 73.

43. For a fascinating account of such rhetoric and its persistence into the early modern and modern periods with its origins in late medieval religious attempts at reform, see Giles Constable, *The Reformation of the Twelfth Century* (New York: Cambridge University Press, 1996), 125–67. Constable concludes that "the spiritual teaching of the *Imitation of Christ* and of the *Devotio Moderna* derived from the twelfth century" (327).

44. Astell and Norris, *Letters Concerning the Love of God,* b6. In *A Serious Proposal* Astell urged women "to revive the ancient Spirit of Piety in the World and to transmit it to succeeding Generations" (18).

45. Astell, *Serious Proposal,* 5, 20, 21.

46. Astell, *Serious Proposal, Part II,* 72.

47. Perry, *The Celebrated Mary Astell,* 405.

48. Astell, *Serious Proposal,* 23.

49. Perry, *The Celebrated Mary Astell,* 405.

50. Astell, *Serious Proposal, Part II,* 69.

51. Astell, *Some Reflections upon Marriage,* 38–39. I thank George Starr for bringing this passage to my attention.

52. Norris and Astell, *Letters Concerning the Love of God,* 126. This is Norris's characterization; Astell adapted the idea for her own purposes. She later repeated her ideas in *The Christian Religion as Profess'd By a Daughter of the Church* (1705). Norris on occasion returned to the fire metaphor and at one point sought to warn Astell against being drawn too closely to others: "The Movements of the Body may be determined by those Objects which environ it, and so by those Movements we may unite our selves to those things which are the natural or occasional Causes of our Pleasure. Thus because we find Pleasure from the Fire, this is Warrant enough to approach it by a Bodily Movement, but we must not therefore *love* it" (*Letters Concerning the Love of God,* 75–76).

53. Astell, *Serious Proposal,* 27.

54. John Norris, *Practical Discourses upon Several Divine Subjects,* (London: Samuel Manship, 1693), 3:17.

55. Perry, *The Celebrated Mary Astell* 135–36, 123, 14; Springborg, "Introduction," in Astell, *Serious Proposal,* esp. xvii and xxiii.

56. The following discussion relies on R. R. Post, *The Modern Devotion: Confrontation with Reformation and Humanism* (Leiden: E. J. Brill, 1968); Albert Hyma, *The Brethren of the Common Life* (Grand Rapids: Eerdmans, 1950); and Gerhard Rehm, *Die Schwestern vom gemeinsamen Leben im nordwestlichen Deutschland* (Berlin: Duncker and Humblot, 1985). Post (341) and Hyma (11) explain that Gerlach Peters, a mystical writer associated with the Modern Devotion, was author of *Soliloquium,* which exerted substantial influence over the Port Royalists.

57. Rehm says, however, that the evidence concerning northern German houses of Sisters suggests that they did give up personal property (*Schwestern vom gemeinsamen Leben,* 34–35).

58. Hyma, *Brethren,* 49. For distinctions between the Sisters and the Beguins as well as other female religious groups, see Rehm, *Schwestern,* 40.

59. Rehm, *Schwestern,* 61.

60. Relevant passages in the *Serious Proposal* include: "your Retreat shall be so manag'd as not to exclude the good Works of an *Active,* from the pleasure and serenity of a *contemplative* Life" (21); "one great end of this institution, shall be to expel that cloud of Ignorance, which Custom has involv'd us in, to furnish our minds with a stock of solid and useful Knowledge" (21); "there shall be no Vows or irrevocable Obligations" (29); "Here will be no impertinent Visits, no foolish Amours, no idle Amusements to distract our Thoughts, and waste our precious time" (29); and, "We will not . . . pretend to be walking Libraries, provided they'll but allow us a competent Knowledge of the Books of GOD" (Astell, *Serious Proposal, Part II,* 180).

61. See Perry, *The Celebrated Mary Astell,* 136–48, for a discussion of the monastery as a space for female friendship. Perry's discussion, including its consideration of Astell's poetry, has greatly influenced my interpretation of Astell's developing ideas about relationships. I am, however, emphasizing the spiritual ideas that *drew* Astell to characterizations so filled with individual longing: the strong mystical Christian element in her thinking that inspired her desire for intimacy, her missionary spirit, and her feminist politics. Perry tends to lend weight to arguments about the social contexts concerning women that led Astell to *flee* conventional women's roles and seek out female companionship: for instance, the fear of childbearing, the onus of housekeeping, and the tyranny of men, all situated within a more accepting general social attitude in the seventeenth century toward women's "spiritualized friendships" (140).

62. Astell, *Serious Proposal,* 37. Perry notes that Astell's enemies-as-friends idea "can be found in the writings of the Cambridge Platonists" (*The Celebrated Mary Astell,* 480n15). Giles Constable discusses ideals of monastic friendship articulated in the late middle ages (*Reformation,* 138); see also Brian Patrick McGuire, *Friendship and Community: The Monastic Experience 350–1250* (Kalamazoo: Cistercian Publications, 1988), who sees changing ideas of friendship arising with the "new humanism" in the late middle ages: "Fourteenth century authors . . . no longer showed the same concern for friendship in terms of its place in enriching communities," and he notes in particular that the influential *Imitation of Christ,* like John Norris, warned against friendships distracting people "from finding the only true friend, Jesus Christ" (414).

63. Perry, *The Celebrated Mary Astell,* 434.

64. Ibid., 451–52.

65. Ibid., 404.

66. Ibid., 452.

67. Astell, *Serious Proposal,* 37.

68. At one point in the *Serious Proposal,* Astell, defining what true friendship is not, suggests that it belongs in the realm of apostolical piety: "But by Friendship I do not mean any thing like those intimacies that are abroad in the world, which are often combinations in evil and at best but insignificant dearnesses; as little resembling true Friendship, as modern Practice does Primitive Christianity" (36).

69. Astell, *Serious Proposal,* 20, 27 and 37, 20, 36, 37.

70. Ibid., 35–36, emphasis added.

71. As Perry points out, the admired author who talks about friendship as contracted charity is Jeremy Taylor, whose *Holy Living* was an immensely influential devotional tract (*The Celebrated Mary Astell*, 140).

72. Jean-Michel Racault, *L'Utopie narrative en France et en Angleterre, 1675–1761* (Oxford: Voltaire Foundation, 1991), 147.

73. Defoe, *An Essay upon Projects*, 8–11.

Chapter 2: Feminist Utopia and the New Commercialism

1. Nancy Armstrong, *Desire and Domestic Fiction: A Political History of the Novel* (New York: Oxford University Press, 1987).

2. Gregory Claeys, "Introduction," in *Utopias of the British Enlightenment*, ed. Gregory Claeys (New York: Cambridge University Press, 1994), x. One mark of women's variation is their move away from radical republicanism.

3. Valerie Bryson, *Feminist Political Theory: An Introduction* (New York: Paragon House, 1992), 17, 18; Jane Spencer, *The Rise of the Woman Novelist: From Aphra Behn to Jane Austen* (Oxford: Basil Blackwell, 1986), 108; Hilda L. Smith, *Reason's Disciples: Seventeenth-Century English Feminists* (Urbana: University of Illinois Press, 1982), 207. Countering such assertions are Alice Browne, *The Eighteenth-Century Feminist Mind* (Brighton: Harvester Press, 1987); Moira Ferguson, "Introduction," in *First Feminists: British Women Writers, 1578–1799* (Bloomington: Indiana University Press, 1985), 1–50; Gary Kelly, "Introduction," in *Bluestocking Feminism: Writings of the Bluestocking Circle, 1738–1785*, 6 vols. (London: Pickering and Chatto, 1999); Gary Kelly, "Introduction," in Sarah Scott, *Millenium Hall* (Peterborough, Ont.: Broadview Press, 1995), 11–46; and Katharine M. Rogers, *Feminism in Eighteenth-Century England* (Urbana: University of Illinois Press, 1982).

4. See especially the essays in Istvan Hont and Michael Ignatieff, eds., *Wealth and Virtue: The Shaping of Political Economy in the Scottish Enlightenment* (New York: Cambridge University Press, 1983); and J. G. A. Pocock, *Virtue, Commerce, and History: Essays on Political Thought and History, Chiefly in the Eighteenth Century* (New York: Cambridge University Press, 1985); J. G. A. Pocock, *The Machiavellian Moment: Florentine Political Thought and the Atlantic Republican Tradition* (Princeton: Princeton University Press, 1975); and Donald Winch, *Riches and Poverty: An Intellectual History of Political Economy in Britain, 1750–1834* (New York: Cambridge University Press, 1996). Other essays on Scottish economic ideas can be found in *The Scottish Contribution to Modern Economic Thought*, ed. Douglas Mair (Aberdeen: Aberdeen University Press, 1990).

By saying that the ideologies contend with one another, I do not mean to imply that they are mutually exclusive. For one thing, both currents were influenced by some of the same thinkers. The impact of Samuel Pufendorf would appear to be an important example. See *Samuel von Pufendorf, 1632–1982*, ed. Kjell Å. Modéer, vol. 12 of Rättshistorika Studier (Lund: Bloms Boktryckeri, 1986), which includes essays by Alfred Dufour ("Pufendorf's Ausstrahlung im französischen und im anglo-amerikanischen Kulturraum"), which traces Pufendorf's popularity as a thinker, and Thomas Mautner ("Pufendorf and Eighteenth-Century Scottish Philosophy"), which explains the nature of Pufendorf's influence on Gerschom Carmichael and Francis Hutcheson. See also Wolfgang Leidhold, who argues that "es war nämlich vor allem das Naturrecht Pufendorfs, das Hutcheson zu seinem systematischen Grundgerüst machte" in *Ethik und Politik bei Francis Hutcheson* (Frankfurt: Suhrkamp, 1979), and Michael P. Zuckert, *Natural Rights and the New Republicanism* (Princeton: Princeton University Press, 1994). Both Leidhold and Zuckert demonstrate the influence of natural-law philsophers Grotius and Pufendorf on Lockean liberalism.

5. Pocock, *Virtue, Commerce, and History,* 110; J. G. A. Pocock, "Cambridge Paradigms and Scotch Philosophers: A Study of the Relations between the Civic Humanist and the Civil Jurisprudential Interpretation of Eighteenth-Century Social Thought," in *Wealth and Virtue,* ed. Hont and Ignatieff, 235–52, quotation, 235–36.

6. Sarah Scott, *The History of Sir George Ellison,* ed. Betty Rizzo (Lexington: University Press of Kentucky, 1996), further citations are noted by page number in the text; Sarah Scott [Henry Augustus Raymond], *The History of Gustavus Ericson* (London: A. Millar, 1761); Sarah Scott, *The Life of Theodore Agrippa D'Aubigné* (London: Edward and Charles Dilly, 1772).

7. Jeanne Marie Leprince de Beaumont, *The New Clarissa: A True History,* 2 vols. (London: J. Nourse, 1768), 2:207. Further citations are noted by page number in the text.

8. For ancient through Renaissance theories of friendship, see Reginald Hyatte, *The Arts of Friendship: The Idealization of Friendship in Medieval and Early Renaissance Literature* (Leiden: E. J. Brill, 1994), who discusses Cicero on the relationship of friendship and the state (30). Christian ideals of friendship (chapter 1) are also broached in chapter 3; also see Brian McGuire, *Friendship and Community: The Monastic Experience 350–1250,* Cistercian Studies Series 95 (Kalamazoo: Cistercian Publications, 1988); Adele Fiske, *Friends and Friendship in the Monastic Tradition* (Cuernavaca, Mex.: Centro Intercultural de Documentacion, 1970); and Giles Constable, *The Reformation of the Twelfth Century* (New York: Cambridge University Press, 1996).

9. Lawrence E. Klein, *Shaftesbury and the Culture of Politeness: Moral Discourse and Cultural Politics in Early Eighteenth-Century England* (New York: Cambridge University Press, 1994).

10. Pocock explains that "the child of jurisprudence is liberalism" and contends that "the liberal paradigm . . . made its appearance in answer to the civic" ("Cambridge Paradigms," 249, 241). For a parsing of liberalism's derivation from jurisprudential thinkers, see Zuckert, *Natural Rights;* see also Hans Medick, *Naturzustand und Naturgeschichte der bürgerlichen Sozialtheorie als Geschichtsphilosophie und Sozialwissenschaft bei Samuel Pufendorf, John Locke, und Adam Smith* (Göttingen: Vandenhoeck and Ruprecht, 1973).

11. I say "to a good extent" because these philosophers were influenced by the civic-humanist model as well; Francis Hutcheson's focus on questions of virtue is a case in point. Jane Rendall, "Virtue and Commerce: Women in the Making of Adam Smith's Political Economy," in *Women in Western Political Philosophy: Kant to Nietzsche,* ed. Ellen Kennedy and Susan Mendus (Brighton: Wheatsheaf, 1987), 44–77.

12. Pocock, "Cambridge Paradigms," 243. Pocock also predicts that future research will show the civic and jurisprudential models to be less mutually exclusive than current scholarship suggests (see esp. 245–52); with its synthetic tendencies, eighteenth-century feminist utopianism buttresses such a supposition. I follow Pocock's distinction between paradigms as a way of clarifying where feminist utopists stand and because it allows me to respond more effectively, especially in chapter 4, to critics who exclusively support the civic-humanist thesis.

13. Pocock, *Virtue, Commerce, and History,* 118.

14. Pocock, *Virtue, Commerce, and History,* 118.

15. Catherine Gallagher, *Nobody's Story: The Vanishing Acts of Women Writers in the Marketplace, 1670–1820* (Berkeley: University of California Press, 1994), 107–10.

16. John Millar, *Observations Concerning the Distinction of Ranks in Society* (London: John Murray, 1771). For commentary on Millar, see Michael Ignatieff, "John Millar and Individualism," in *Wealth and Virtue,* ed. Hont and Ignatieff, 317–43.

17. On the Bluestockings, see Sylvia Harcstark Myers, *The Bluestocking Circle: Women, Friendship, and the Life of the Mind in Eighteenth-Century England* (New York: Oxford University Press, 1990); Betty Rizzo, *Companions without Vows: Relationships among Eighteenth-Century British Women* (Athens: University of Georgia Press, 1994); and Kelly, gen. ed., *Bluestocking Feminism.* On the public praise of women writers, see Harriet Guest, *Small Change: Women, Learning, Patriotism, 1750–1810* (Chicago: University of Chicago Press, 2000); Elizabeth Eger, "Representing Culture: 'The Nine Living Muses of Great Britain' (1779)," in *Women, Writing and the Public Sphere, 1700–1830,* ed. Elizabeth Eger et al. (New York: Cambridge University Press, 2001), 104–32; and Charlotte Grant, "The Choice of Hercules: The Polite Arts and 'Female Excellence' in Eighteenth-Century London," in *Women, Writing and the Public Sphere,* ed. Elizabeth Eger et al., 75–103.

18. Istvan Hont and Michael Ignatieff, "Needs and Justice in the *Wealth of Nations:* An Introductory Essay," in *Wealth and Virtue,* ed. Hont and Ignatieff, 1–44, quotations, 2, 44; Adam Smith, *An Inquiry into the Nature and Causes of the Wealth of Nations,* ed. R. H. Campbell and A. S. Skinner, 2 vols. (New York: Oxford University Press, 1976), 1:24. Smith echoes John Locke's *Second Treatise of Government,* para. 41.

19. Scott, *Sir George Ellison,* 16–17.

20. Sarah Fielding, *The Adventures of David Simple,* ed. Peter Sabor (1744, repr. Lexington: University Press of Kentucky, 1998), 89.

21. Armstrong explains that bifurcation and its impact on literature in *Desire and Domestic Fiction;* see also James Thompson, *Models of Value: Eighteenth-Century Political Economy and the Novel* (Durham: Duke University Press, 1996).

22. By the time Adam Smith wrote the *Weath of Nations,* he did not rely on the idea of the social contract (Winch, *Riches and Poverty*). At mid-century, however, when Sarah Fielding and Sarah Scott were pondering these notions, philosophers continued to invoke it. See, for example, Francis Hutcheson, *A System of Moral Philosophy,* 2 vols. (Glasgow: R. and A. Foulis, 1755), 2:225; and Jean-Jacques Rousseau, *The Social Contract,* trans. and intro. by Maurice Cranston (Harmondsworth: Penguin, 1968).

23. Pocock, *Virtue, Commerce, and History,* 106.

24. John Locke, *Two Treatises of Government,* intro. by W. S. Carpenter (1924, repr. London: Dent, 1990); Melissa A. Butler, "Early Liberal Roots of Feminism: John Locke and the Attack on Patriarchy," in *Feminist Interpretations and Political Theory,* ed. Mary Lyndon Shanley and Carole Pateman (Cambridge: Polity Press, 1991), 74–94; Hutcheson, *System,* 2:226.

25. Diana Coole, *Women in Political Theory,* 2d ed. (New York: Harvester/Wheatsheaf, 1993), 104. For further explanations of Smith on wages, see Winch, *Riches and Poverty,* 81, 111.

26. Thomas Hobbes, *Leviathan* (1651), ed. and intro. by C. B. Macpherson (Harmonds-

worth: Penguin, 1985), pt. 1, ch. 11, p. 162. My thanks to Hanna Pitkin for bringing the Hobbes passage to my attention.

27. See also Butler, "Early Liberal Roots," 80: "[Liberal theorists] maintained that the obligation of disenfranchised groups stemmed from their nurture, from the debt of gratitude owed to the government for their upbringing and education. Members of these groups had no actual voice and were themselves never expected to give free consent to their government. Yet still they were held to be obliged—out of gratitude." Sarah Fielding discusses this subject in *David Simple* and *Volume the Last,* analyzed in chapter 3 of this volume.

28. Adam Smith, *The Theory of Moral Sentiments,* ed. D. D. Raphael and A. L. Macfie (New York: Oxford University Press, 1976), 85–86. Further citations are noted by page number in the text. For a discussion see Winch, *Riches and Poverty,* 97–100.

29. Smith cites an earlier, although less famous, example from Lord Kames, who observes that benevolence and generosity, "not being so necessary to the support of society, they are left upon the general footing of approbatory pleasure; while justice, faith, truth, without which society could not at all subsist, are the objects of the above peculiar feeling [necessity], to take away all shadow of liberty, and to put us under a necessity of performance." Henry Home, Lord Kames, *Essays on the Principles of Morality and Natural Religion* (Edinburgh: R. Fleming, A. Kincaid, A. Donaldson, 1751), 60–73, quotation, 61.

30. Susan Staves, *Married Women's Separate Property in England, 1660–1833* (Cambridge: Harvard University Press, 1990).

31. Pocock, "Cambridge Paradigms," 236–37.

32. Sarah Scott, *A Journey through Every Stage of Life,* in *Bluestocking Feminism,* gen. ed. Kelly, 5:66.

33. Mary Astell, *Some Reflections upon Marriage* (London: John Nutt, 1700), 4th ed. reprinted (New York: Source Book Press, 1970), 128.

Chapter 3: Sarah Fielding

1. Betty Rizzo, *Companions without Vows: Relationships among Eighteenth-Century British Women* (Athens: University of Georgia Press, 1994), 45; Gillian Skinner, *Sensibility and Economics in the Novel, 1740–1800: The Price of a Tear* (London: Macmillan and New York: St. Martin's, 1999), 15.

2. The editions of Sarah Fielding's works to which I will refer are: *The Adventures of David Simple* and *Volume the Last,* ed. Peter Sabor (1744, 1752, repr. Lexington: University Press of Kentucky, 1998); *Familiar Letters between the Principal Characters in David Simple,* 2 vols. (London: A. Millar, 1747); *The Governess; or, Little Female Academy* (1749, repr. London: Pandora, 1987); *Remarks on Clarissa,* ed. Peter Sabor (1749, repr. Los Angeles: Augustan Reprint Society, 1985); *The Cry: A New Dramatic Fable,* 3 vols. (London: R. and J. Dodsley, 1754); *The Lives of Cleopatra and Octavia,* ed. R. Brimley Johnson (1757, repr. London: Scholartis Press, 1928); *The History of the Countess of Dellwyn,* 2 vols. (London: A. Millar, 1759); *The History of Ophelia,* 2 vols. (London: R. Baldwin, 1760); and *Xenophon's Memoirs of Socrates, with the Defence of Socrates, before His Judges,* trans. Sarah Fielding (Bath: C. Pope, 1762). Further citations are noted by page number in the text.

3. Other examples: "What he felt during that Interval, is not to be expressed or under-

stood, but by the few who are capable of real Tenderness" (14); and emotions felt "can only be imagined by those People, who know what it is to have a Passion" (135). Betty Schellenberg also draws attention to the fact that "the reader is encouraged to align her- or himself with the imitators of David Simple, thereby becoming part of a community with the author and her characters." Betty A. Schellenberg, *The Conversational Circle: Rereading the English Novel, 1740–1775* (Lexington: University Press of Kentucky, 1996), 127.

4. George Starr, "Sentimental Novels of the Later Eighteenth Century," in *The Columbia History of the British Novel,* ed. John Richetti (New York: Columbia University Press, 1994), 181–98; George Starr, "'Only a Boy': Notes on Sentimental Novels," *Genre* 10 (1977): 501–27; Gerard A. Barker, "*David Simple:* The Novel of Sensibility in Embryo," *Modern Language Studies* 12, no. 2 (1982): 69–80.

5. Starr, "Sentimental Novels," 184.

6. John Worthington, "Preface To the Reader," in [Thomas à Kempis], *The Christians Pattern; or, A Divine Treatise of the Imitation of Christ* (London: John Williams, 1677), a3v–a4. Worthington—indeed, all the writers I discuss—assumes a Christian audience.

7. Michel de Certeau, *The Practice of Everyday Life,* trans. Steven F. Rendall (Berkeley: University of California Press, 1984), 166.

8. Hilda L. Smith, *Reason's Disciples: Seventeenth-Century English Feminists* (Urbana: University of Illinois Press, 1982); Margaret J. M. Ezell, *The Patriarch's Wife: Literary Evidence and the History of the Family* (Chapel Hill: University of North Carolina Press, 1987).

9. Linda Bree points out that educating children by means of fantasy was controversial in this period because some religious groups "saw little distinction between fantasy and the sin of lying," and some among the commercial classes "distrusted fantasy as an unproductive waste of time" (*Sarah Fielding* [New York: Twayne, 1996], 58–72, quotation, 66). Bree also discusses *The Governess* in "Sisterhood and Sarah Fielding," in *Female Communities 1600–1800: Literary Visions and Cultural Realities,* ed. Rebecca D'Monté and Nicole Pohl (London: Macmillan, 2000), 184–98.

10. Consider, for instance, the stories of Cynthia and Camilla, which move David to come to their aid (80–95, 104–34), and the way readers must take in those texts. They are interpreted—through David's response—much as the fables of *The Governess* are carefully construed for Mrs. Teachum's charges.

11. The desire to "pass through life unnoted" echoes the *Imitation of Christ* (ch. 1): "If thou wilt learn and know any thing profitably, love to be unknown and to be accounted as naught" (*The Consolation of Philosophy,* intro. by Irwin Edman [New York: Modern Library, 1943], pt. 1, ch. 2, p. 132). Both the old and the new Clarissa along with Mary Astell, who has been claimed as a pattern for Richardson's heroine, deeply absorbed this devotional tradition. For Astell as model, see Ruth Perry, *The Celebrated Mary Astell* (Chicago: University of Chicago Press, 1986), 100; and Derek Taylor, "Clarissa Harlowe, Mary Astell, and Elizabeth Carter: John Norris of Bemerton's Female 'Descendants,'" *Eighteenth-Century Fiction* 12, no. 1 (1999): 19–38. Catherine Gallagher has argued that women writers in the eighteenth century became "nobodies," and one might conclude that Fielding epitomizes the "vanishing acts" of female authors. However, although she exploited print's possibility of proliferating her "author-self" textually, her grave doubts about the reading abilities of her audience made her a more unusual example of female authorship than the more representative writers Gallagher discusses in *Nobody's Story: The*

Vanishing Acts of Women Writers in the Marketplace 1670–1820 (Berkeley: University of California Press, 1994). As de Certeau suggests, learning to read depended on prior oral instruction: "cultural memory (acquired through listening, through oral tradition) alone makes possible and gradually enriches the strategies of semantic questioning whose expectations the deciphering of a written text refines, clarifies, or corrects. From the child to the scientist, reading is preceded and made possible by oral communication" (*Practice,* 168).

12. Betty Schellenberg maintains that in Fielding's *David Simple* and *Volume the Last,* as well as in Scott's *Millenium Hall,* "earlier portrayals of the community of consensus tend to be more optimistic about the applicability of the model to society at large, while later portrayals increasingly seal off the community from its context, rendering it at best an alternative to, at worst the victim of, a chaotic and irredeemable society." According to Schellenberg this kind of circumscription intensifies "to the point of paralyzing the ideal . . . imitation becomes impossible . . . prescription gives way to description" (*Conversational Circle,* 5, 6). Gillian Skinner concludes that "*David Simple* demonstrates how difficult it is to propose an easy coexistence of the sentimental community and the early modern commercial world" ("'The Price of a Tear': Economic Sense and Sensibility in Sarah Fielding's *David Simple,*" *Literature and History,* 3d ser., 1 [1992]: 16–28, quotation, 26; repeated in Skinner, *Sensibility and Economics,* 30).

Alhough Fielding was never sunny-spirited, her repeated, persistent concern with the question of coexistence reveals its importance to her; the apparently removed community is, by the logic of reproductive utopianism, intended to affect the world at large. A consideration of Fielding's later work, written in the context of the supportive and enterprising Bath Community, demonstrates a shift toward greater hopefulness at the end of her life. That, in turn, testifies to the power of the Astellian model of practical monasticism, which allowed deployment of Christian ideals to critique social custom and the unfair economies of feeling and resources that custom supported.

13. Skinner, *Sensibility and Economics,* 15–36, quotations, 36, 32. She argues, in political-theoretical terms, that Fielding "disapprove[s] strongly of luxury in the civic humanist manner in one breath, while lauding it, in ways reminiscent of Mandeville, as a source of income for women in the next" (32). In *Dellwyn,* Fielding conflates "sensibility and commercial instinct and recruit[s] the resulting combination in defence of the middle classes"; "vice . . . is very much an aristocratic affair" (36).

14. Rizzo, *Companions without Vows,* 307. Hamilton plagiarized Fielding (ch. 5).

15. Plato, *Republic,* trans. Robin Waterfield (New York: Oxford University Press, 1993), 176 (462b).

16. Fielding, trans., *Xenophon's Memoirs of Socrates,* esp. Book 2. In a note to a conversation of Socrates with the courtesan Theodota about snaring admirers, Fielding listed Socrates' friends and the pains and dangers they would endure to see him: "And when, to Friends like these, we may still add many others . . . almost all of them the wisest as well as the best Men of their Age;—who can suspect the Virtue of *Socrates?*—who can doubt his being, a HAPPY MAN!" (228).

17. Terri Nickel, who has looked at the question of affective paradigms through histories of the family and psychoanalytic theory, explains Fielding's "mimetic forms of identification" as "metaphoric incest" necessary before individuals become a part of the com-

munity. Nickel's clever reading accounts for the paradox that Fielding appears to create communities only to destroy them—groups based on metaphoric incest are doomed—but it does not encompass the frequent same-sex attachments in Fielding's texts; interrogate other forms of sympathy, love, and identification that can transcend the fraught and sexualized relations of the family; or account for Fielding's intense interest in ethics. I am, therefore, more inclined to probe the classical and Christian models that were available to Fielding and her readers. Nickel, "'Ingenious Torment': Incest, Family, and the Structure of Community in the Work of Sarah Fielding," *The Eighteenth Century: Theory and Interpretation* 36, no. 3 (1995): 234–47, quotations, 241, 239.

On the issue of incest, see also George E. Haggerty, "Brotherly Love in *David Simple*," in Haggerty, *Unnatural Affections: Women and Fiction in the Later Eighteenth Century* (Bloomington: Indiana University Press, 1998), 23–36; Martin C. Battestin, "Henry Fielding, Sarah Fielding, and 'The Dreadful Sin of Incest,'" *Novel* 13 (1979): 6–18; and Martin C. Battestin, with Ruthe R. Battestin, *Henry Fielding: A Life* (New York: Routledge, 1989), 27–30. On the question of same-sex ties, Bree points out how Fielding all her life was part of communities of women (Bree, *Sarah Fielding*; Bree, "Sisterhood and Sarah Fielding," note 10).

Other scholars see Fielding as a critic of gender ideology, including Deborah Downs-Miers, "Springing the Trap: Subtexts and Subversions," in *Fetter'd or Free? British Women Novelists, 1670–1815*, ed. Mary Anne Schofield and Cecilia Macheski (Athens: Ohio University Press, 1986), 308–23. Carolyn Woodward observes that "centering feminine virtues in a male character serves to defamiliarize them, and we can see that innocence and passivity are, in fact, weaknesses" ("Sarah Fielding's Self-Destructing Utopia: *The Adventures of David Simple*," in *Living by the Pen: Early British Women Writers*, ed. Dale Spender [New York: Teachers College Press, 1992], 65–81, quotation, 74). Harriet Guest sees David Simple's feminization as a product of commercial culture (*Small Change: Women, Learning, Patriotism, 1750–1810* [Chicago: University of Chicago Press, 2000], 31–36); see also Liz Bellamy, *Commerce, Morality and the Eighteenth-Century Novel* (New York: Cambridge University Press, 1998), 131–38. Felicity Nussbaum complicates the question of Fielding's feminism by analyzing the politics of effeminacy. Fielding's novel calls into question "a strictly symmetrical understanding or simple reversal of sexual difference" and outlines the need for the female satirist, a manly woman, to create community and strengthen the nation ("Effeminacy and Femininity: Domestic Prose Satire and *David Simple*," *Eighteenth-Century Fiction* 11, no. 4 [1999]: 421–44, quotation, 425).

18. This has been noted by Skinner (*Sensibility*, 30), who also draws attention, as do I, to Cynthia's overtly Mandevillian view of exchange.

19. See especially *David Simple*, 85–87; Mary Astell, *Reflections upon Marriage* (London: John Nutt, 1700), 4th ed. reprinted (New York: Source Book Press, 1970). Cynthia also resembles Fielding in experience and outlook.

20. Bernard Mandeville, *The Fable of the Bees*, ed. and intro. by Phillip Harth (1714, repr. Harmondsworth: Penguin, 1989).

21. Rizzo, who has analyzed this figure, traces the history of the "toadeater" and uses Jane Collier's *An Essay on the Art of Ingeniously Tormenting* to anatomize the abuse of "the companion-as-victim" (*Companions without Vows*, 41–60, quotation, 47). I will consider the tyranny via the intersecting discourses of philanthropy and political economy throughout Fielding's work. See also Bree, "Sisterhood and Sarah Fielding," 192–97.

22. On how distressing the search for work could become for eighteenth-century Englishwomen, see Bridget Hill, *Women, Work, and Sexual Politics in Eighteenth-Century England* (London: UCL Press, 1994); Olwen Hufton, *The Prospect before Her: A History of Women in Western Europe,* vol. 1: *1500–1800* (London: Fontana Press, 1997); and Paul Langford, *A Polite and Commercial People: England, 1727–1783* (New York: Oxford University Press, 1989).

23. Anthony Ashley Cooper, Third Earl of Shaftesbury, *Characteristics of Men, Manners, Opinions, Times,* 2 vols., ed. John M. Robertson (London: Grant Richards, 1900), 1:315. Further citations are noted by page number in the text. Rizzo points out that in general Fielding "endors[ed] the Shaftesburian or sentimental system" (*Companions without Vows,* 52).

24. Donna T. Andrew, *Philanthropy and Police: London Charity in the Eighteenth Century* (Princeton: Princeton University Press, 1989), especially ch. 1.

25. Andrew, *Philanthropy,* 41, 13.

26. This is the central concern of Jeanne Marie Leprince de Beaumont's *The New Clarissa* (ch. 6).

27. Quoted in Andrew, *Philanthropy,* 31.

28. Ibid., 35.

29. Rizzo, *Companions without Vows,* 41–60. My emphasis will be on double slavery—the way emotions as well as the body are involved in women's dependence. As with my discussion of Astell, which seeks to include love in analyses of power, so, too, in Fielding do I see a need to probe the ways in which feelings helped shape her utopian impulse.

30. Orgueil's tyranny is analyzed in similar, and by now familiar, terms: "Such Dependance is Slavery, worse than working in the Gallies: all Endeavours to please are vain: if you exert yourself, and take any one Step without previously consulting these Patrons, this they condemn as throwing them off, and seeking other Protection: and if you entirely depend upon them, they accuse you of Imprudence, in that you seem to think them bound to provide for you. And the true Source of all this odd Behaviour seems to be, that such Friends do not desire that a Man they chuse for a Slave, should be provided for; but that he should be kept on in a dependent State, with only barely enough to prevent his being starved, and by that means escaping their Power" (302).

31. I thank George Starr for conversations that inspired the following discussion.

32. Samuel Pufendorf, *The Law of Nature and Nations: or, A General System of the Most Important Principles of Morality, Jurisprudence, and Politics, in Eight Books,* 5th ed. (1672 [in Latin], repr. London: J and J Bonwicke et al., 1749). Further citations are noted by page number in the text.

33. For the history of the movement of these ideas, see Wolfgang Leidhold, *Ethik und Politik bei Francis Hutcheson* (Freiburg: Karl Alber, 1985).

34. Shaftesbury impressed George Berkeley, who repeated his ideas in "Friendship and Benevolence," *The Guardian,* no. 126 (Aug. 5, 1713).

35. Francis Hutcheson, *An Essay on the Nature and Conduct of the Passions and Affections; with Illustrations on the Moral Sense,* 3d ed. 1742, intro. by Paul McReynolds (1728, repr. Gainesville: Scholars' Facsimiles and Reprints, 1969), 82.

36. David Marshall, *The Figure of Theater: Shaftesbury, Defoe, Adam Smith, and George Eliot* (New York: Columbia University Press, 1986). Ann Jessie Van Sant discusses "sym-

pathetic visibility" in *Eighteenth-Century Sensibility and the Novel: The Senses in Social Context* (New York: Cambridge University Press, 1993), 16–44.

37. Francis Hutcheson, *A Short Introduction to Moral Philosophy, in Three Books; Containing the Elements of Ethicks, and the Law of Nature* (1747, repr. Hildesheim: Georg Olms Verlagsbuchhandlung, 1969), 145–46.

38. Pufendorf cites Seneca: "The best feature of a kindness is lost if it is brought into court, as if it were a sum of money, or something owed by contract or lease, for it thereupon begins to be a loan; that while it is held to be becoming to feel gratitude, it ceases to be becoming, upon its being necessary" (377). Francis Hutcheson, *A System of Moral Philosophy*, 2 vols. (Glasgow: R and A Foulis, 1755), 1:306.

39. Hutcheson, *System*, 1:307–8.

40. Such a relationship foreshadows Hegel's analyses of interdependence, and these are discussed with reference to women by Jessica Benjamin in *The Bonds of Love: Psychoanalysis, Feminism, and the Problem of Domination* (London: Virago Press, 1990), esp. 31–50, and also in Benjamin, *Like Subjects, Love Objects: Essays on Recognition and Sexual Difference* (New Haven: Yale University Press, 1995), 36–39.

41. Fielding's middle way, between benevolism and realism, has not lost currency; it has reappeared, for example, in Finkielkraut's *The Wisdom of Love*. Like Fielding, Finkielkraut viewed the world through the eyes of the oppressed—in this case victims of the Holocaust—and sought to develop an antitotalitarian philosophy that would alert people to their human responsibilities toward others. Identity politics, he argued, inevitably essentializes because individuals' "faces" are not seen; individuals merely represent the group rather than themselves. (He takes the idea of the "face" from Emmanuel Levinas.) "To be antitotalitarian, philosophy must think of man beyond the totality: not as someone to be liberated but as someone already free."

Like Fielding, therefore, Finkielkraut leaned on jurisprudential discourse to posit the individual as a free creation. He insisted, however, that his philosophy be couched in the realist language of Hobbes rather than the idealist vocabulary of the moral sense philosophers. People, when presented with the "face" of the Other, incur a debt and have an obligation. Evil arises because people try to rebel against the responsibility to which they are obliged by the face of their neighbor. By coming face to face with me, for example, the neighbor forces me from indifference to a state of debt and obligation. Therefore, like Fielding, Finkielkraut did not seek to do away with obligation but to distribute it evenly. If people recognized their condition—that they are all free and that not only the powerless but all people are always in debt—then the need to jockey for position, to force others to bear the weight of obligation, would dissolve. The obligation would be universal. Alain Finkielkraut, *The Wisdom of Love* (*La sagesse de l'amour*), trans. Kevin O'Neill and David Suchoff (1984, repr. Lincoln: University of Nebraska Press, 1997), quotations, 86, 96.

Feminist political theorists advocating an ethic of care similarly emphasize, as does Fielding, the fact of human interdependence and the universal obligation to mutual aid. Seyla Benhabib describes a middle way between the particular and the universal as she urges us to see simultaneously a "generalized" and a "concrete other." Benhabib, *Situating the Self: Gender, Community and Postmodernism in Contemporary Ethics* (Cambridge: Polity Press, 1992), 148; the essay appears also in *Feminism as Critique: On the Politics of*

Gender, ed. Seyla Benhabib and Drucilla Cornell (Minneapolis: University of Minnesota Press, 1987), 77–95. See also Joan C. Tronto, *Moral Boundaries: A Political Argument for an Ethic of Care* (New York: Routledge, 1993).

42. A short explanation of Bloch's definitions is in the Introduction to this volume.

43. Carolyn Woodward first drew attention to this episode in "'Feminine Virtue, Ladylike Disguise, Women of Community': Sarah Fielding and the Female I Am at Mid-Century," *Transactions of the Samuel Johnson Society of the Northwest* 15 (1984): 57–71.

44. Hannah More echoes the link of commerce and conversation in her poem, *The Bas-Bleu: or, Conversation:* "But 'tis thy commerce, Conversation, / Must give it use by circulation; / That noblest commerce of mankind, / Whose precious merchandise is MIND!" (li. 248–51) (*Selected Writings of Hannah More*, ed., intro., and notes by Robert Hole [London: William Pickering, 1996], 25–35, quotation, 32). Schellenberg's reading of the intellectual context, in which "the metaphor of commerce becomes ideal for the description of language as an exchange of signs," emphasizes how words, potentially arbitrary signs, "can be employed for the purposes of moral obscurity and personal gain as much as for mutual benefit." She emphasizes how they require a closed conversational circle to ensure "agreed-upon" values or some "mutually acceptable foundation for authority" (*Conversational Circle*, 12–13, 21). *Dellwyn* offers a more sanguine view, where the efforts of the paragon can under certain circumstances meet with success.

45. Woodward, "Feminine Virtue," 62.

46. M. J. Daunton, *Progress and Poverty: An Economic and Social History of Britain, 1700–1850* (New York: Oxford University Press, 1995); David Owen, *English Philanthropy 1660–1960* (Cambridge: Harvard University Press, 1964); Andrew, *Philanthropy*.

47. Rizzo, *Companions without Vows*, 23; Johanna M. Smith, "Philanthropic Community in *Millenium Hall* and the York Ladies Committee," *The Eighteenth Century: Theory and Interpretation* 36 (1995): 266–82; see also Edith Sedgwick Larson, "A Measure of Power: The Personal Charity of Elizabeth Montagu," *Studies in Eighteenth-Century Culture* 16 (1986): 197–210. Cf. Dorice Williams Elliott, "Sarah Scott's *Millenium Hall* and Female Philanthropy," *Studies in English Literature* 35 (1995): 535–53, who argues that "the developing ideology of domesticity threatened to make women's active participation in newer businesslike charities seem inappropriate and improper," 536.

48. Rizzo, *Companions without Vows*, 307–14, quotations, 311, 307.

Chapter 4: Reconceiving the Contract

1. Betty Rizzo, *Companions without Vows: Relationships among Eighteenth-Century British Women* (Athens: University of Georgia Press, 1994), 317–19; Linda Bree, *Sarah Fielding* (New York: Twayne Publishers, 1996), 22–28.

2. Gary Kelly, "Introduction," in *A Description of Millenium Hall*, ed. Gary Kelly (Peterborough, Ont.: Broadview Press, 1995), 11–46, quotations, 19, 37, 30–34; Gary Kelly, "General Introduction," in *Bluestocking Feminism: Writings of the Bluestocking Circle, 1738–1785*, gen. ed. Gary Kelly, 6 vols. (London: Pickering and Chatto, 1999), 1:xiii; Harriet Guest, *Small Change: Women, Learning, Patriotism, 1750–1810* (Chicago: University of Chicago Press, 2000), 44–45; Alfred Lutz, "Commercial Capitalism, Classical Republicanism, and

the Man of Sensibility in *The History of Sir George Ellison,*" *Studies in English Literature* 39 (1999): 557–74, quotation, 557.

3. Ruth Perry, "Mary Astell and the Feminist Critique of Possessive Individualism," *Eighteenth-Century Studies* 23, no. 4 (1990): 444–57, quotation, 448.

4. Carole Pateman, *The Sexual Contract* (Cambridge: Polity Press, 1988); see also Diana Coole, *Women in Political Theory: From Ancient Misogyny to Contemporary Feminism,* 2d ed. (New York: Harvester Wheatsheaf, 1993); Diana H. Coole, "Women, Gender, and Contract: Feminist Interpretations," in *The Social Contract from Hobbes to Rawls,* ed. David Boucher and Paul Kelly (New York: Routledge, 1994), 191–210; Valerie Bryson, *Feminist Political Theory: An Introduction* (New York: Paragon House, 1992); Judith Squires, *Gender in Political Theory* (Cambridge: Polity Press, 1999); and Penny A. Weiss, *Conversations with Feminism: Political Theory and Practice* (Lanham: Rowman and Littlefield, 1998). Anthologies with relevant articles include Mary Lyndon Shanley and Carole Pateman, eds., *Feminist Interpretations and Political Theory* (Cambridge: Polity Press, 1991); Cass R. Sunstein, ed., *Feminism and Political Theory* (Chicago: University of Chicago Press, 1990); Gisela Bock and Susan James, eds., *Beyond Equality and Difference: Citizenship, Feminist Politics and Female Subjectivity* (New York: Routledge, 1992); Tjitske Akkerman and Siep Stuurman, eds., *Perspectives on Feminist Political Thought in European History: From the Middle Ages to the Present* (New York: Routledge, 1998); and Anne Phillips, ed., *Feminism and Politics* (New York: Oxford University Press, 1998). Gayle Rubin forcefully brings feminist theory to notions of the contract by drawing on Levi-Strauss and Freud in "The Traffic in Women: Notes on the 'Political Economy' of Sex," in *Toward an Anthropology of Women,* ed. Rayna R. Reiter (New York: Monthly Review Press, 1975), 157–210. I am following Pateman in viewing "contract as a principle of social association and one of the most important means of creating social relationships, such as the relation between husband and wife or capitalist and worker" (*Sexual Contract,* 5).

P. S. Atiyah writes that in the eighteenth century "the relationship between social contract ideas and 'ordinary' contractual ideas was so close that any historical study of contractual theory requires some exploration of this theme," which Atiyah goes on to do in *The Rise and Fall of Freedom of Contract* (New York: Oxford University Press, 1979), quotation 39. See also P. S. Atiyah, *An Introduction to the Law of Contract,* 4th ed. (New York: Oxford University Press, 1989).

5. Thomas Hobbes, *Leviathan,* ed. and intro. by C. B. Macpherson (Harmondsworth: Penguin, 1985); John Locke, *Two Treatises of Government,* intro. by W. S. Carpenter (London: Dent, 1990); Martha C. Nussbaum, *Sex and Social Justice* (New York: Oxford University Press, 1999), 33, see also 55–80 for a response to "the feminist critique of liberalism."

6. Sarah Scott, *A Description of Millenium Hall,* ed. Gary Kelly (1762, repr. Peterborough: Broadview, 1995), 111. Further citations are noted by page number in the text.

7. See Rizzo, *Companions without Vows,* 296–306, for Scott's troubles getting support from her father. In a letter of June 16, 1762 (MO 5791, Montagu Papers, Huntington Library), Elizabeth Montagu recounts an unpleasant argument with their father about providing 20 pounds a year to Sarah, which would have been matched by Mr. Montagu; Mr. Robinson simply became irate. All quotations from the Montagu Papers are made by permission of the Huntington Library, San Marino, Calif.

8. Sarah Scott to Elizabeth Montagu, letter dated March 13, 1762 (the publication year of *Millenium Hall*), MO 5290, Montagu Papers. In Sarah Fielding's translation of Xenophon's *Memoirs of Socrates,* to which Scott subscribed, Socrates is recorded to have insisted that if people wish to be respected by their families "they might urge their Claim on the Account of *Merit;* and not owe the *Whole,* only to *Consanguinity*" (Sarah Fielding, trans., *Xenophon's Memoirs of Socrates. With the Defence of Socrates, before His Judges* [Bath: C. Pope, and London: A. Millar, 1762], 42). Another Socratic anticonsanguinity idea that would have appealed to Scott involves relieving children from the inadequate moral education offered by their parents (see note 25 below).

9. Sarah Scott to Elizabeth Montagu, letter dated Nov. 30, 1763, MO 5407, Montagu Papers.

10. Sarah Scott, *The Test of Filial Duty* (1772), in *Bluestocking Feminism,* gen. ed. Kelly, 6:113–14. Further citations are noted by page number in the text.

11. Sarah Scott, *The History of Sir George Ellison,* ed. Betty Rizzo (1766, repr. Lexington: University Press of Kentucky, 1996), 16–17. Further citations are noted by page number in the text.

12. Eve W. Stoddard, "A Serious Proposal for Slavery Reform: Sarah Scott's *Sir George Ellison,*" *Eighteenth-Century Studies* 28 (1995): 379–96, quotation, 383.

13. Rizzo, "Introduction," in Scott, *Sir George Ellison,* xxxi–xxxii.

14. Markman Ellis, *The Politics of Sensibility: Race, Gender, and Commerce in the Sentimental Novel* (New York: Cambridge University Press, 1996), esp. 87–114, quotation, 87.

15. Ellis, *Politics,* 105. Sentimentalism in Scott is a complicated issue; her novels simultaneously promote and satirize sensibility. Janet Todd distinguishes sentimental modes in *Millenium Hall;* in analyzing female friendship she has emphasized the limits of Scott's sentimentalism (*Women's Friendship in Literature* [New York: Columbia University Press, 1980], 346–47), whereas the novel's focus on altruism, she feels, renders it more sentimental than Astell's female monastery (*The Sign of Angellica: Women, Writing, and Fiction, 1660–1800* [London: Virago Press, 1989], 115).

16. Felicity Nussbaum, "Women and Race: 'A Difference of Complexion,'" in *Women and Literature in Britain, 1700–1800,* ed. Vivien Jones (New York: Cambridge University Press, 2000), 69–88, quotation, 78. See also Moira Ferguson, *Subject to Others: British Women Writers and Colonial Slavery, 1670–1834* (New York: Routledge, 1992), and, for contextual materials on the construction of race, the volume of Aphra Behn's *Oroonoko* edited by Catherine Gallagher and Simon Stern (Boston: St. Martin's, 2000).

17. Rizzo has observed that Scott's "plea for slaves is . . . of a piece with her implicit plea for wives" (*Companions without Vows,* 316). In an analysis of *Millenium Hall* and three other eighteenth-century utopian texts, Perry concludes that "gender is key in determining how radical the utopian vision actually is," with Scott's and Mary Hamilton's visions critiquing "existing forms of social domination" and Samuel Jackson Pratt's *Shenstone-Green* and Robert Bage's *Mt. Henneth* reinscribing "the existing social relations of class, gender, and colonialism" ("Bluestockings in Utopia," in *History, Gender and Eighteenth-Century Literature,* ed. Beth Fowkes Tobin [Athens: University of Georgia Press, 1994], 159–78, quotation, 176).

18. Lord Bolingbroke, *Letters on the Spirit of Patriotism and on the Idea of a Patriot King,* intro. A. Hassall (New York: Oxford University Press, 1917), 84–85. Gerrard argues that at

this time Bolingbroke saw his book "not so much as a political manifesto" but "as an imaginative vision designed to inspire and invigorate a political opposition centred on the [Hanoverian] heir to the throne"; "Jacobitism and Whig Patriotism . . . shared an overlapping set of political idioms and a similar language of redemptive kingship" (*Patriot Opposition,* 208, 206).

19. Christine Gerrard, *The Patriot Opposition to Walpole: Politics, Poetry, and National Myth, 1725–1742* (New York: Oxford University Press, 1994), 208.

20. Sarah Scott [Henry Augustus Raymond], *The History of Gustavus Ericson* (London: A. Millar, 1761), 232–33. Further citations are noted by page number in the text.

21. Gustavus Ericson, generally known as Gustavus Vasa, was not an obscure figure; Scott's treatment of the illustrious Swedish king joined a substantial tradition of Gustavus representations. The Abbé Vertot's *History of the Revolutions in Sweden* was translated in 1696 and appeared in many editions in the first quarter of the eighteenth century, and Samuel Pufendorf's *Compleat History of Sweden, from Its Origin to This Time* appeared in translation in 1702. Drawing on these works in 1706, Catherine Trotter wrote *The Revolution of Sweden: A Tragedy,* although she emphasized the critical roles played by female characters, the heroines Christina and Constantia.

Henry Brooke's treatment of the theme, *Gustavus Vasa, the Deliverer of His Country,* is notable because it was the first play suppressed by the censor under the new Licensing Act of 1737. The drama, which creates a parallel between the villain Trollio and Walpole to expose the English minister's underhandedness and further the cause of the opposition, was published two years later. Hundreds subscribed. Jonathan Swift ordered ten copies, and Samuel Johnson not only subscribed but also published his own satirical response to the suppression: *A Compleat Vindication of the Licensers of the Stage, from the Malicious and Scandalous Aspersions of Mr. Brooke, Author of Gustavus Vasa* (1739).

A later but noteworthy example is *The Interesting Narrative of the Life of Olaudah Equiano; or, Gustavus Vassa, the African* (1789), in which Equiano draws on the literary tradition of Gustavus. Like the Swedish liberator, Equiano escapes captivity and moves not from the dark mines of Dalecarlia but from the depths of the slave ship to emerge as a deliverer of his people. Although the name "Gustavus Vasa" is foisted on Equiano and intended ironically, his narrative is structured by moments he interprets as signs of God's providence. Equiano calls himself a "predestinarian," and his story of narrow escapes, abuse, witty defiance, hard work, and heroism emphasizes the ways he fulfills his God-given destiny as African counterpart to the Swedish emancipator.

The Gustavus tradition therefore suggests that the figure provided writers of different political persuasions with an image of virtue, strength, and liberation wielded in order to expose tyranny, justify the struggle against it, and persuade others to join in the fight for a freer future. Scott's history fits into this tradition by emphasizing the power and desirability of the reformer. Gary Kelly has argued, however, that Scott's *Gustavus Ericson,* in its intention to instruct the new king George III and criticize Pitt as a warmonger, was "characteristic of historiography written by eighteenth-century commonwealthmen and classical republicans like Conyers Middleton" ("Introduction," in *Millenium Hall,* 23). Scott's representation might well have been influenced by such historiography but is likely not determined by it. Scott cited primarily the Abbé Vertot and Pufendorf, a jurisprudential philosopher who deeply influenced the Scottish school, and she emphasized Gustavus's religious endeavors. The varied nature of the tradition, including Trotter's feminist intervention, suggests that the image of Gustavus was deployed to a plethora of political ends.

22. "Once in a century perhaps . . . a man may arise whose single voice will have more weight than that of hundreds" (Scott, *Sir George Ellison,* 132). "The whole course of a century will scarcely produce half a dozen men of such superior abilities" (ibid., 41).

23. Pateman discusses this split throughout *The Sexual Contract;* see also Nancy Armstrong, *Desire and Domestic Fiction* (New York: Oxford University Press, 1987), Jane Spencer, *The Rise of the Woman Novelist* (Oxford: Basil Blackwell, 1986), and Guest, *Small Change.*

24. Scott, *Sir George Ellison,* 92–100.

25. Socrates was the most famous example of a teacher displacing and challenging the influence of parents. Sarah Fielding's translation of Xenophon's *Defense of Socrates* contains a passage in which Socrates argues against accusations that he has corrupted youth. Melitus suggests that Socrates' alleged corruption has nothing to do with ruining of morals but that "thou hast persuaded [them] to obey thee, rather than their *Parents.*" "With good Reason," Socrates replies, "when the Point in Question concerned Education; since no Man but knows that I made this my chief Study: And which of you, if sick, prefers not the Advice of the Physician to his Parents? . . . I . . . am persecuted even to Death, because I am thought by many to have excelled in that Employment which is the most noble; and which hath for its Aim the greatest Good to Mankind; by instructing our Youth in the Knowledge of their Duty; and planting in the Mind each virtuous Principle!" (12–13). It is a sentiment Scott would have applauded.

26. Sarah Scott to Elizabeth Montagu, July 30, 1756 (?), MO 5256, Montagu Papers; see also Sarah Scott to Elizabeth Montagu, June 12 (?), 1756: "I am much better able to bear a misfortune that happens suddenly, than one which I have been prepar'd for by expectation" (MO 5254).

27. Scott, *Gustavus Ericson,* iii–xiv. Scott engaged a larger debate on historiography. Samuel Johnson, for example, advocated biographical history in *The Rambler* 60 (Oct. 13, 1750), and Henry Mackenzie discerned more utility in biography because it exists "to prompt the conduct of the bulk of mankind . . . [and] to excite the useful though less splendid virtues of private and domestic life" (*The Lounger,* no. 29, reprinted in *The Lounger: A Periodical Paper,* 2 vols., 6th ed. [New York: Samuel Campbell, 1789], 1:179). In the period, general history began to gain favor, as evidenced in David Hume's *History of England* (completed in 1762) and Edward Gibbon's *Decline and Fall of the Roman Empire* (1776–88), works that treat of large forces and grand events and employ a theory of inevitable political and social currents. In the words of one contemporary observer, general or philosophical history suggests that "nations like individuals, have their infancy, maturity, decline and extinction; and that in their gradual establishment and various revolutions, immediate causes springing from the actions and characters of individuals, and even all the wisdom and foresight of man, have had but a very slender share, in comparison of the influence of general and unavoidable circumstances" (*The Lounger* 5 [1785], 1:27–28).

28. Scott, *Gustavus Ericson,* iii–ix.

29. Scott's idea of what is "scarcely perceptible" might be related to what Harriet Guest

has called "small change," "the quotidian, . . . the minutiae of private life," those elements ignored in large cultural transactions that nonetheless give them "current value" (*Small Change,* 2). Scott, however, self-consciously moved beyond the circumscribed "femininity" seen as characterizing eighteenth-century conceptions. Her utopianism, like Fielding's, allowed her to look past the gendered and hierarchized ordering of separated private and public spheres. She fashioned a view of the "scarcely perceptible" that, through accumulation and replication, had the power to reform the nation and alter the course of history.

Guest makes a similar argument about the gendered nature of biography by pointing to the ways its details suggest feminization and debasement through "its mundanity" (49–56, quotation, 56). Although Scott may have desired to further moral instruction, however, her aim was to include men and women in a historical quest for truths beyond the scope of the domestic or the national. The epistemological and ethical stakes, for Scott, were enormous, and the breadth of her vision anticipated the foundations of later feminist and radical arguments at the end of the century.

Guest quotes a letter of Elizabeth Carter to Elizabeth Montagu in 1772 that, a decade later, echoed on a spiritual level Scott's idea about the "scarcely perceptible." Carter suggested that this sentiment may have circulated as an element of a Bluestocking creed: "All external performances derive their true value, with respect to the soul, from the disposition from which they proceed, with regard to the Supreme Being. Wherever his will and his approbation are made the supreme object, all talents, all opportunities, however different in their appearances, become equal possibilities for the acquirement of virtue and happiness. The most insignificant action, the most unobserved motion of the mind, upon this principle, become great and important, and extend their consequences to eternity" (*Small Change,* 140). Again, the stakes are not regarded as "small change"; the implications are immense—indeed, infinite.

30. Caroline Gonda, *Reading Daughters' Fictions, 1709–1834: Novels and Society from Manley to Edgeworth* (New York: Cambridge University Press, 1996), 105–10.

31. Amanda Vickery has suggested, based on her work on women's diaries and letters, how girls generally succeeded at bringing parents and families around to accept their desired fiancees (*The Gentleman's Daughter: Women's Lives in Georgian England* [New Haven: Yale University Press, 1998]).

32. Marilyn Friedman, "Feminism and Modern Friendship: Dislocating the Community," in *Feminism and Political Theory,* ed. Cass R. Sunstein (Chicago: University of Chicago Press, 1990), 143–58, quotations, 154.

33. Friedman, "Feminism and Modern Friendship," 155.

34. Lillian Faderman, *Surpassing the Love of Men: Romantic Friendship and Love between Women from the Renaissance to the Present* (London: The Women's Press, 1981), 103ff. Emma Donoghue (*Passions between Women: British Lesbian Culture, 1668–1801* [London: Scarlet Press, 1993]) argues that commentators have glossed over the love between women in Scott's novels, and she critiques Faderman for understating the sexual content of romantic friendship and looking past women's communities while focusing too closely on exclusive pair-bonds. I concur that women's love of women, including its physical expression, has not received enough attention in Scott criticism, but Faderman's focus on couples is well founded. That view is supported by George Haggerty in "Romantic

Friendship in *Millenium Hall,*" in Haggerty, *Unnatural Affections: Women and Fiction in the Later Eighteenth Century* (Bloomington: Indiana University Press, 1998), 88–102. See also Felicity Nussbaum, *Torrid Zones: Maternity, Sexuality, and Empire in Eighteenth-Century English Narratives* (Baltimore: Johns Hopkins University Press, 1995), 135–62.

35. Sarah Scott, *The History of Cornelia* (Dublin: John Smith, 1750), 171. Further citations are noted by page number in the text.

36. Haggerty, *Unnatural Affections,* 96, 97. Cf. Nussbaum, for whom d'Avora represents "the mediating eunuch" (*Torrid Zones,* 243n42).

37. Sarah Scott to Elizabeth Montagu, MO 5308, Montagu Papers.

38. Sarah Scott to Elizabeth Montagu, May 26, 1763, MO 5302, Montagu Papers.

39. Emily Climenson, ed., *Elizabeth Montagu, the Queen of the Blue-Stockings: Her Correspondence from 1720–1761,* 2 vols. (New York: Dutton, 1906), 2:78–79.

40. Sarah Scott to William Robinson, May 26, 1762, HM 17438, Montagu Papers.

41. Thomas Hobbes, *Leviathan,* pt. 1, ch. 11, p. 162.

42. Marcel Mauss, *The Gift: The Form and Reason for Exchange in Archaic Societies,* trans. W. D. Halls (1950, repr. London: Routledge, 1990), 3; Annette B. Weiner, *Women of Value, Men of Renown: New Perspectives in Trobriand Exchange* (Austin: University of Texas Press, 1976), 14–15; Natalie Zemon Davis, *The Gift in Sixteenth-Century France* (Madison: University of Wisconsin Press, 2000).

43. Sarah Scott to Elizabeth Montagu, May 11, 1754, MO 5241, Montagu Papers.

44. Sarah Scott to Elizabeth Montagu, Sept 14, 1752, MO 5222, Montagu Papers.

45. Sarah Scott to Elizabeth Montagu, July 30, 1756, MO 5256, Montagu Papers.

46. Susan Moller Okin, "Gender, the Public, and the Private," in *Feminism and Politics,* ed. Anne Phillips (New York: Oxford University Press, 1998), 116–41; see also "Humanist Liberalism," in *Liberalism and the Moral Life,* ed. Nancy L. Rosenblum (Cambridge: Harvard University Press, 1989), 39–53.

47. Christine Rees notes, "As befits a Christian community, [Millenium Hall's] social relations are predicated on respect for others and a sense of reciprocity of rights and obligations" (*Utopian Imagination and Eighteenth-Century Fiction* [London: Longman, 1996], 219).

48. Sarah Scott, *A Journey through Every Stage of Life* (1754), in *Bluestocking Feminism,* gen. ed. Kelly, 5:69. The relevant passage from Luke 6:29 reads: "And unto him that smiteth thee on the one cheek offer also the other; and him that taketh away thy cloke forbid not to take thy coat also."

49. Sarah Scott to Elizabeth Montagu, April 1754 (?), MO 5240, Montagu Papers.

50. Vincent Carretta, "Utopia Limited: Sarah Scott's *Millenium Hall* and *The History of Sir George Ellison,*" *Age of Johnson* 5 (1992): 303–25; Betty A. Schellenberg, *The Conversational Circle: Rereading the English Novel, 1740–1775* (Lexington: University Press of Kentucky, 1996), 101; Guest, *Small Change,* 45.

Chapter 5: Mary Hamilton

1. Mary Walker Hamilton, *Letters from the Duchess de Crui and Others, on Subjects Moral and Entertaining, Wherein the Character of the Female Sex, with Their Rank, Importance, and Consequence, Is Stated, and Their Relative Duties in Life Are Enforced,* 2d ed. (London:

Robson, 1777), 1:3. Because Hamilton's works are largely unknown and difficult of access, I will quote extensively from them in this chapter. Further citations to *Letters from the Duchess de Crui* are noted by page number in the text, with volume and page number preceded by *D*.

2. Michel de Certeau, *The Practice of Everyday Life*, trans. Steven F. Rendall (Berkeley: University of California Press, 1984), xiii–xiv.

3. John Brewer, *The Pleasures of the Imagination: English Culture in the Eighteenth Century* (New York: Farrar Straus Giroux, 1997), 429, 441.

4. Brewer, *Pleasures of the Imagination*, 463.

5. Mary Walker Hamilton, *Memoirs of the Marchioness de Louvoi, in Letters*, 3 vols. (London: Robson, 1777), 1:24. Further citations to *Memoirs of the Marchioness* are noted by page number in the text, with volume and page numbers preceded by *M*.

6. Clare Brant, "Varieties of Women's Writing," in *Women and Literature in Britain, 1700–1800*, ed. Vivien Jones (New York: Cambridge University Press, 2000), 287.

7. Mary Hamilton, *Munster Village*, intro. by Sarah Baylis (1778, repr. London: Pandora, 1987), 32–33. Further citations are noted by page number in the text, with page numbers preceded by *MV*.

8. Daniel Defoe, *The History of the Devil, as Well Ancient as Modern: In Two Parts* (London, 1726), 378–80. Further citations are noted by page number in the text.

9. Virginia Blain, Patricia Clements, and Isobel Grundy, eds., *The Feminist Companion to Literature in English: Women Writers from the Middle Ages to the Present* (New Haven: Yale University Press, 1990), 480–81.

10. H. M. Paull, *Literary Ethics: A Study in the Growth of the Literary Conscience* (1928, repr. Port Washington: Kennikat Press, 1968), 111; Mark Rose, "The Author as Proprietor: *Donaldson v. Becket* and the Genealogy of Modern Authorship," *Representations* 23 (Summer 1988): 51–85; Mark Rose, *Authors and Owners: The Invention of Copyright* (Cambridge: Harvard University Press, 1993); Brewer, *Pleasures of the Imagination*, 476–89.

11. For a complete list of Defoe's work, including some erroneously attributed to him, see John Robert Moore, *A Checklist of the Writings of Daniel Defoe* (Bloomington: Indiana University Press, 1960). For arguments about criteria to be employed in establishing Defoe's authorship, see P. N. Furbank and W. R. Owens, *The Canonisation of Daniel Defoe* (New Haven: Yale University Press, 1988), and P. N. Furbank and W. R. Owens, *Defoe De-Attributions* (London: Hambledon Press, 1994).

12. T. L. DeVinne, *The Invention of Printing* (1876, repr. Detroit: Gale Research Company Book Tower, 1969), 466. I take "John Walchius" to be Johann Walch and have not succeeded in tracing the story in his writings.

13. John Bagford, *An Essay on the Invention of Printing* (Chicago: Committee on Invention of Printing, 1940), transcribed from the *Philosophical Transactions of the Royal Society* 25 (1706–7): 2397–407.

14. "Sur quoy nous devons premierement remarquer que le charactere dont fut composée cette Bible . . . estoit si semblable à l'escriture de main que l'on faisoit en ce temps-là, que ledit Iean Fust en ayant apporté grand nombre à Paris pour les distribuer, la pluspart desquelles aussi estoient sur du velin, & ornées de grandes lettres & vignettes d'or, il les vendit au commencement pour manuscriptes, & ne les bailloit à moins de soixante escus piece: mais venant par apres à les lascher à vingt ou trente, & ceux qui en avoient

acheté de premieres s'estant apperceus qu'elles estoient en trop grand nombre & trop semblables pour estre escrites à la main, ils intenterent action de survente contre luy, & le poursuivirent si chaudement que s'estant sauvé de Paris à Maience, & ne s'y trouvant pas en assez grande seureté, il passa à Strasbourg où il demeura quelque temps, & enseigna son art à Iean Mentelin habitant de ladite ville." Gabriel Naudé, *Addition à l'histoire de Louys XI* (Paris: François Targa, 1630), 290–91. In this account, those who first bought the book at the higher price commenced an *"action de survente"* against Fust for cheating them; there is no mention of sorcery. Naudé wrote an entire book on men who had been wrongly suspected of magic: *Apologie pour tous les grands personnages qui ont esté faussement soupçonnez de magie* (Paris: François Targa, 1625). Defoe, however, does not appear to have mined it for his own writings on the supernatural.

15. Bagford, *Invention of Printing,* 5. The biography of Faust to which Bagford refers is *The Historie of the Damnable Life and Deserved Death of Doctor John Faustus* (1592), which had been reprinted in 1674 and is a sensational pamphlet about the German magician. Bagford pointed to a parallel that could explain the Fust/Faust confusion: "We have another Example of the like nature for our famous Roger Bacon, tho' some Centuries of Years before, who had the like Fate" (5–6). That is, Bacon was tried and confined for sorcery because he attempted new experiments. Another explanation for the confusion could come from an attempted pun on the Latin, *faustus* (happy) made by Junius (DeVinne, *The Invention of Printing,* 331). The German writer Maximilian Klinger (1752–1831) knowingly perpetuated the Fust/Faust confusion in his novel *Fausts Leben, Taten und Höllenfahrt* (1791) to highlight sixteenth-century wariness about magic and the pursuit and distribution of knowledge.

16. Jean-Michel Sallmann, "Witches," trans. Arthur Goldhammer, in *A History of Women: Renaissance and Enlightenment Paradoxes,* ed. Natalie Zemon Davis and Arlette Farge (Cambridge: Harvard University Press, 1993), 444–57.

17. Daniel Defoe, *A System of Magick; or, A History of the Black Art* (London: J. Roberts, 1727); Daniel Defoe, *An Essay on the History and Reality of Apparitions* (London: J. Roberts, 1727); Daniel Defoe, *A Journal of the Plague Year* (London: E. Nutt, 1722). Further citations are noted by page number in the text.

18. The most noteworthy examples in eighteenth-century English literary life include Samuel Richardson's theft of Elizabeth Carter's "Ode to Wisdom," for which he commissioned music and then engraved it in order to adorn the text of *Clarissa* (Richardson, *Clarissa; or, The History of a Young Lady,* ed. Angus Ross [Harmondsworth: Penguin, 1985], 231–34, 1514, 1534). Richardson's attention to the comments of his female readers is, of course, well known. Scholars are also assessing, with the aid of computers, the extent to which Sarah Fielding and Henry Fielding collaborated (J. F. Burrows and A. J. Hassall, "*Anna Boleyn* and the Authenticity of Fielding's Feminine Narratives," *Eighteenth-Century Studies* 21 [1988]: 427–53). Samuel Johnson's and Samuel Richardson's alleged contributions to Charlotte Lennox's *The Female Quixote* have been debated for some time (Charlotte Lennox, *The Female Quixote; or, The Adventures of Arabella,* ed. Margaret Dalziel [New York: Oxford University Press, 1989], 414–15, 419–28).

19. Nicole Pohl, in an analysis of the social meaning of architecture in *Munster Village,* argues that "gender equality is sacrificed to the stability of the whole," although that does not lessen her obvious interest in the fates of innocent female protagonists. Nicole Pohl,

"Gender and Utopian Space in Women's Literature, 1660–1789," Ph.D. diss., University of London, 1997, 224.

20. Mary Astell ridiculed Locke's state of nature, which, she maintained, obscured the role of mothers, as though "men sprung up like so many Mushrooms" ("A Prefatory Discourse to Dr. D'Avenant," in *Moderation Truly Stated* [London: Wilkin, 1704], xxxv).

21. Mary Wollstonecraft, *A Vindication of the Rights of Woman,* ed. and intro. by Miriam Brody Kramnick (1792, repr. Harmondsworth: Penguin, 1983), 253.

22. This echoes Defoe. In *Roxana* (1724) the Dutch Merchant offers Roxana a prenuptial agreement that would allow her control of her assets, as does Lord Darnley, but she, like Lady Frances after her, refuses. Daniel Defoe, *Roxana, the Fortunate Mistress,* ed. David Blewett (London: Penguin, 1987), 186.

23. Hamilton repeats Fénelon but tellingly alters the gender valence. Fénelon writes: "What revolutions in state have been all caused merely or chiefly by the irregularities of women!" François de Salignac de La Mothe-Fénelon, *Instructions for the Education of Daughters,* trans. George Hickes (Glasgow: Foulis, 1750), 4, quoted in Devoney Looser, *British Women Writers and the Writing of History, 1670–1820* (Baltimore: Johns Hopkins University Press, 2000), 17. See also Hamilton, *Memoirs of the Marchioness,* 1:179, for epistemological arguments about the need to look beyond surface appearances to discern "secret springs" and perceive the truth.

24. Sarah Fielding, *The Adventures of David Simple,* ed. Peter Sabor (1744, repr. Lexington: University Press of Kentucky, 1998), 91. Fielding's passage is quoted in chapter 3 of this volume.

25. This interest may derive from Locke. On Locke's attention to "theatrical education," see Richard Barney, *Plots of Enlightenment: Education and the Novel in Eighteenth-Century England* (Stanford: Stanford University Press, 1999), ch. 2, 81–122.

26. Sarah Scott, *A Journey through Every Stage of Life,* in *Bluestocking Feminism: Writings of the Bluestocking Circle, 1738–1785,* gen. ed. Gary Kelly, 6 vols. (London: Pickering and Chatto, 1999), 5:67.

27. Scott, *A Journey,* 5:67.

28. "The principal advantage of an Academy is, that, besides furnishing able men to direct the Student, it will be a repository for the great examples of the art. . . . By studying these authentick models that idea of excellence which is the result of the accumulated experience of past ages, may be at once acquired." Joshua Reynolds, *Discourses on Art,* ed. Robert R. Wark (San Marino: Huntington Library, 1959), first discourse, Jan. 2, 1769, 15. Hamilton praised one indigenous artistic achievement: the fresco of Sir James Thornhill at Greenwich, an allegory on the ceiling of the Upper Hall of the Royal Naval Hospital that celebrates the navy's role in promoting trade and commerce (*M* 3:42). Given her interest in trade, it is not surprising that this work in particular would have merited her attention.

29. Iain Pears, *The Discovery of Painting: The Growth of Interest in the Arts in England, 1680–1768* (New Haven: Yale University Press, 1988), 52–57. Hamilton implied that the lack of national education in appreciating art leaves the English "to be dupes to the *picture jobbers from abroad*"; moreover, "would gentlemen but venture to see with their own eyes, these impositions would be prevented" (*M* 2:69, 71).

30. This evaluation echoes that of James Barry, who in a 1766 letter to Burke called the

cartoons "the best of Raffael's works." *The Works of James Barry Esq.* (London, 1809), 68–69, quoted in John Shearman, *Raphael's Cartoons in the Collection of Her Majesty the Queen and the Tapestries for the Sistine Chapel* (London: Phaidon, 1972), 153.

31. Shearman, *Raphael's Cartoons,* 152.

32. Productive imitation is distinguished from slavish copying. One heroine denounces modern sculptors, saying that "their greatest perfection [is] a servile imitation of the antique" (*M* 2:62). An artist must contribute something novel rather than endlessly duplicate classical patterns, otherwise there is nothing useful about the work. Sir John Bolton employs the same argument to denigrate an excess of speculative learning that "is of no farther use than to form us for action." Those who dwell solely in speculative realms "are ever chained down to imitation," whereas that study is justifiable that "may best supply contemplation with hints for the oeconomy of common life" (*M* 1:101–2).

33. Christine Rees, *Utopian Imagination and Eighteenth-Century Fiction* (London: Longman, 1996), 234.

34. Ruth Perry, "Bluestockings in Utopia," in *History, Gender, and Eighteenth-Century Literature,* ed. Beth Fowkes Tobin (Athens: University of Georgia Press, 1994), 159–78, quotation, 164.

35. Brewer, *Pleasures of the Imagination,* 427–489.

36. Alexander Pope, *An Essay on Criticism* in *The Twickenham Edition of the Poems of Alexander Pope,* gen. ed. John Butt (London: Methuen, 1939), pt. 2, li. 140.

37. Edward Young's *Conjectures on Original Composition* anticipated the organic metaphor of Romanticism: "An *Original* may be said to be of a *vegetable* nature; it rises spontaneously from the vital root of Genius; it *grows,* it is not *made: Imitations* are often a sort of *Manufacture* wrought up by those *Mechanics, Art,* and *Labour,* out of pre-existent materials not their own." Although he praised originality, Young was not opposed to finding inspiration in the authors of classical antiquity: "Let our Understandings feed on theirs; they afford the noblest nourishment: But let them nourish, not annihilate, our own. When we read, let our Imagination kindle at their Charms; when we write, let our Judgment shut them out of our Thoughts." Edward Young, *Conjectures on Original Composition in a Letter to the Author of Sir Charles Grandison* (Dublin: P. Wilson, 1759), 8–9, 12–13.

Other commentators include William Duff, who recognized variance among disciplines. Poetry thrives best "in the early and uncultivated periods of social life" because, among poets, imitation stifles "the wild exuberance and plastic force of Genius." However, "There never arose an eminent Painter, Orator, Musician, Architect or Philosopher, in any age, completely self-taught, without being indebted to his predecessors in the art or science he professed." Even "the *Italian* Masters, though they had none of the ancient paintings to serve them as models, had however some admirable remains both of the *Grecian* and *Roman* statuary, which, by heightening their ideas of excellence in its sister art, and kindling their ambition, contributed greatly to the perfection of their works." William Duff, *An Essay on Original Genius* (London: Edward and Charles Dilly, 1767), 296, 263.

Robert Wood reached similar conclusions about the excellence of early poetry and the reason for its excellence. The much-imitated Homer exhibits genius because he does not imitate other authors. His poetry results from an "unbiassed investigation of the different powers of Nature, and the various springs of action, not as they are fancied in the Closet, transcribed from speculative Systems, and copied from books; but as they were seen exerted in real life." Robert Wood, *An Essay on the Original Genius and Writings of Homer* (London: H. Hughs, 1775), 298.

38. Lisa Kozlowski, "A Source for Ann Radcliffe's *The Mysteries of Udolpho*," *Notes and Queries* 242 (1997): 228–30; Anne K. Mellor, *Romanticism and Gender* (New York: Routledge, 1993), 53–54.

Chapter 6: Reproducing Utopia beyond Britain

1. Barbara Becker-Cantarino, "Sophie von La Roche (1730–1807): Kommentiertes Werkverzeichnis," *Das Achtzehnte Jahrhundert* 17 (1993): 28–49.

2. Pierre de la Place was best known for his success in popularizing English literature in France. His translations were compiled in the eight-volume *Collection de romans et contes, imités de l'anglois* (Paris: Cussac, 1788) and included work by Aphra Behn, Sarah Fielding, and Clara Reeve. Lillian Cobb, *Pierre-Antoine de la Place: Sa vie et son oeuvre, 1707–1793* (Paris: Boccard, 1928).

3. Sarah Scott to Elizabeth Montagu, letter dated 1763 (?), MO 5308, Montagu Papers, Huntington Library.

4. Sophie von La Roche, *Pomona für Teutschlands Töchter* 4 (1783): 323 ff., esp. 342–87; for the translation of Knight, see 6 (1783): 583. See also Monika Nenon, *Autorschaft und Frauenbildung: Das Beispiel Sophie von La Roche* (Würzburg: Königshausen and Neumann, 1988), 147.

5. Volume 4 (April 1783) of *Pomona für Teutschlands Töchter* offers ample evidence: "In der neuen Geschichte giebt uns Engelland die Gefühle von Grösse und Macht, welche man in dem Lesen der alten Weltbegebenheiten von Rom bekommt" (324). La Roche praised English scholars and artists, merchants and manufacturers, and was happy to claim that the German spirit is closer to that of the British than that of the French (325–26).

6. For her part, Burney felt La Roche was too effusive: "I could really like Madame la Roche, were she less flattering." When a mutual friend asked Burney to give her a lock of hair to send on to La Roche, Burney declined, "thinking so little as I think of Madame de la Roche, it would have been a species of falsehood to send such a gift." Frances Burney, *Diary and Letters of Madame d'Arblay (1778–1840)*, ed. Charlotte Barrett, 6 vols. (London: Macmillan, 1905), see esp. 3:23 ff. and 3:53 ff., quotations, 3:54, 3:351.

7. Angelika Bammer, *Partial Visions: Feminism and Utopianism in the 1970s* (New York: Routledge, 1991). Bammer is discussed in the introduction to this volume.

8. Leprince de Beaumont's life is not well documented, but information can be found in Patricia A. Clancy, "A French Writer and Educator in England: Mme Le Prince de Beaumont," *Studies on Voltaire and the Eighteenth Century* 201 (1982): 195–208, and Alix Deguise, "Madame Leprince de Beaumont: Conteuse ou moraliste?" in *Femmes savantes et femmes d'esprit: Women Intellectuals of the French Eighteenth Century*, ed. Roland Bonnel and Catherine Rubinger (New York: Peter Lang, 1994), 155–82.

9. M. A. Reynaud, *Mme LePrince de Beaumont: Vie et oeuvre d'une éducatrice*, Bibliothèque Nationale, 2 vols., typescript, deposited June 25, 1971, 1:145 ff., 1:170; Deguise, "Madame Leprince de Beaumont," 164, quoting Grace Gill-Mark, *Une femme de lettres au XVIIIe siècle, Anne-Marie du Boccage*, Bibliothèque de la Revue de Littérature Comparée (Paris: Librairie Ancienne Honoré Champion, 1927), 41:62.

10. Jacques Barchilon, "A Note on the Original Text of 'Beauty and the Beast,'" *MLR* 56 (1961): 81–82.

11. See also Joan Hinde Stewart, *Gynographs: French Novels by Women of the Late Eighteenth Century* (Lincoln: University of Nebraska Press, 1993), 24–49.

12. Jeanne Marie Leprince de Beaumont, *The New Clarissa: A True History,* 2 vols. (London: J. Nourse, 1768). The novel was first published in French a year earlier by the same bookseller: *La nouvelle Clarice, histoire véritable,* 2 vols. (London: J. Nourse, Libraire du Roi, 1767). Regarding this earlier text, see Anna Striedter, "Women Writers and the Epistolary Novel: Gender, Genre, and Ideology in Eighteenth-Century Fiction," Ph.D. diss., University of California, San Diego, 1994, 57–61. Further citations to the English edition are noted by page number preceded by volume number in the text.

13. Michel Foucault, *The History of Sexuality,* vol. 1, trans. Robert Hurley (New York: Vintage, 1990), 23 ff.

14. James C. Riley, *The Seven Years War and the Old Regime in France: The Economic and Financial Toll* (Princeton: Princeton University Press, 1986), 192 ff.; see also James C. Riley, *Population Thought in the Age of the Demographic Revolution* (Durham: Carolina Academic Press, 1985).

15. She may also have been responding to followers of Montesquieu, such as Etienne Noël Damilaville, who composed the *Encyclopédie* essay on "Population" (13:88–103). Other followers on this issue include Mirabeau, the Physiocratic writers, the Abbé Coyer, Jean Auffray, Rousseau, and Maurice de Saxe (Riley, *Population Thought,* 53).

16. The French reads: "A quoi doit-on attribuer le progrès du commerce en Angleterre? A la destruction du préjugé, qui fait regarder le commerce comme une profession indigne de la noblesse. Un négociant honnête et laborieux peut prétendre à tout. Le duc, le comte, ne rougissent point de s'allier avec lui, de le traiter avec distinction, de lui montrer des égards. Les motifs les plus puissans sur l'esprit de l'homme se réunissent donc pour faire fleurir le commerce, l'intérêt et l'amour-propre. Il conduit à la fortune et à la considération. L'Anglais fait plus: l'agriculture conduit au même but, lorsqu'on se distingue en la faisant fleurir. Un fermier qui a su s'enrichir par son industrie a rang parmi les gentilshommes: le lord l'admet à sa table, à son amitié, à ses plaisirs. Si j'etais distributrice des marques d'honneur, je ne balancerais pas à accorder une statue au premier homme qui a eu le courage de s'élever au-dessus du préjugé ridicule qui fait mépriser le commerce et l'agriculture: cet homme a plus fait pour son pays que s'il eût gagné dix batailles: il a fait jaillir des sources abondantes de richesses réelles." Madame Leprince de Beaumont, *Le Magasin des Enfans* (Paris: Garnery, n.d. [ca. 1800]), "Avertissement," 15–16. Thanks to Daniel Gordon for translating this passage and for editorial suggestions on the topic of Leprince.

17. Nina Rattner Gelbart, *The King's Midwife: A History and Mystery of Madame du Coudray* (Berkeley: University of California Press, 1998).

18. Although Joan Hinde Stewart considers novels other than *The New Clarissa,* she concludes that "the feminism of eighteenth-century authors is not necessarily congruent with our own. . . . the interest of these fictions lies not in outright demonstrations of revolt, but in a subtle questioning of social institutions, in a sometimes almost imperceptible slippage in terms, or in the overt revision of conventional plot elements. In these allegories about personal fulfilment, displays of rebellion may take shapes that suggest ambiguous relations to social and literary convention" (*Gynographs,* 48).

19. I discuss this point, made repeatedly by feminists across the centuries, at greater length in the Afterword.

20. Joachim Heinrich Campe, *Bibliothèque géographique et instructive des jeunes gens, ou recueil de voyages intérressants dans toutes les parties du monde, pour l'instruction et l'amusement de la jeunesse,* trans. J. B. J. Breton de la Martinière, 12 vols. (Paris: J. E. G. Dufour, 1802–n.d.). "Voyage au Lac Oneida" appeared in volume 10 (1803). Alexis's brother's name apppears on a subscription list. André Jardin, *Tocqueville: A Biography* (New York: Farrar Straus Giroux, 1988), 123.

21. Jeannine Blackwell, "Sophie von La Roche," *Dictionary of Literary Biography* (New York: Bruccoli Clark and Gale, 1990), 94:154–61.

22. Sophie von La Roche, *The History of Lady Sophia Sternheim,* trans. and intro. by Christa Baguss Britt (1771, repr. Albany: State University of New York Press, 1991), 66. In the original: "Gerechtigkeit und Wohltätigkeit wurde[n] in dem kleinen Umkreis ihrer Herrschaft in gleichem Maße ausgeübt." Sophie von La Roche, *Geschichte des Fräuleins von Sternheim,* ed. Barbara Becker-Cantarino (1771, repr. Stuttgart: Reclam, 1983), 45. Further citations to the translation are noted by page number in the text; citations to the Becker-Cantarino edition appear in the notes.

23. *"ein Gesindhaus* . . . worin arme Mädchen zu guten und geschickten Dienstmädchen gezogen würden" (238). "Mylord will ein Schulhaus und ein Hospital nach der Einrichtung der Sternheimischen erbauen lassen" (346).

24. Barbara Becker-Cantarino, "Nachwort" to von La Roche, *Geschichte des Fräuleins von Sternheim,* 415. Rita Calabrese Conte concurs. She sees a utopian tendency in La Roche's dynamic reconciliation of cultural opposites, of "sentimenti e realismo, aristocrazia e borghesia, uomo e donna, dove la donna è 'genio femminile,' attiva e consapevole nell'organizzare e reggere una vera e propria comunità." Rita Calabrese Conte, "L'Utopia femminile in *Fräulein von Sternheim* di Sophie von La Roche," *Comunità: Revista mensiale di informazione culturale* 40 (1986): 379–402. For Ruth-Ellen Joeres, the "utopian vision" concluding the novel consists in the ménage a trois ruled by Sophie as matriarch. Ruth-Ellen Joeres, "'That Girl Is an Entirely Different Character!' Yes, but Is She a Feminist?: Observations on Sophie von La Roche's *Geschichte des Fräuleins von Sternheim,*" in *German Women in the Eighteenth and Nineteenth Centuries: A Social and Literary History,* ed. Ruth-Ellen Joeres and Mary Jo Maynes (Bloomington: Indiana University Press, 1986), 137–56, see esp. 153. See also Barbara Becker-Cantarino, "Freundschaftsutopie: Die Fiktionen der Sophie La Roche," in *Untersuchungen zum Roman von Frauen um 1800,* ed. Helga Gallas and Magdalena Heuser (Tübingen: Max Niemeyer, 1990), 92–113; Jeannine Blackwell and Susanne Zantop, eds. and intro., *Bitter Healing: German Women Writers, 1700–1830* (Lincoln: University of Nebraska Press, 1990); and Charlotte Craig, "Sophie von La Roche's Enlightened Anglophilia," *Germanic Notes* 8 (1977): 34–40.

25. Sophie von La Roche, *Erscheinungen am See Oneida,* 3 vols. (Leipzig: Heinrich Gräff, 1798): "Anfang und Fortgang des Anbaues der Vernunft und der Erde zu sehen" (1:4); "um Natur und Kunst an ihren Gränzen zu vergleichen" (3:27). Translations are my own throughout.

26. I am indebted to Alan Taylor for bringing to my attention the accounts of Oneida Lake travelers discussed here. Francis Adrian Van der Kemp, "Journey to Lake Ontario" (June 1792), *Publications of the Buffalo Historical Society* (Buffalo: Bigelow Brothers, 1880),

2:80–85, 2:97–99, quotation, 80. For references to accounts, see Victor Lange, "Visitors to Lake Oneida: An Account of the Background of Sophie von La Roche's Novel, *Erscheinungen am See Oneida*," in *Deutschlands Literarisches Amerikabild: Neuere Forschungen zur Amerikarezeption der Deutschen Literatur,* ed. Alexander Ritter (Hildesheim: George Olms Verlag, 1977), 92–122, esp. 112–13n2e.

27. Quoted in the *Castorland Journal,* reproduced by permission of the Massachusetts Historical Society. "Typewritten version of the longhand translation by Mr. Franklin B. Hough of the journal recording the experiences, observations, and events noted by Simon Desjardins and Pierre Pharoux, Commissaires, and Geoffrey Desjardins, Secretary, of 'New York Company,' for the period July 1, 1793–April 10, 1797, during survey of a tract of 220,500 acres on the north side of Black River in the present Lewis and Jefferson Counties, State of New York" (Dec. 1980), 69–70. See also Fr[ançois] A. F. Duc de La Rochefoucauld Liancourt, *Voyage dans les États-Unis d'Amérique, fait en 1795, 1796, et 1797* (Paris, 1799), 2:256–61.

28. *Castorland Journal,* 67–70, 103–6, quotations, 68, 103–4. My thanks to Alan Taylor for providing the transcript of this fascinating source, along with the report of Des Wattines by Elkanah Watson, "Journal of Travels, Principally by Water, from Albany to the Seneca Lake" (1791), in *In Mohawk Country: Early Narratives about a Native People,* ed. Dean R. Snow, Charles T. Gehring, and William A. Starna (Syracuse: Syracuse University Press, 1996), 345. See also DeWitt Clinton, Journal (1810) in William W. Campbell, *The Life and Writings of DeWitt Clinton* (New York: Baker and Scribner, 1849), esp. 64–66; J. V. H. Clark, "History of Onondaga County," *Castorland Journal* 2:177; and C. Johnson, *History of Oswego County, New York* (Philadelphia, 1877), 44–51. Lange in an appendix offers a partial transcript of the French version of the *Castorland Journal* ("Visitors to Lake Oneida," 119–22).

29. "Wir fangen mit harter Arbeit an, wissen aber, daß es für uns ist, und arbeiten um so ämsiger, immer das Auge auf die Zukunft des Genusses geheftet, wie wir andre den Erfolg ihres Fleißes genießen sahen; denn diese Ideen und Gefühle verlieren sich nie. Und warum sollen wir für das Vergnügen einer philosophischen Phantasie immer nur die Rollen der ersten Scene der Cultur durchspielen?" (1:53).

30. "Dieses werden wir bey der Erziehung unserer Kinder thun, indem wir soviel [wie] möglich ihrer Vernunft zu den Kräften helfen wollen, Schiff und Seegel, bey Wind und Ruhe, nach dem bestimmten Hafen zu bringen" (1:55).

31. La Rochefoucauld quoted in *Castorland Journal,* 70.

32. "Waren nicht die Oneidas, bey welchen ich Schutz und Hülfe gefunden hatte, Engel gegen das Volk der Pariser?" (2:163); "Aber entsagen auf Wissen, auf verbesserte Sitten, und zurückgehen auf die niederste Stufe der Vernunft,—o nein, nein, lieber sterben, als erworbne Kenntnisse verlieren" (2:164–65).

33. Mary Louise Pratt, *Imperial Eyes: Travel Writing and Transculturation* (London: Routledge, 1993, 1992), 168.

34. "Wenn sie nicht von den Europäern ausgerottet werden" (2:159).

35. Michael Maurer, "Sophie von La Roche und die Französische Revolution," in *Wieland-Studien II,* ed. Klaus Manger (Sigmaringen: Jan Thorbecke Verlag, 1994), 130–55; Monika Nenon, "Social Theory and Human Welfare: The Political Stance of Sophie von La Roche in Her Novels," *Lessing Yearbook* 23 (1991): 159–74, esp. 168. Maurer and Nenon

underscore La Roche's belief in education without considering the conflict that the desire for simplicity, figured in the parallel between the Indians' and the Wattineses' circumstances and austere existences, raises in the text.

36. "Wo Menschen sind, ist Unvollkommenheit" (1:57); "das wirkliche Leben leidet darunter; wir . . . werden ungerecht und strenge gegen unsern Nächsten und unser Schicksal, und was das schlimmste ist, man stiftet selten Gutes" (1:57–58).

37. Mary Walker Hamilton, *Letters from the Duchess de Crui and Others, on Subjects Moral and Entertaining, Wherein the Character of the Female Sex, with Their Rank, Importance, and Consequence, Is Stated, and Their Relative Duties in Life Are Enforced,* 2d ed. (London: Robson, 1777), 1:19–20.

38. "Wenigstens wünsche ich seit Jahren, daß nur Poeten und Künstler, die gefährlichen Reitze der Fähigkeit Ideale zu schaffen kennen möchten, weil diese ihr Glück dadurch gründen, und das Vergnügen der andern, durch Darstellung schöner Bilder befördern" (1:58).

39. For Schiller's relationship to women writers, see Katherine R. Goodman and Edith Waldstein, "Introduction," in *In the Shadow of Olympus: German Women Writers around 1800,* ed. and intro. by Katherine R. Goodman and Edith Waldstein (Albany: State University of New York Press, 1992), 1–27, esp. 13–18.

40. Margrit Langner also comments on Emilie's sense of initiative in contrast to Virginie (*Sophie von La Roche—die empfindsame Realistin* [Heidelberg: C. Winter, 1995], 291).

41. "Ach! nur in den Gefühlen und Bedürfnissen der Natur ist sie, die wahre einzige Gleichheit, welche Frankreichs neue Philosophen durch das ganze Leben und in allen Verhältnissen der Menschen haben wollen" (2:146).

42. "wo der Name Colonist, jedem gleiche Rechte und gleiche Pflichten gebe"; "das sicherste Verwahrungsmittel gegen diese Gefahr [liegt] in dem Festhalten und Einprägen der englischen Grundgesetze. . . . Freyheit zu lassen, mit sich und seinem Eigenthume zu thun was man will, nur nichts gegen das gemeine Beste und gegen andre. Dieses würde alle und jeden glücklich machen" (3:117–18).

43. Maurer, "Sophie von La Roche und die französische Revolution," 134–35; Michael Maurer, "Einleitung," to Sophie von La Roche, *Ich bin mehr Herz als Kopf: Sophie von La Roche, ein Lebensbild in Briefen* (Munich: C. H. Beck, 1983), 32. See also Michael Maurer, *Aufklärung und Anglophilie in Deutschland* (Göttingen: Vandenhoeck and Ruprecht, 1987), and Nenon, "Social Theory," 169.

44. "Unser Carmil soll hier nie von dem Adel seines Names sprechen, aber den moralischen Adel der Seele in Wissenschaft und männlicher Tugend beweisen" (3:161). Nenon ("Social Theory") views La Roche's emphases on bourgeois virtues as the core of her political vision.

45. In her analysis of *Erscheinungen,* Ute Brandes emphasizes that La Roche endorsed "new middle-class patterns of strictly polarized male and female attitudes." Ute Brandes, "Escape to America: Social Reality and Utopian Schemes in German Women's Novels Around 1800," in *In the Shadow of Olympus,* 157–71, quotation, 168.

46. Bernd Heidenreich, *Sophie von La Roche—eine Werkbiographie* (Frankfurt: Peter Lang, 1986), 181.

47. Lange, "Visitors to Lake Oneida," 105; Nenon, "Social Theory," 170n8.

48. Alexis de Tocqueville, "Journey to Lake Oneida," in *Journey to America,* ed. J. P.

Mayer, trans. George Lawrence (New Haven: Yale University Press, 1960), 321–27, quotation, 326.

49. Tocqueville, "Journey," 326.

50. Gustave de Beaumont to his sister Eugenie, letter dated July 14, 1831, quoted in George Wilson Pierson, *Tocqueville and Beaumont in America* (New York: Oxford University Press, 1938), 204, unnumbered note.

51. Tocqueville, "Journey," 323.

52. Tocqueville, *Journey to America,* 130–31, quoted also in Pierson, *Tocqueville and Beaumont,* 205, and André Jardin, *Tocqueville: A Biography,* trans. Lydia Davis with Robert Hemenway (New York: Farrar Straus Giroux, 1988), 125.

53. Matthew Mancini argues for the importance of the "Journey to Lake Oneida" in revealing Tocqueville's early interest in the sublime, saying that the episode "demonstrates his recognition of the modern necessity of separating politics from aesthetics, power from beauty." Matthew Mancini, *Alexis de Tocqueville* (New York: Twayne, 1994), 24.

54. Alexis de Tocqueville, *Democracy in America,* ed. Phillips Bradley (New York: Alfred A. Knopf, 1951), 1:296.

55. Nenon, "Social Theory," 163.

56. For further information about the Oneida Community, see George Wallingford Noyes, compiler, *Free Love in Utopia: John Humphrey Noyes and the Origin of the Oneida Community,* ed. Lawrence Foster (Urbana: University of Illinois Press, 2001).

Afterword

1. Michel de Certeau, *The Practice of Everyday Life,* trans. Steven F. Rendall (Berkeley: University of California Press, 1984).

2. Seyla Benhabib, *Situating the Self: Gender, Community and Postmodernism in Contemporary Ethics* (Cambridge: Polity Press, 1992), 243.

3. Gary Kelly, "Women's Provi(de)nce: Religion and Bluestocking Feminism in Sarah Scott's *Millenium Hall,*" in *Female Communities, 1600–1800: Literary Visions and Cultural Realities,* ed. Rebecca D'Monté and Nicole Pohl (London: Macmillan, and New York: St. Martin's, 2000), 166–83, quotation, 170.

4. Jeanne Marie Leprince de Beaumont, *The New Clarissa: A True History,* 2 vols. (London: J. Nourse, 1768), 2:165–66.

5. Mary Astell, *A Serious Proposal to the Ladies, Part II,* ed. and intro. by Patricia Springborg (London: Pickering and Chatto, 1997), 150; Virginia Woolf, *Three Guineas* (1938, repr. London: Hogarth Press, 1952), 197.

6. Rosi Braidotti, *Nomadic Subjects: Embodiment and Sexual Difference in Contemporary Feminist Theory* (New York: Columbia University Press, 1994), 32.

7. Seyla Benhabib, "Sexual Difference and Collective Identities: The New Global Constellation," *Signs: Journal of Women in Culture and Society* 24, no. 2 (1999): 335–61, quotation, 355.

8. Nancy Fraser, *Justice Interruptus: Critical Reflections on the "Postsocialist" Condition* (New York: Routledge, 1997), 82.

9. See, for example, Vincent Carretta, "Utopia Limited: Sarah Scott's *Millenium Hall* and *The History of Sir George Ellison,*" *Age of Johnson* 5 (1992): 303–25. In *The Conversa-*

tional Circle: Rereading the English Novel, 1740–1775 (Lexington: University Press of Kentucky, 1996), Betty A. Schellenberg argues that conversational novels "increasingly seal off the community from its context, rendering it at best an alternative to, at worst the victim of, a chaotic and irredeemable society" (5).

10. Fraser, *Justice Interruptus,* 82.

11. David Harvey, *Spaces of Hope* (Berkeley: University of California Press, 2000), 163, 159. Elizabeth Faue similarly urged women in particular "to take time out to dream, imaginatively construct alternative futures, and creatively sketch out paths to reach them." Elizabeth Faue, "Women's History in the New Millennium: A Conversation across Three 'Generations': Part 2," *Journal of Women's History* 11, no. 2 (1999): 9–30, 199–220, quotation, 211.

12. Ruth Perry, *The Celebrated Mary Astell* (Chicago: University of Chicago Press, 1986); Mary Astell, *A Serious Proposal to the Ladies, Parts I and II,* ed. and intro. by Patricia Springborg (London: Pickering and Chatto, 1997); Mary Astell, *Political Writings,* ed. and intro. by Patricia Springborg (New York: Cambridge University Press, 1996).

13. Betty Rizzo, *Companions without Vows: Relationships among Eighteenth-Century British Women* (Athens: University of Georgia Press, 1994); "Introduction," in Sarah Scott, *The History of Sir George Ellison,* ed. Betty Rizzo (Lexington: University Press of Kentucky, 1996).

14. Scott, *The History of Sir George Ellison,* 223, preface note 3.

15. James Burgh, *An Account of the Cessares,* in *Utopias of the British Enlightenment,* ed. Gregory Claeys (New York: Cambridge University Press, 1994), 71–136, quotation, 92.

16. Claire Tomalin, *The Life and Death of Mary Wollstonecraft,* rev. ed. (London: Penguin, 1992), 47, 51, passim; Gary Kelly, *Revolutionary Feminism: The Mind and Career of Mary Wollstonecraft* (London: Macmillan, 1992), esp. 28, 91; Janet Todd, *Mary Wollstonecraft: A Revolutionary Life* (London: Weidenfeld and Nicolson, 2000).

17. Barbara Taylor, *Eve and the New Jerusalem: Socialism and Feminism in the Nineteenth Century* (London: Virago Press, 1983). Closer examination of the utopian influences of mid-eighteenth-century women on the English Jacobins would repay investigation. The need for such a project is underscored by the work of April London, who argues that radical utopists of the 1790s repudiated "the determining influence of the past" and instead invited readers to create "individual and political virtue." The break she discusses between their texts and traditional utopias parallels the disjunction I have described in the introduction to this volume and thus begs the question of feminist utopists' direct influence. April London, "Clock Time and Utopia's Time in Novels of the 1790s," *Studies in English Literature* 40, no. 3 (2000): 539–60, quotation, 540.

18. For commentary see Taylor, *Eve and the New Jerusalem,* esp. chs. 1–3.

19. Darby Lewes, *Dream Revisionaries: Gender and Genre in Women's Utopian Fiction, 1870–1920* (Tuscaloosa: University of Alabama Press, 1995). On Fanny Wright, see Celia Morris, *Fanny Wright: Rebel in America* (Urbana: University of Illinois Press, 1992). On Flora Tristan, see *Flora Tristan, Utopian Feminist: Her Travel Diaries and Personal Crusade,* ed. and intro. by Doris Beik and Paul Beik (Bloomington: Indiana University Press, 1993).

Index

ALESSA JOHNS is an associate professor of English at the University of California, Davis. She has edited *Dreadful Visitations: Confronting Natural Catastrophe in the Age of Enlightenment* (1999).

The University of Illinois Press
is a founding member of the
Association of American University Presses.

University of Illinois Press
1325 South Oak Street
Champaign, IL 61820-6903
www.press.uillinois.edu